D1224362

Cognitive Schemas
and Core Beliefs
in Psychological
Problems

Cognitive Schemas and Core Beliefs in Psychological Problems

A Scientist–Practitioner Guide

Edited by
Lawrence P. Riso, Pieter L. du Toit,
Dan J. Stein, and Jeffrey E. Young

AMERICAN PSYCHOLOGICAL ASSOCIATION • WASHINGTON, DC

Published by
American Psychological Association
750 First Street, NE
Washington, DC 20002
www.apa.org

To order
APA Order Department
P.O. Box 92984
Washington, DC 20090-2984
Tel: (800) 374-2721
Direct: (202) 336-5510
Fax: (202) 336-5502
TDD/TTY: (202) 336-6123
Online: www.apa.org/books/
E-mail: order@apa.org

In the U.K., Europe, Africa, and the Middle East, copies may be ordered from
American Psychological Association
3 Henrietta Street
Covent Garden, London
WC2E 8LU England

Typeset in Goudy by World Composition Services, Inc., Sterling, VA

Printer: Edwards Brothers, Inc., Ann Arbor, MI
Cover Designer: Mercury Publishing Services, Rockville, MD
Technical/Production Editor: Tiffany L. Klaff

The opinions and statements published are the responsibility of the authors, and such opinions and statements do not necessarily represent the policies of the American Psychological Association.

Library of Congress Cataloging-in-Publication Data

Cognitive schemas and core beliefs in psychological problems : a scientist-practitioner guide / edited by Lawrence P. Riso . . . [et al.].— 1st ed.
p. ; cm.
Includes bibliographical references and index.
ISBN-13: 978-1-59147-782-2
ISBN-10: 1-59147-782-4
1. Cognitive therapy. 2. Schemas (Psychology) I. Riso, Lawrence P. II. American Psychological Association.
[DNLM: 1. Cognitive Therapy. 2. Mental Disorders—therapy. 3. Psychological Theory. WM 425.5.C6 C6777 2007]

RC489.C63C645 2007
616.89'142—dc22   2006035438

British Library Cataloguing-in-Publication Data
A CIP record is available from the British Library.

Printed in the United States of America
First Edition

To Lisa, Alana, Hannah, and Alec
Lawrence P. Riso

To Karen and Tashi
Pieter L. Du Toit

To Heather, Gabriella, Joshua, and Sarah
Dan J. Stein

To my close circle of friends over so many years
Jeffrey E. Young

CONTENTS

CONTRIBUTORS

Samuel A. Ball, PhD, Associate Professor of Psychiatry, Yale University School of Medicine, Division of Substance Abuse, New Haven, CT

Pieter L. du Toit, MA, Psychologist, National Health Service in the United Kingdom, Cambridge, England

Peter Farvolden, PhD, Assistant Professor of Psychiatry, Centre for Addiction and Mental Health, Toronto, Ontario, Canada

Matt J. Gray, PhD, Assistant Professor of Psychology, University of Wyoming, Laramie

Helen Kennerley, PhD, Consultant and Clinical Psychologist, Oxford Cognitive Therapy Centre, Warneford Hospital, Oxford, England

Brett T. Litz, PhD, Professor, Boston Veterans Affairs Health Care System and Boston University School of Medicine, Boston, MA

Rachel E. Maddux, MA, Georgia State University, Atlanta

Shira Maguen, PhD, Psychologist, San Francisco Veterans Administration Medical Center, San Francisco, CA

Carolina McBride, PhD, Research Director, Interpersonal Psychotherapy Clinic, Department of Psychiatry, University of Toronto, Ontario, Canada

Anthony P. Morrison, PhD, Senior Lecturer, University of Manchester, Manchester, England

Vartouhi Ohanian, PhD, Lakeside Mental Health Unit, West London Mental Health NHS Trust, West Middlesex University Hospital, Middlesex, England

Gilbert Pinard, MD, Professor of Psychiatry, McGill University Health Centre, Montreal, Quebec, Canada

Lawrence P. Riso, PhD, Associate Professor, American School of Professional Psychology, Argosy University/Washington, DC

Noelle Turini Santorelli, MA, Georgia State University, Atlanta

Debbie Sookman, PhD, Associate Professor of Psychiatry and Director, Obsessive–Compulsive Disorder Clinic, McGill University Health Centre, Montreal, Quebec, Canada

Dan J. Stein, MD, PhD, Professor and Chair, Department of Psychiatry and Mental Health, University of Cape Town; Director, Medical Research Council Unit on Anxiety Disorders, Cape Town, South Africa; Mt. Sinai School of Medicine, New York, NY

Stephen R. Swallow, PhD, Psychologist, Oakville Centre for Cognitive Therapy, Oakville, Ontario, Canada

Lisa A. Uebelacker, PhD, Brown University Medical School and Butler Hospital, Providence, RI

Glenn Waller, PhD, Professor, Eating Disorders Section, Institute of Psychiatry, King's College London; Vincent Square Clinic, Central and North West London Mental Health Trust, London, England

Mark A. Whisman, PhD, Associate Professor, Department of Psychology, University of Colorado, Boulder

Jeffrey E. Young, PhD, Founder and Director, Cognitive Therapy Centers of New York and the Schema Therapy Institute, New York, NY; Department of Psychiatry, Columbia University College of Physicians and Surgeons, New York, NY

ACKNOWLEDGMENTS

The editors would like to thank and acknowledge Ms. Tiffany L. Klaff for her help in preparation of the manuscript.

Cognitive Schemas and Core Beliefs in Psychological Problems

1

INTRODUCTION: A RETURN TO A FOCUS ON COGNITIVE SCHEMAS

LAWRENCE P. RISO AND CAROLINA McBRIDE

More than 30 years ago, Aaron T. Beck (1967, 1976) emphasized the operation of cognitive schemas as the most fundamental factor in his theories of emotional disorders. Schemas, accordingly, played a principal role in the development and maintenance of psychological disorders as well as in the recurrence and relapse of episodes.

Despite the central place of cognitive schemas in the earliest writings of cognitive therapy, the cognitive techniques and therapeutic approaches that later emerged tended to address cognition at the level of automatic negative thoughts, intermediate beliefs, and attributional style. In a similar way, the psychotherapy protocols that developed tended to be short term. Relatively less attention was paid to schema-level processes.

In most accounts of clinical cognitive theory, cognition can be divided into different levels of generality (Clark & Beck, 1999). Automatic thoughts (ATs) are at the most specific or superficial level. Automatic thoughts are moment-to-moment cognitions that occur without effort, or spontaneously, in response to specific situations. They are readily accessible and represent conscious cognitions. Examples of ATs include "I'm going to fail this test," "She thinks I'm really boring," or "Now I'll never get a job." ATs are often negatively distorted, representing, for instance, catastrophizing, personalization, or minimization. They are significant in that they are tightly linked to both the individual's mood and his or her behavioral responses to situations.

Beliefs at an intermediate level (termed *intermediate beliefs* or *conditional assumptions*) are in the form of "if . . . then" rules. Examples of intermediate beliefs include "If I do whatever people want, then they will like me" and "If I trust others, I'll get hurt."

At the highest level of generality are cognitive schemas. Negative automatic thoughts and intermediate beliefs are heavily influenced by underlying cognitive schemas, particularly when these schemas are activated. In cognitive psychology, the notion of cognitive schemas has played an important role in the understanding of learning and memory. For clinical contexts, A. T. Beck (1967) described a cognitive schema as "a cognitive structure for screening, coding, and evaluating the stimuli that impinge on the organism . . ." (p. 283).

A number of authors have returned recently to Beck's original notions of the need to conceptualize patients in terms of their cognitive schemas (see, for instance, Young, 1995, and Safran, Vallis, Segal, & Shaw, 1986). Jeffrey Young (1995; Young, Klosko, & Weishaar, 2003) has been one of the more influential proponents of a schema-focused clinical approach. Noting limitations of traditional cognitive therapy, Young (1995) suggested that a focus on schemas was often necessary because some patients have poor access to moment-to-moment changes in affect, making a primary focus on ATs unproductive. Other patients are readily able to recognize the irrationality of their thoughts in therapy, but then report that they still "feel" bad. Still others are unable to establish a productive and collaborative working alliance that is required for more symptom-focused work. Finally, Young noted that patients seen in the community are often much more complex and chronic than are those enrolled in clinical trials with 3-month cognitive therapy protocols. As a consequence, the need to focus on underlying schemas has begun to influence the practice of cognitive therapy. In this volume, we have compiled work by a number of authors who tailor the schema-focused approach to the understanding and treatment of specific clinical problems.

The increased interest in cognitive schemas parallels the search for underlying dimensions of vulnerability to psychopathology. The search for these underlying processes includes factors such as temperament, personality, and personality disorders. Schema-focused approaches also represent a return to an interest in developmental antecedents of psychopathology.

The concept of schemas has a rich ancestry in psychology deriving from cognitive psychology, cognitive development, self-psychology, and attachment theory. Within the cognitive therapy literature, the term *cognitive schema* has had multiple meanings (James, Southam, & Blackburn, 2004;

Segal, 1988; Young et al., 2003). These definitions vary in the extent to which schemas are accessible or inaccessible cognitive structures. Nearly all definitions, however, maintain that cognitive schemas represent highly generalized superordinate-level cognition, that schemas are resistant to change, and that they exert a powerful influence over cognition and affect. As in psychoanalytic theory, the notion of cognitive schemas suggests the power of unconscious processes in influencing thought, affect, and behavior. However, unlike the psychodynamic unconscious, schemas exert their influence through unconscious information processing, rather than through unconscious motivation and instinctual drives.

Early attempts to study cognitive schemas used paper-and-pencil measures such as the Dysfunctional Attitudes Scale (Weissman & Beck, 1978). Numerous studies found that currently ill individuals consistently scored higher on self-report inventories purportedly measuring dysfunctional schemas than did control participants who were never depressed (see Segal, 1988, for review). However, subsequent research demonstrated that these elevated scores normalized with symptomatic recovery (Blackburn, Jones, & Lewin, 1986; Giles & Rush, 1983; Haaga, Dyck, & Ernst, 1991; Hollon, Kendall, & Lumry, 1986, Silverman, Silverman, & Eardley, 1984). The explanation for these findings, from a schema-theory perspective, was that following recovery, cognitive schemas became dormant and thus difficult to detect.

Therefore, the next generation of research examined cognitive schemas using information-processing tasks. It was assumed that information tasks would be less prone to reporting biases and more able to detect latent schemas, particularly when these tasks were accompanied by an effort to prime or activate the schema. In one such task, individuals made judgments of whether a number of positive and negative personal adjectives were self-descriptive, followed by an incidental recall test. Results indicated that not only were individuals with depression biased toward recall of negative self-referent information (Derry & Kuiper, 1981; Dobson & Shaw, 1987) but also, and perhaps more importantly, these formerly depressed individuals were biased in their recall after undergoing a sad mood induction (Hedlund & Rude, 1995; Teasdale & Dent, 1987). In other work, individuals who had recovered from depression made more tracking errors during dichotic listening tasks than did control participants, who were never depressed, after they underwent a sad mood induction (Ingram, Bernet, & McLaughlin, 1994). Finally, Miranda and colleagues (Miranda, Gross, Persons, & Hahn, 1998; Miranda, Persons, & Byers, 1990) assessed dysfunctional attitudes in formerly depressed versus never depressed individuals. Although the groups exhibited similar levels of dysfunctional attitudes before any mood induction, following the mood induction procedure only the formerly depressed group showed increases in their reporting of dysfunctional attitudes. These and other studies substantiated the notion that schemas are latent during non-symptomatic periods and become accessible and impact cognitive processing when they are activated.

The importance of schemas in the development and maintenance of psychopathology, as well as the role of schemas in treatment resistance, has much in common with the *Diagnostic and Statistical Manual of Mental Disorders* (4th ed.; *DSM–IV*; American Psychiatric Association, 1994) Axis II personality disorders. Like personality disorders, schemas represent purportedly stable generalized themes that develop early in life and are important considerations for understanding and treating a wide range of psychopathological conditions. Unlike personality disorders, however, schemas are dimensional rather than categorical, are more cognitive–affective than behavioral, and were derived from the traditions of personality psychology and cognitive phenomenology, rather than the traditions of operationalized psychiatric nomenclature and descriptive psychopathology.

Given the accelerating interests in personality, temperament, and developmental antecedents of psychopathology as well as schema theory, we thought that a volume devoted to schema theory and schema-focused approaches to clinical problems would be a timely and important contribution. Our volume examines how the general principles of schema theory can be applied to specific clinical problems. The chapters in this volume cover several major psychological problems including depression, eating disorders, posttraumatic stress disorder, substance use disorders, obsessive–compulsive disorder, and schizophrenia, as well as couple distress. Each chapter begins with basic research on schema processes and issues in the assessment of schemas for that particular disorder, followed by a description of the clinical application of the schema-focused approach. Each chapter describes the implications of a schema-focused approach for theory, research, and practice. Thus, this volume is intended for either a scholar–practitioner or a practitioner–scholar with at least some familiarity with the cognitive therapy literature. The contributing authors range from clinic directors to faculty members at universities and university medical schools, and all have developed innovative treatment models that combine science with practice.

In this volume, several of the chapters (i.e., chaps. 1, 2, 5, 6, and 8) draw heavily on Young's (1995; Young et al., 2003) notion of early maladaptive schemas (EMS). Young (1995) described EMS as "extremely stable and enduring themes that develop during childhood and are elaborated upon throughout an individual's lifetime" (p. 9). EMS, which contain underlying life themes and are assessed with self-report instruments, differ somewhat from other definitions of schemas that emphasize an implicit structure and organization of cognitive and affective elements (Segal, 1988; Segal, Gemar, Truchon, Guirguis, & Horowitz, 1995). According to the more "structural" perspective, the existence of a cognitive schema can be demonstrated only with information-processing tasks.

By contrast, the 16 rationally derived EMS are assessed with the Young Schema Questionnaire (YSQ; Young, 1995). Examples of EMS include failure to achieve, vulnerability to harm, and emotional deprivation. There is generally good support for the YSQ's factor structure (Lee, Taylor, & Dunn, 1999; Schmidt, Joiner, Young, & Telch, 1995) and long-term stability (Riso et al., in press). EMS capture the verbal content of schemas and are therefore more accessible than are some other definitions primarily emphasizing structure. The accessibility of EMS is a desirable quality from a clinical standpoint as they are available for scrutiny in psychotherapy (Elliot & Lassen, 1997). As accessible structures that reside at the level of awareness, EMS fit closely with the notion of core beliefs, which have been described as the cognitive content or verbal representation of schemas (J. S. Beck, 1995; Clark & Beck, 1999; James et al., 2004). Both core beliefs and schemas are defined as stable, overgeneralized belief structures. They influence both the selection and interpretation of incoming information, have varying levels of prepotence or activation, and contain stored affects and cognition. Because of a lack of adequate theoretical and empirical work to justify a sharp distinction between them, the terms are sometimes used interchangeably. We refer to both terms in the title of this volume and both are used in the chapters herein.

The concept of cognitive schemas was initially developed and researched in the effort to understand depressive disorders. Thus, this volume begins with a chapter on cognitive schemas and major depressive disorder. A chapter on chronic depression (chap. 2) is included because there is now considerable research documenting important differences between chronic and nonchronic depression. Moreover, as described in chapter 2, there is now good evidence that dysfunctional schemas are particularly related to chronic forms of depression.

Other chapters adapting Young's (1995) general approach to specific clinical problems include chapter 6 in which the activation of painful EMS is described as a risk factor for relapse in substance-related disorders. In chapter 7, Waller and colleagues describe how the reaction to EMS can in part determine the form of an eating pathology. Chapter 8 describes how underlying schemas may impact the form of psychotic symptoms. A method of case formulation and specific interventions are then described for individuals with schizophrenia and other forms of psychosis.

Chapters 4, 5, and 9 (on posttraumatic stress disorder, obsessive–compulsive disorder, and couple distress, respectively) focus more on theoretical issues and directions for future research as there has been less effort to translate theory and research into clinical guidelines in these areas.

Chapter 4 discusses the struggles faced by trauma victims as they try to fit their traumatic experiences into existing schemas of self, world, and future. Chapter 5 describes a subset of individuals with resistant obsessive–compulsive disorder for which schema-focused strategies may significantly augment standard exposure and response prevention treatment. Finally, chapter 9 examines perhaps the newest clinical application of schema theory—the treatment of couple distress. Topics discussed include the use of attachment theory, relationship scripts, and Young's (1995) EMS in understanding and treating discordant couples. We conclude this volume with an afterword discussing the strengths and limitations of the schema approach, unanswered questions, and directions for additional work.

REFERENCES

American Psychiatric Association. (1994). *Diagnostic and statistical manual of mental disorders* (4th ed.). Washington, DC: Author.

Beck, A. T. (1967). *Depression: Clinical, experimental, and theoretical aspects.* New York: Hoeber.

Beck, A. T. (1976). *Cognitive therapy and the emotional disorders.* New York: International Universities Press.

Beck, J. S. (1995). *Cognitive therapy: Basics and beyond.* New York: Guilford Press.

Blackburn, I. M., Jones, S., & Lewin, R. J. (1986). Cognitive style in depression. *British Journal of Clinical Psychology, 25,* 241–251.

Clark, D. A., & Beck, A. T. (1999). *Scientific foundations of cognitive theory and therapy of depression.* New York: Wiley.

Derry, P. A., & Kuiper, N. A. (1981). Schematic processing and self-reference in clinical depression. *Journal of Abnormal Psychology, 90,* 286–297.

Dobson, K. S., & Shaw, B. F. (1987). Specificity and stability of self-referent encoding in clinical depression. *Journal of Abnormal Psychology, 96,* 34–40.

Elliott, C. H., & Lassen, M. K. (1997). A schema polarity model for case conceptualization, intervention, and research. *Clinical Psychology: Science and Practice, 4,* 12–28.

Giles, D. E., & Rush, A. J. (1983). Cognitions, schemas, and depressive symptomatology. In M. Rosenbaum, C. M. Franks, & Y. Jaffe (Eds.), *Perspectives on behaviour therapy* (pp. 184–199). New York: Springer Publishing Company.

Haaga, D. A., Dyck, M. J., & Ernst, D. (1991). Empirical status of cognitive theory of depression. *Psychological Bulletin, 110,* 215–236.

Hedlund, S., & Rude, S. S. (1995). Evidence of latent depressive schemas in formerly depressed individuals. *Journal of Abnormal Psychology, 104,* 517–525.

Hollon, S. D., Kendall, P. C., & Lumry, A. (1986). Specificity of depressotypic cognitions in clinical depression. *Journal of Abnormal Psychology, 9,* 52–59.

Ingram, R. E., Bernet, C. Z., & McLaughlin, S. C. (1994). Attentional allocation processes in individuals at risk for depression. *Cognitive Therapy and Research, 18*, 317–332.

James, I. A., Southam, L., & Blackburn, M. (2004). Schemas revisited. *Clinical Psychology and Psychotherapy, 11*, 369–377.

Lee, C. W., Taylor, G., & Dunn, J. (1999). Factor structure of the schema questionnaire in a large clinical sample. *Cognitive Therapy and Research, 23*, 441–451.

Miranda, J., Gross, J. J., Persons, J. B., & Hahn, J. (1998). Mood matters: Negative mood induction activates dysfunctional attitudes in women vulnerable to depression. *Cognitive Therapy and Research, 22*, 363–376.

Miranda, J., Persons, J. B., & Byers, C. N. (1990). Endorsement of dysfunctional beliefs depends on current mood state. *Journal of Abnormal Psychology, 99*, 237–241.

Riso, L. P., Froman, S. E., Raouf, M., Gable, P., Maddux, R. E., Turini-Santorelli, N., et al. (in press). The long-term stability of early maladaptive schemas. *Cognitive Therapy and Research*.

Safran, J. D., Vallis, T. M., Segal, Z. V., & Shaw, B. F. (1986). Assessment of core cognitive processes in cognitive therapy. *Cognitive Therapy and Research, 10*, 509–526.

Schmidt, N. B., Joiner, T. E., Young, J. E., & Telch, M. J. (1995). The schema questionnaire: Investigation of psychometric properties and the hierarchical structure of a measure of maladaptive schemas. *Cognitive Therapy and Research, 3*, 295–321.

Segal, Z. V. (1988). Appraisal of the self-schema construct in cognitive models of depression. *Psychological Bulletin, 103*, 147–162.

Segal, Z. V., Gemar, M., Truchon, C., Guirguis, M., & Horowitz, L. M. (1995). A priming methodology for studying self-representation in major depressive disorder. *Journal of Abnormal Psychology, 104*, 205–213.

Silverman, J. S., Silverman, J. A., & Eardley, D. A. (1984). Do maladaptive attitudes cause depression? *Archives of General Psychiatry, 41*, 28–30.

Teasdale, J. D., & Dent, J. (1987). Cognitive vulnerability to depression: An investigation of two hypotheses. *British Journal of Clinical Psychology, 26*, 113–126.

Weissman, A. N., & Beck, A. T. (1978). *Development and validation of the Dysfunctional Attitude Scale: A preliminary investigation.* Paper presented at the Annual Meeting of the American Educational Research Association, Toronto, Ontario, Canada.

Young, J. E. (1995). *Cognitive therapy for personality disorders: A schema-focused approach.* Sarasota, FL: Professional Resource Exchange.

Young, J. E., Klosko, J. S., & Weishaar, M. E. (2003). *Schema therapy: A practitioner's guide.* New York: Guilford Press.

2

MAJOR DEPRESSIVE DISORDER AND COGNITIVE SCHEMAS

CAROLINA McBRIDE, PETER FARVOLDEN,
AND STEPHEN R. SWALLOW

The past 3 decades have witnessed a significant growth in the status of cognitive theory and practice of cognitive therapy in the treatment of depression. Although a number of authors have discussed how cognitive therapy (CT) can be modified and refined, all current variations share a conceptual framework that emphasizes the role of dysfunctional schemas in the onset and course of depression. It follows, then, that schema change is a central goal for the treatment of depression. In this chapter we present a brief description of the role of cognitive schemas in cognitive theory, an overview of research supporting the concept of cognitive schemas, and a number of strategies and techniques for schema identification and change.

Negative automatic thoughts (ATs) are the observable, often conscious, products of errors in processing through which perceptions and interpretations of experience are distorted. Examples include "My life is meaningless" or "Nobody cares about me." These thoughts are automatic insofar as they are not readily controllable (A. T. Beck, 1963).

Underlying negative ATs are inferred errors in information processing that bias and distort the meaning attached to experiences. Errors in processing include an emphasis on the negative aspects of life events, a pervasive preoccupation with the possible adverse meanings of events, and self-attribution and self-blame for problems across all situations (A. T. Beck, 2002).

Negative ATs and errors in processing are both byproducts of underlying cognitive schemas, which can be defined as cognitive structures that screen, code, and evaluate incoming information (A. T. Beck, 1967). Attention is necessarily selective as it would be impossible to process all information gathered from the senses, and schemas act as screening templates to determine what is processed and what is not. Although all cognitive theories of depression assume the existence of schemas (e.g., Abramson, Metalsky, & Alloy, 1989; Abramson, Seligman, & Teasdale, 1978; A. T. Beck, 1967; Young, 1990), the definitions and descriptions of schemas vary considerably. Dysfunctional schemas are generally believed to develop early in life and, once activated, negatively distort and bias the categorization and interpretation of information, bringing about depression (A. T. Beck, 1967; Young, 1994).

A key postulate of cognitive theory is that depressive schemas are stable cognitive structures that become latent during times of symptomatic recovery (A. T. Beck, 2002). These latent structures become activated by stressful life events and provide access to a tightly organized network of stored personal information that is mostly unfavorable, precipitating the depression (A. T. Beck, Rush, Shaw, & Emery, 1979; Segal & Shaw, 1986).

According to A. T. Beck (1987, 2002), two specific personality types, sociotropic and autonomous, may render an individual more vulnerable to depression. Highly sociotropic individuals are excessively concerned about and sensitive to the possibility of disapproval from others whereas autonomous individuals have a need for independence and goal achievement. The interaction between negative life events and a congruent sociotropic or autonomous personality activates dysfunctional schemas and precipitates depression (a diathesis–stress model).

To characterize the interpersonal nature of the self, Safran (1990; Safran, Vallis, Segal, & Shaw, 1986) introduced the notion of the *interpersonal schema*. Interpersonal schemas are generalized cognitive representations of interactions with others that initially develop from patterns of interactions with attachment figures, and allow an individual to predict interactions with significant others and maximize the probability of maintaining interpersonal relatedness (Hill & Safran, 1994). These representations contain information in this form: "If I do X, others will do Y" (e.g., "If I assert myself, others will put me down").

The introduction to this volume (chap. 1) describes the progression of research and thought in measuring schemas. In summary, early efforts to measure schemas used self-report questionnaires. Although these studies found elevations of dysfunctional schemas while individuals were acutely symptomatic, these elevations tended to normalize with symptomatic improvement. The next generation of research used information-processing paradigms (e.g., memory, modified Stroop, and dichotic listening tasks). This next wave of studies found that existence of dysfunctional schemas could be demonstrated in both acutely ill and recovered individuals. When induced into a negative mood, recovered individuals exhibited dysfunctional schematic processing. Overall, the results of this series of studies suggested that cognitive schemas are stable structures that lie dormant until activated, and, once activated, they negatively bias attention, memory, and perception.

A novel application of the mood-priming paradigm to schema research in major depressive disorder (MDD) has been to test whether cognitive reactivity (e.g., to negative mood) can be differentially reduced according to treatment and is predictive of relapse (Segal, Gemar, & Williams, 1999). Segal and colleagues compared dysfunctional attitudes before and after a negative mood induction for patients who had recovered from major depression through either CT or pharmacotherapy. Patients who were treated pharmacologically and had recovered from depression showed significantly larger increases in dysfunctional cognitions (i.e., greater cognitive reactivity) compared with patients who were treated with CT. Moreover, patients' reactions to the mood induction procedure were predictive of subsequent depressive relapse, with greater levels of cognitive reactivity being associated with increased risk. Although these results have considerable implications, it should be noted that the conclusions are limited by the fact that the groups were not randomly assigned to treatment conditions, which introduced the possibility of some unassessed variables serving as confounds. Segal and colleagues have recently completed a study that specifically addresses this limitation.

In the remainder of this chapter, we present the clinical application of the schema concept in the treatment of MDD. The following two cases help illustrate schema assessment, case formulation, and schema change interventions.

> **Case 1:** Stephanie, a 21-year-old woman, presents with depression-related symptoms including loss of interest and pleasure, feelings of worthlessness and low self-esteem, memory and concentration difficulties, extreme fatigue, and social withdrawal. She often cries, for no apparent reason, and has lost 10 pounds in the past month. She is no longer attending classes at the university, and tends to spend her days sleeping. Her friends and family are concerned and have noticed her restlessness and irritation. Stephanie was referred for cognitive therapy by her family doctor, and she reported in the initial assessment interview

that her mood started to change noticeably approximately 6 months ago, after her boyfriend of 2 years broke up with her.

Case 2: Andrew, a 34-year-old married man with a 14-month-old child, presents with depression-related symptoms including lack of motivation and flat affect. He continues to go to work as a consultant for a large firm but finds that he can't "deal with people anymore." His libido is down, and he is more irritable with his wife. Andrew's sleep has been affected, and he finds that he wakes up at least four or five times a night. He is tired and agitated during the day, and he finds that he is making mistakes at work. Andrew describes himself as a perfectionist and notes that he has always been highly self-critical. At intake, he reported a change in his mood dating to 1 year ago, which coincided with the merger of his company with another consulting firm. He also cites ongoing marital problems as a stressor, especially since the birth of his son.

COGNITIVE ASSESSMENT AND CASE FORMULATION

Conducting effective CT requires an ongoing cognitive assessment to aid in the development of a specific case formulation about the nature of the patient's problems. Despite some variation in methods for arriving at and using case formulations, the key aspect of the assessment is that it ties together all of a patient's problems and provides a guide for understanding and treating the patient's current difficulties (Persons, 1989). The case formulation sheet (Appendix 2.1) can be used multiple times during the assessment phase of treatment to construct, discuss, and modify the case formulation with the client and collaboratively determine treatment goals. An example of a completed case formulation is presented in Appendix 2.2.

The schema concept is fundamental to the case formulation, as schemas are the hypothesized underlying mechanism responsible for the patient's overt problem. A good working hypothesis of the relationship between a client's overt difficulties and the underlying schemas helps the therapist understand the association between problems endorsed by the individual, predict behavior, decide on a treatment plan, and choose appropriate interventions. The process of developing hypotheses about underlying schemas is challenging, partly because schemas are not readily accessible to conscious thought. From the outset of treatment a number of methods are available to clinicians to help them generate hypotheses regarding the idiographic schemas of the patient and arrive at a case formulation. Developing the case formulation together with the client helps to strengthen the therapeutic alliance and engage the client in the therapeutic process.

Examining Automatic Thoughts

Automatic thoughts are the first and most easily accessible level of cognition that can provide clues to the activated schemas. One standard and reliable way to elicit ATs is to ask the patient to think of an emotionally charged situation and, through Socratic questioning, probe for the "hot" thoughts: What was going through your mind when you started to feel this way? What did the situation mean to you? What does it say about you? Your world? Others? Your future? What images or memories do you have from this situation? Questioning the meaning of high-affect events soon leads to the identification of schemas, especially if the affect is reproduced in session. If the client has difficulty with this exercise, the therapist may wish to get him or her to track mood changes during the week and write down thoughts during or immediately after an emotionally charged situation. Appendix 2.3 shows an example of an automatic thought record (ATR) that can be given to the client as homework between sessions, and the therapist can use the downward arrow technique (Appendix 2.4) in conjunction with the thought record to elicit core beliefs.

The therapist can also use in-session fluctuations in mood to probe for ATs.

Therapist: Did you notice any fluctuations in your mood this week, Andrew?

Andrew: Yes, I felt really depressed all day Tuesday.

Therapist: Did anything in particular happen on Tuesday that affected your mood?

Andrew: Well, in the morning my supervisor came by my desk and handed me a new project to work on.

Therapist: Can you describe how you felt when he handed you the new project?

Andrew: I don't know. I guess I felt a lot of pressure. I felt overwhelmed.

Therapist: I notice that you are clenching your fist. What are you feeling right now as you think of the new project assigned to you?

Andrew: I'm feeling that sense of pressure all over again. Like there's a lot of pressure for me to perform.

Therapist: Let's examine the thoughts that are connected to that sense of pressure. What is going through your mind right now as you think about the project?

> *Andrew:* I doubt whether or not I can do a good job. I really need to impress my supervisor so that I can get a promotion at work and make more money and I'm not sure if I can do it. I guess I'm expecting to fail.

From Andrew's ATs, the therapist might begin to theorize that a general theme of inadequacy, incompetence, inferiority, competitive loss, and social defeat might be central to his underlying schemas. It might also be hypothesized that Andrew has a stronger predisposition toward an autonomous personality style, resulting in the need for independence and goal achievement and an overwhelming concern regarding the possibility of failure.

Examining Cognitive Processes

The next level of cognition consists of attitudes ("Being single is a sign of inferiority"), rules ("I should always appear in control"), expectations ("I will be mocked if I assert myself"), and assumptions ("If I'm not perfect, I won't be liked") that are less accessible and malleable than automatic thoughts, but are one step closer to the schemas that drive information processing. Therapists work in various ways to access this level of cognition. One popular technique is to have patients complete conditional statements:

> *Therapist:* You said you felt depressed and hopeless after you and Michael broke up.
>
> *Stephanie:* Yes, I just can't understand what happened or what I did wrong. I really thought it was going to work out this time. But instead I drove him away, and now I'm alone again.
>
> *Therapist:* How would you finish this statement? "Being alone means _____."
>
> *Stephanie:* It means that there's something wrong with me. That I'm a loser, and I'll always be alone.

Ascertaining the patient's automatic thoughts and interpretation of events during the cognitive assessment is key, not only because they are indicators of underlying schemas, but also because they will become one of the initial targets for therapy. According to Padesky (1994), schema work is most effective if it's done after having focused cognitive interventions on automatic thoughts and interpretations.

Determining the Life Events Linked to the Onset of the Depression

Another important way to uncover activated schemas is to explore life events that occurred around the time the individual became depressed, to assess for congruency between what precipitated the depression and an individual's specific vulnerability. For Stephanie, depression followed a relationship breakup, whereas Andrew became depressed following workplace changes. These findings suggest that interpersonal relatedness is a central theme in Stephanie's core schemas, and achievement striving is a central theme in Andrew's core schemas. However, it is important to look for both autonomous and sociotropic concerns for each patient, and discern the extent to which either relatedness or achievement striving, or both, are central to that person's experiences. Andrew also endorsed marital difficulties as a stressor, which suggests that schemas about relatedness might also be activated and maintaining his depressed state.

Examining Early Childhood Experiences

Cognitive theorists (A. T. Beck, 2002; Young, Klosko, & Weishaar, 2003) have argued that maladaptive schemas that develop the earliest (i.e., within the nuclear family) are the strongest, whereas schemas developed later in life from other influences such as peers and school are somewhat less pervasive and powerful. A careful examination of early childhood experiences, therefore, can be a useful aid during the cognitive formulation.

> Stephanie was raised in an intact nuclear middle-class family. She described her parents as "simple folk" and has always had very different interests, often feeling guilty and conflicted about their differences. She depicted a difficult relationship with her mother since childhood, whom she described as controlling, stubborn, and domineering. Areas of conflict between them often related to privacy and independence issues. Memories of her childhood and adolescence included her mother reading her diary, criticizing her choices of friends, and throwing out her possessions without consulting her first. Her father, described as passive and uncommunicative, often acted as a mediator and tried to buffer the conflict. However, this would lead to marital distress and Stephanie would inevitably be blamed. Her parents frequently argued, threatened divorce, and competed against one another for Stephanie's attention. Despite all the conflict with her mother, she also described her mother as being emotionally dependent and doting. This left Stephanie with the sense that her mother's identity depended exclusively on her, and Stephanie would often feel guilty if she disagreed with her mother. Stephanie's chief conflict while growing up was between wanting to please her mother and wanting to assert her own independence.

From this description, the therapist can theorize that Stephanie's childhood experiences led to the development of schemas of instability and abandonment in relationships, and to schemas of the self as unlovable. "If I assert myself, I will disappoint others," "My decisions are wrong," and

"Others disapprove of me" were some schemas that the therapist and Stephanie formulated together.

Formulating Interpersonal Schemas

In addition to exploring the history of significant relationships and patterns in past and current relationships outside of therapy, the therapeutic relationship itself can provide important opportunities for understanding and modifying interpersonal schemas (Safran & Segal, 1990).

> Andrew described his father as a "tyrannical" figure who was easily provoked and, as a result, the family "walked on eggshells" when his father was around. He was also a highly critical and overly expectant father who was never satisfied with Andrew's achievements, particularly in the academic realm. Andrew's personal, social, and employment history revealed disputes with others as a recurrent theme. He described numerous conflicts at work over the years, remarking that he had no tolerance for people who treated him dismissively, and his expectation was that others were continually trying to take advantage of him. He also noted sensitivity to interpersonal rejection, admitting that he had difficulty concealing his emotions in such instances, and he described a fundamentally competitive relationship with coworkers, which led to strained relations and an impoverished social network. In session, his interpersonal style was abrupt and aggressive.

Andrew's relationship history revealed a pattern of feelings of anger and resentment, particularly toward authority figures. He was particularly sensitive to criticism and often perceived injustices when there were none. Instability in interpersonal relationships was apparent. Interpersonal schemas that were hypothesized for Andrew included "If I fail, I will be criticized and rejected" and "If I let my guard down, others will take advantage of me."

Attachment (Bowlby, 1982), defined as the tendency to seek the proximity and care of a specific person whenever one is vulnerable or distressed, can also provide useful information about a patient's interpersonal schema (Liotti, 2002). According to Liotti (2002), those with an avoidant attachment style construct interpersonal schemas in which the self is portrayed as bound to loneliness and others are portrayed as unwilling to provide comfort. Anxiously attached individuals, in contrast, construct self–other working models in which the self is viewed as helpless and others are viewed as unpredictable and intrusive. Finally, the interpersonal schema of those with a disorganized or disoriented pattern of attachment portrays both self and other as unavailable in times of distress. Appendix 2.5 features a worksheet that the therapist can use when trying to assess interpersonal schemas.

Assessing Implicit Schemas

There has been an increasing realization that core cognitive structures and processes are largely outside the realm of overt awareness and are implicit in nature (Dowd & Courchaine, 2002). Implicit learning has been described as having several properties including being (a) robust and resistant to degradation, (b) phylogenetically older, (c) resistant to consciousness, and (d) less available than explicit knowledge (Schacter, 1987). If core structures are implicit in nature, it follows that they are more robust, less available, and less easily recalled than is explicit knowledge, and may require repeated cognitive challenges and corrective emotional experiences for change (Dowd & Courchaine, 2002). Theory and research on implicit learning can assist cognitive therapists in the development of new assessment and intervention techniques. However, this area is relatively new and much work remains to be done regarding the role of implicit learning in schema theory.

INTERVENTION AND TECHNIQUES

Once maladaptive schemas have been identified and an initial case conceptualization has been developed, schema change can begin. A first step toward schema change is for therapist and client to develop more adaptive alternative schemas. According to Padesky (1994), clinical methods for schema change are more effective if the alternative, more adaptive schema rather than the maladaptive schema is the focus of evaluation. To identify alternative schemas Padesky (1994) suggested asking clients specific questions using constructive language such as "How would you like to be?" or "What would you like other people to be like?" A number of methods are available for schema change. Usually involving a simultaneous weakening of old maladaptive schemas and a strengthening of new adaptive schemas, they include continuum methods (Padesky, 1994), positive data log (Padesky, 1994), historical test of schemas (Young, 1999), and the Core Belief Worksheet (J. S. Beck, 1995).

Continuum Methods

A main purpose of a continuum is to shift maladaptive absolute beliefs (e.g., "I am unlovable") to more balanced beliefs. In basic terms, the continuum method involves creating a chart on which maladaptive schemas lie on one end (failure 100%) and more adaptive schemas lie on the other end (success 100%). Clients are initially asked to place themselves on the continuum, and through questioning the evidence for his or her choice and searching for alternative evidence using the standard techniques of CT, the client slowly shifts his or her self-evaluations toward a more adaptive stance.

Padesky (1994) developed a number of strategies to maximize the effectiveness of continua work, including charting on the adaptive continuum, constructing criteria continua, using two-dimensional charting of continua, and using a two-dimensional continuum graphs. Because of space limitations, we present only the process of charting on the adaptive continuum simultaneously with constructing continua criteria using Stephanie's case to illustrate the method (Appendix 2.6).

Stephanie and her therapist began the continuum method by identifying her maladaptive schema ("I'm unlovable"). Her desired alternative schema was "I'm lovable." When she was asked to rate herself on a continuum ranging from 0% to 100% for the adaptive schema, she rated herself as 5% lovable and marked this point on the continuum with an X. The next step involved asking Stephanie to develop specific criteria for evaluating the target schema.

The rationale behind constructing specific criteria is that schemas, by nature, are abstract and global, which increases the chances that clients will rate themselves in extreme terms. Reducing the global nature of schemas to specific and concrete criteria decreases the probability that clients will rate themselves in these extremist forms. Stephanie, for example, was quick to judge herself as 5% unlovable; however, once she had dissected 0% lovable to include "not having any friends," "never caring for others," and "hurting other's feelings," she was able to recognize that she did not meet the these criteria, which forced her to increase her lovability rating. Developing specific criteria for schemas is not an easy task for clients, however, and the therapist must be aware of distortions. Stephanie, for example, initially developed criteria for 0% lovable that included "being fat" and "being ugly." Once Stephanie and her therapist completed the task of identifying specific criteria, the therapist asked her to place an X on each continuum according to how she rated herself. Through this exercise Stephanie was able to begin the shift in her negative self-perspective by recognizing that on some of the criteria she endorsed as part of being lovable she actually rated herself quite favorably.

Positive Data Log

The positive data log (Appendix 2.7) helps to strengthen new adaptive schemas by correcting information-processing errors (Padesky, 1994). The first step is to provide a clear rationale for the task to the client by explaining how maladaptive schemas are maintained. Padesky (1991) recommended using the idea of prejudice as a metaphor to explain the idea that schemas, like prejudices, are maintained by discounting, distorting, and ignoring information that is not consistent with them. For example, Andrew's schema "I'm a failure" was maintained by his overevaluation of mistakes, misinterpretation of people's comments, and discounting of successes. The positive data log is set up as a task to encourage the client to actively look for information to support the new and more adaptive schema "I'm successful." The client is encouraged to observe and record on a daily basis information that is consistent with the new schema, no matter how small or insignificant it might seem. As noted by Padesky (1994), the therapist can assume that the client will discount, distort, and resist information that is not consistent with the old schema, and the challenge for the therapist is to support and encourage the client to perceive and record data the client does not believe exist. Persons, Davidson, and Tompkins (2001) offered some helpful hints to ensure that the benefits of this task are maximized:

- start the log early in treatment and during a session;
- reward small steps;
- add items to the log during sessions;
- review obstacles to use of the log;
- review rationale for the log;
- suggest particular life areas to monitor;
- revisit the case formulation with the client;
- treat the task as an experiment; and
- use a thought record to restructure negative expectations about the usefulness of the log.

Historical Test of Schemas

The Historical Test of Schemas (Appendix 2.8), developed by Jeffrey Young (1994), is another useful intervention to alter maladaptive schemas. The rationale behind this intervention is that schemas are formed in response to experiences throughout one's life and can be restructured through a systematic and realistic review of the evidence from life experiences. The first task involves identifying a maladaptive schema and helping the client list both confirming and disconfirming evidence for this core belief that spans the client's lifetime. For each period specified by the client (e.g., 0–2 years of age), the client and therapist write a summary of the data collected as it pertains to the schema. It is recommended that the historical test of the schema begin with the infancy period, as clients will be less likely to judge themselves harshly during this time period. (See Appendix 2.9 for a section of Andrew's historical review.)

Core Belief Worksheets

J. S. Beck (1995) developed a Core Belief Worksheet, which asks clients to write down their old maladaptive schemas and their new adaptive schemas and rate the believability (from 0%–100%) of each on a weekly basis. As homework, the client collects evidence that supports the new belief and evidence that seems to support the old belief but, given an alternative explanation, could be consistent with the new belief. A client with an old schema of "I'm not terribly intelligent," for example, could write down "I passed the exam" as evidence to support the new belief "I'm intelligent." Evidence such as "I don't know the answer to this question" might be written down as "In the past I would have taken not knowing the answer as proof that I am not intelligent. Not knowing, however, could also be viewed as a challenge and as a way of learning, and as having nothing to do with intelligence." A version of a Core Belief Worksheet is shown in Appendix 2.10.

Irrespective of what method is used to change schemas, some type of written record to document the client's schema learning is recommended (Padesky, 1994). Writing down the learning experience helps the client consolidate the information, increasing the likelihood that the new schema will begin to direct information processing.

Outcome Research

Research suggests that CT is as effective as pharmacotherapy in treating acute episodes of depression, even if severe, and is better at preventing relapse (Antonuccio, Thomas, & Danton, 1997; DeRubeis, Gelfand, Tang, & Simons, 1999; Segal et al., 1999). These findings are consistent with the view that the active mechanisms of CT are the interventions aimed at the core schemas and that schema change can reduce risk of relapse (A. T. Beck et al., 1979).

Some empirical evidence suggests that CT produces schema change, and that schema change reduces relapse (Segal et al., 1999). Segal and colleagues found that patients who were treated with pharmacotherapy and recovered showed a significant increase in dysfunctional cognitions compared with patients treated and recovered with CT. Moreover, a link was found between this cognitive reactivity to mood induction and later relapse.

There is little direct evidence, however, that the actual schema interventions result in schema change. Jacobson and colleagues (Jacobson et al., 1996, 2000) have completed a number of studies in which they have dismantled CT and examined which component of the therapy is related to outcome. In one study, they randomly assigned 150 patients with MDD to a treatment focused exclusively on the behavioral activation (BA) component, a treatment that included both BA and the teaching of skills to modify automatic thoughts but excluding the components of CT focused on core schema, or the full CT treatment. They found that both component groups improved as much as did those who received interventions aimed at modifying underlying schemas; this finding raised questions as to the necessary and sufficient conditions for change in CT. Follow-up data they are collecting will answer questions as to the relative effectiveness of schema change interventions compared with the components of CT to prevent relapse and recurrence.

CONCLUSION

Schema concept has played a pivotal role in both research and clinical treatment of major depression. It provides a useful framework from which to understand the development, maintenance, and high relapse rate in depression, and has led to the development of an array of clinical tools and techniques aimed at treating depression through schema change. As our research knowledge accumulates, researchers and clinicians are beginning to understand more clearly the usefulness as well as the limitations of the schema concept as it applies to the treatment of MDD. The importance of social environment and attachment security in depression, for example, has necessitated a greater differentiation of schema type and greater attention to developmental and interpersonal issues in schema formation and maintenance. Researchers and clinicians are also beginning to understand similarities and differences in women's and men's accounts of depression and how these apply to the schema model. More work, however, is needed to extend the schema model of depression and clinical interventions to include the importance of both relatedness and autonomy concerns for men and women, and take into account individual differences in the extent to which either relatedness or autonomy is central to that person's experiences. From a clinical perspective, therapies that include interventions aimed at schema change have been found to result in lower relapse rates. However, additional studies are needed to better understand the efficacy and mechanism of schema change.

As a descriptive model of how individuals with depression think, the schema concept of cognitive theory has served an important heuristic function, generating research of considerable clinical usefulness. Moreover, the therapeutic application of the model (cognitive theory) is one of the most effective treatments for depression. Nevertheless, schema concept and cognitive theory are vulnerable to a number of criticisms that will likely promote continued evolution of the theory.

One critique of cognitive theory is that researchers interested in the primacy of schemas in depression have not adequately integrated other approaches that emphasize relevant research regarding the neurophysiological substrate of depression. For example, although research has demonstrated that CT effects significant change in the neurobiology of depression (e.g., Joffe, Segal, & Singer, 1996), the model does not currently specify the mechanisms by which schema change effects neurophysiological change and vice versa. Other evidence calls into question the primacy of schemas in the onset and course of MDD. First, it is now an established fact that the dysfunctional schemas thought to underlie depressive cognition are mood-state dependent, and are activated only in the presence of negative affect (Ingram, Miranda, & Segal, 1998; Miranda, Gross, Persons, & Hahn, 1998). Second, cognitive theory does not adequately take into account abundant neurobiological evidence regarding the affective responses that operate prior to the involvement of cognitive processing (Shean, 2001). Third, some evidence suggests that the behavioral component of CT appears to have the greatest effect on changes in depression scores at the end of treatment and at subsequent follow-up (e.g., Dobson & Khatri, 2000; Gortner, Gollan, Dobson, & Jacobson, 1998; Jacobson et al., 1996). If dysfunctional schemas cause depression, then presumably treatments targeting maladaptive cognitions and schema change should increase efficacy over and above behavioral treatment alone. Such data suggest that depressive schemas are one component of a more complex system involving synchronous and reciprocal relations among affect, behavior, and cognition (Swallow, 2000).

A second major criticism of the cognitive model relates to its failure to address adequately the question of why individuals with depression and individuals vulnerable to depression think the way they do (D. T. Gilbert, 1992). Some cognitive theorists invoke Piagetian learning concepts to explain the development and persistence of depressive thinking, and propose that individuals generate idiosyncratic schemas as a result of interacting with their environment. However, such a view neglects the inherently purposive nature of human activity and the degree to which schemas may be the product of evolutionary history as well as the learning history of the individual (Swallow, 2000). A third major criticism of cognitive theory and schema concept is the tendency to localize the cause of depression within the individual, and to pay relatively less attention to the broader social, economic, and interpersonal context of depression (e.g., Coyne, 1976; Joiner & Coyne, 1999).

In an attempt to address these criticisms, a number of theorists (P. Gilbert & Allan, 1998; Price, 1972; Swallow, 2000) have proposed a model in which depression is conceptualized as the outworking of a biologically hardwired response pattern that has evolved to inhibit aggression and promote reconciliation following hierarchical or competitive defeat. An involuntary defeat strategy (IDS) is triggered and inhibits anger when one senses that one is losing (or will lose) an agonistic encounter with another person by generating a powerful affective state of inferiority, shame, worthlessness, sadness, hopelessness, helplessness, anhedonia, and anergia (depression). Escape from this negative state (and deactivation of the IDS response) is possible through flight or acceptance of defeat or subordinate status. However, when escape is blocked, the IDS may continue to intensify, resulting in an intense and prolonged depressive response (P. Gilbert & Allan, 1998; Swallow, 2000). In summary, according to this view, some very general schemas, such as the IDS, are hardwired products of evolutionary history as well as the learning history of the individual. Such an account implies that the maladaptive schemas observed in depression are part of an evolved submissive defense response designed to terminate the motive to keep trying to win in a no-win situation, with the general goal of self-protection in agonistic encounters with other people (Swallow, 2000).

It is important to note that although new ideas, such as ideas about IDS, may contribute to the further development of schema concept, cognitive theory, and clinical applications, it is clear that cognitive models have been responsive to the criticisms leveled at them and adapted as a result. For instance, consider the increasing recognition of the importance of emotional activation in CT so that schemas can be effectively targeted as well as recent attention to the importance of the interpersonal aspect of CT (e.g., Safran & Segal, 1996).

APPENDIX 2.1

Case Formulation Sheet

Name of client: _____

Name of therapist: _____

Problem list: _____

Date of formulation: _____

Step 1: Questions to elicit core schemas

Automatic thoughts

Can you think of one or two specific situations in which you felt a change in mood?

Describe situation:

Type of situation: work _____ relationship _____ other _____

Describe your thoughts in the situation:

Underlying assumptions, expectations, attitudes

What attitude or expectations do you hold about yourself, others, and the world in work, relationships, and other situations?

Finish these sentences:

If I do _____, others will do _____.

I am _____.

People are _____.

The world is _____.

It is important to (be/do/have) _____.

Early life experiences and life events

What early childhood experiences do you think are relevant?

Describe what was going on around the time you became depressed.

Relatedness and achievement themes

How important is it to you to be in a relationship?

How important is it to you to be successful?

Step 2: Hypothesized underlying schemas

Self:

Other:

World:

Future:

Interpersonal:

Step 3: Events that trigger schemas
Step 4: Automatic thoughts triggered by schemas
Step 5: Behavior triggered by schemas
Step 6: Ways in which schemas are maintained
Summary of working hypothesis:

APPENDIX 2.2

Stephanie's Case Formulation Sheet

Name of client: *Stephanie*
Name of therapist: *Dr. Jones*
Problem list: *Depression, social withdrawal*
Date of formulation: *May 5, 2003*

Step 1: Questions to elicit core schemas
Automatic thoughts
Can you think of one or two specific situations in which you felt a change in mood?
Saturday night
Describe situation: *was alone, writing in diary, started thinking of ex-boyfriend*
Type of situation: work _____ relationship _____ other ___X___
Describe your thoughts in the situation: *Why did he break up with me? I'll always be alone. I wasn't good enough for him.*

Underlying assumptions, expectations, attitudes
What attitude or expectations do you hold about yourself, others, and the world in work, relationships, and other situations?
If you're not in a relationship, then you're a loser.
Others are better than me.
You have to be smart, pretty, and athletic to be liked.
Finish these sentences:
    If I _____, others will _____.
    I am *not good enough.*
    People *are better than me.*
    The world is *a game.*
    It is important to (be/do/have) *loved.*

Early life experiences and life events
What early childhood experiences do you think are relevant?
Parents fought a lot; mother was intrusive and controlling.
Describe what was going on around the time you became depressed.
Boyfriend dumped me.

Relatedness and achievement themes
How important is it to you to be in a relationship? *Extremely important*
How important is it to you to be successful? *Pretty important*

Step 2: Hypothesized underlying schemas
Self: *I am unlovable.*
Other: *Others are better than me. Others' needs are more important.*
World: *The world is competitive.*
Future: *I am destined to be alone.*
Interpersonal: *If I assert myself, I'll be put down.*

Step 3: Events that trigger schema
Relationship breakup.

Step 4: Automatic thoughts triggered by schema
I'm not good enough.
I'll always be alone.
I'm a loser.

Step 5: Behavior triggered by schema
Submissiveness in relationships.
Social withdrawal.
Not able to express anger.
Tends to please others.

Step 6: Ways in which schema is maintained
Doesn't assert her needs, so others respond by being dominating and controlling.
Tends to be taken advantage of in relationships. Confirms her view that she is not good enough.

Summary of working hypothesis:

Automatic Thought Record

Situation	Mood	Thoughts
Describe what was going on when you noticed a change in your mood. Type of situation: Work _____ School _____ Home _____ Relationship _____ Other _____	Describe what you were feeling in the situation, and rate the intensity of the feeling on a scale of 0 to 100.	What was going through your mind? What did the situation say about you? What did the situation say about others? What did the situation say about your future? What did the situation say about the world? What did the situation say about your relationship? Describe any images that came to mind.

APPENDIX 2.4

Downward Arrow Technique Identifying Core Beliefs

1. About the self

Situation (from thought record)

_____

What does this say about me?

↓

_____

What does this say about me?

↓

_____

What does this say about me?

2. About others

Situation (from thought record)

_____

What does this say about other people?

↓

_____

What does this say about other people?

↓

_____

What does this say about other people?

3. About the world

Situation (from thought record)

_____

What does this say about the world?

↓

_____

What does this say about the world?

↓

_____

What does this say about the world?

From *Mind Over Mood: Change How You Feel by Changing How You Think* (pp. 136–138), by D. Greenberger and C. A. Padesky, 1995, New York: Guilford Press. Copyright 1995 by Guilford Press. Reprinted with permission.

APPENDIX 2.5

Interpersonal Schema Formulation Sheet

Step 1: Ask the client to think of people in his or her life that have made an impact (either positive or negative) on who he or she is today and explore the nature of the relationship, focusing on what the client learned as a result of the interaction.

Example:
Person: Harry
Relationship to Client: brother
Impact: I need to work harder than others do to succeed.

Step 2: Write down patterns noticed in relationships (e.g., lack of assertion, difficulty communicating conflict).

Step 3: What is the client's hypothesized attachment security? Choose from the following:

Secure: "I am OK; others are OK."
Anxious ambivalent: "I am not OK; others are OK."
Anxious avoidant: "I am OK; others are not OK."
Disorganized: "I am not OK; others are not OK."

Step 4: On Kiesler's interpersonal circumplex, where would you place the client's main interpersonal style? On this basis, what reactions are expected from those who interact with client?

Step 5: Create a working hypothesis of interpersonal schemas and how they are maintained.

APPENDIX 2.6

Stephanie's Continuum

Maladaptive schema: *I'm unlovable.*
Adaptive schema: *I'm lovable.*

Step 1: Rate yourself on the adaptive schema continuum.

X = 5%
_____

| 0% | 100% |
| Lovable | Lovable |

Step 2: Specify specific criteria for each endpoint of the adaptive schema.

0%	100%
Lovable	Lovable
▪ Not having any friends	▪ Having friends
▪ Never caring for others	▪ Being generous toward others
▪ Hurting others' feelings	▪ Being kind

Step 3: Rate yourself on each of the criteria specified.

X = 80%
_____

| 0% | 100% |
| Not having any friends | Having friends |

X = 50%
_____

| 0% | 100% |
| Never caring for others | Being generous toward others |

X = 75%
_____

| 0% | 100% |
| Hurting others' feelings | Being kind |

Step 3: Rerate yourself on the adaptive schema continuum.

X = 65%
_____

| 0% | 100% |
| Lovable | Lovable |

APPENDIX 2.7

Positive Data Log

Instructions: Describe your maladaptive schema and alternative schema in the space provided. Then, write down each piece of evidence in support of your alternate schema and the date and time when you observed the evidence. Be as specific as you can, and remember to write down all evidence in support of your alternative schema, regardless of how small or insignificant you might think it is.

Maladaptive schema: _____

Adaptive schema: _____

Date and time	Evidence in support of alternative schema

APPENDIX 2.8

Historical Test of Schema

Instructions:

1. For each period of your life, list the evidence that supports your maladaptive schema, and the evidence that does not support your maladaptive schema. Be as specific as possible.
2. Review the evidence, both supporting and not supporting, and write down a brief summary of what the evidence suggests.
3. Remember that perception, assumptions, and feelings are not evidence.

Maladaptive schema: _____

Age range: _____	
Evidence that supports maladaptive schema	**Evidence that does not support maladaptive schema**
Summary of evidence	

Age range: _____	
Evidence that supports maladaptive schema	**Evidence that does not support maladaptive schema**
Summary of evidence	

APPENDIX 2.9

Excerpt From Andrew's Historical Test of Schema

Instructions:
1. For each period of your life, list the evidence that supports your maladaptive schema, and the evidence that does not support your maladaptive schema. Be as specific as possible.
2. Review the evidence, both supporting and not supporting, and write down a brief summary of what the evidence suggests.
3. Remember that perception, assumptions, and feelings are not evidence.

Maladaptive schema: _____"I'm a failure."_____

Age range: 14 to 16	
Evidence that supports maladaptive schema	**Evidence that does not support maladaptive schema**
I didn't win the math competition. My father would always tell me that I could do better.	I received mostly As on my report card. I joined the football team. I had lots of friends.
Summary of evidence Between the ages of 14 and 16, my father's expectations of me were quite high, and I always felt I disappointed him. However, I actually accomplished a lot during that time period.	

APPENDIX 2.10

Core Belief Worksheet

Old core belief:

New belief:

Evidence that contradicts old core belief and supports new belief	Evidence that supports old core belief with reframe

REFERENCES

Abramson, L. Y., Metalsky, G. I., & Alloy, L. B. (1989). Hopelessness depression: A theory-based subtype of depression. *Psychological Review, 96,* 358–372.

Abramson, L. Y., Seligman, M. E., & Teasdale, J. (1978). Learned helplessness in humans: Critique and reformulation. *Journal of Abnormal Psychology, 87,* 49–74.

Antonuccio, D. O., Thomas, M., & Danton, W. G. (1997). A cost-effectiveness analysis of cognitive behavior therapy and fluoxetine (Prozac) in the treatment of depression. *Behavior Therapy, 28,* 187–210.

Beck, A. T. (1963). Thinking and depression: 1. Idiosyncratic content and cognitive distortions. *Archives of General Psychiatry, 9,* 324–333.

Beck, A. T. (1967). *Depression: Clinical experimental and theoretical aspects.* New York: Harper & Row.

Beck, A. T. (1987). Cognitive model of depression. *Journal of Cognitive Psychotherapy, 1,* 2–27.

Beck, A. T. (2002). Cognitive models of depression. In R. L. Leahy & T. E. Dowd (Eds.), *Clinical advances in cognitive psychotherapy: Theory and application* (pp. 29–61). New York: Springer Publishing Company.

Beck, A.T., Rush, J., Shaw, B. F., & Emery, G. (1979). *Cognitive therapy of depression.* New York: Guilford Press.

Beck, J. S. (1995). *Cognitive therapy: Basics and beyond.* New York: Guilford Press.

Bowlby, J. (1982). Attachment and loss: Retrospect and prospect. *American Journal of Orthopsychiatry, 52,* 664–678.

Coyne, J. C. (1976). Toward an interactional description of depression. *Journal for the Study of Interpersonal Processes, 39,* 28–40.

DeRubeis, R. J., Gelfand, L. A., Tang, T. Z., & Simons, A. D. (1999). Medications versus cognitive behavior therapy for severely depressed outpatients: Mega-analysis of four randomized comparisons. *American Journal of Psychiatry, 156,* 1007–1013.

Dobson, K. S., & Khatri, N. (2000). Cognitive therapy: Looking backward, looking forward. *Journal of Clinical Psychology, 56,* 907–923.

Dowd, E. T., & Courchaine, K. (2002). Implicit learning, tacit knowledge, and implications for stasis and change in cognitive psychotherapy. In R. L. Leahy & E. T. Dowd (Eds.), *Clinical advances in cognitive psychotherapy: Theory and application* (pp. 325–344). New York: Springer Publishing Company.

Gilbert, D. T. (1992). "How mental system believe": Reply. *American Psychologist, 47,* 670–671.

Gilbert, P., & Allan, S. (1998). The role of defeat and entrapment (arrested flight) in depression: An exploration of an evolutionary view. *Psychological Medicine, 28,* 585–598.

Gortner, E. T., Gollan, J. K., Dobson, K. S., & Jacobson, N. S. (1998). Cognitive–behavioral treatment for depression: Relapse prevention. *Journal of Consulting and Clinical Psychology, 66,* 377–384.

Greenberger, D., & Padesky, C. A. (1995). *Mind over mood: Change how you feel by changing how you think*. New York: Guilford Press.

Hill, C. R., & Safran, J. D. (1994). Assessing interpersonal schemas: Anticipated responses of significant others. *Journal of Social and Clinical Psychology, 13,* 366–379.

Ingram, R. E., Miranda, J., & Segal, Z. V. (1998). *Cognitive vulnerability to depression*. New York: Guilford Press.

Jacobson, N. S., Dobson, K. S., Truax, P. A., Addis, M. E., Koerner, K., Gollan, J. K., et al. (1996). A component analysis of cognitive–behavioral treatment for depression. *Journal of Consulting and Clinical Psychology, 64,* 295–304.

Jacobson, N. S., Dobson, K. S., Truax, P. A., Addis, M. E., Koerner, K., Gollan, J. K., et al. (2000, June 2). Do cognitive change strategies matter in cognitive therapy? *Prevention & Treatment, 3,* Article 25. Retrieved September 19, 2006, from http://journals.apa.org/prevention/volume3/pre0030025c.html

Joffe, R., Segal, Z., & Singer, W. (1996). Change in thyroid hormone levels following response to cognitive therapy for major depression. *American Journal of Psychiatry, 153,* 411–413.

Joiner, T., & Coyne, J. C. (1999). *The interactional nature of depression: Advances in interpersonal approaches*. Washington, DC: American Psychological Association.

Liotti, G. (2002). Patterns of attachment and the assessment of interpersonal schemata: Understanding and changing difficult patient-therapist relationships in cognitive psychotherapy. In R. L. Leahy & T. E. Dowd (Eds.), *Clinical advances in cognitive psychotherapy: Theory and application* (pp. 377–388). New York: Springer Publishing Company.

Miranda, J., Gross, J. J., Persons, J. B., & Hahn, J. (1998). Mood matters: Negative mood induction activates dysfunctional attitudes in women vulnerable to depression. *Cognitive Therapy and Research, 22,* 363–376.

Padesky, C. A. (1991). *International Cognitive Therapy Newsletter, 6,* 6–7.

Padesky, C. A. (1994). Schema change processes in cognitive therapy. *Clinical Psychology and Psychotherapy, 1,* 267–278.

Persons, J. B. (1989). *Cognitive therapy in practice: A case formulation approach*. New York: Norton.

Persons, J. B., Davidson, J., & Tompkins, M. A. (2001). *Essential components of cognitive–behavior therapy for depression*. Washington, DC: American Psychological Association.

Price, J. S. (1972). Genetic and phylogenetic aspects of mood variation. *International Journal of Mental Health, 1*(1–2), 124–144.

Safran, J. D. (1990). Towards a refinement of cognitive therapy in light of interpersonal theory: I. Theory. *Clinical Psychology Review, 10,* 87–105.

Safran, J. D., & Segal, Z. V. (1990). *Interpersonal process in cognitive therapy*. Northvale, NJ: Jason Aronson.

Safran, J., & Segal, Z. V. (1996). *Interpersonal process in cognitive therapy*. New York: Jason Aronson.

Safran, J. D., Vallis, T. M., Segal, Z. V., & Shaw, B. F. (1986). Assessment of core cognitive processes in cognitive therapy. *Cognitive Therapy and Research, 10,* 509–526.

Schacter, D. L. (1987). Implicit expressions of memory in organic amnesia: Learning of new facts and associations. *Human Neurobiology, 6,* 107–118.

Segal, Z. V., Gemar, M., & Williams, S. (1999). Differential cognitive response to a mood challenge following successful cognitive therapy of pharmacotherapy for unipolar depression. *Journal of Abnormal Psychology, 108,* 3–10.

Segal, Z. V., & Shaw, B. F. (1986). Cognition in depression: A reappraisal of Coyne and Gotlib's critique. *Cognitive Therapy and Research, 10,* 671–693.

Shean, G. (2001). A critical look at the assumptions of cognitive therapy. *Psychiatry, 64,* 158–164.

Swallow, S. R. (2000). A cognitive behavioural perspective on the involuntary defeat strategy. In L. Sloman & P. Gilbert (Eds.), *Subordination and defeat: An evolutionary approach to mood disorders and their therapy* (pp. 181–198). Mahwah, NJ: Erlbaum.

Young, J. E. (1990). *Cognitive therapy for personality disorders: A schema-focused approach*. Sarasota, FL: Professional Resource Press.

Young, J. E. (1994). *Cognitive therapy for personality disorders: A schema-focused approach*. Sarasota, FL: Professional Resource Press.

Young, J. E. (1999). *Cognitive therapy for personality disorders: A schema-focused approach* (3rd ed.). Sarasota, FL: Professional Resource Press.

Young, J. E., Klosko, J. S., & Weishaar, M. E. (2003). *Schema therapy: A practitioner's guide*. New York: Guilford Press.

3

EARLY MALADAPTIVE SCHEMAS IN CHRONIC DEPRESSION

LAWRENCE P. RISO, RACHEL E. MADDUX, AND
NOELLE TURINI SANTORELLI

"I've been depressed as long as I can remember."

"Everyone says I'm a depressive."

"I'm not sure what you mean by *normal mood*. I've always been this way."

"Somehow I've managed to get by at work, but deep down I am always depressed and unhappy."

"Over the past 10 years, I haven't been without my depression for more than a week or two. It's always there in the background."

Chronic depression is common (19% of depressed patients; Keller & Hanks, 1995), difficult to treat (Howland, 2004; Keitner & Cardemil, 2004), and a significant public health problem (Howland, 1993). Once of limited interest to psychiatry and psychology, chronic depression is now a problem receiving considerable attention in the literature. For instance, a computerized PsycINFO search revealed more than 400 journal articles addressing some aspect of chronic depression and three edited books focusing on chronic depression specifically (Akiskal & Cassano, 1997; Alpert & Fava, 2004; Kocsis & Klein, 1995). In this chapter, we describe the different forms of chronic depression, review the distinction between chronic depression and nonchronic depression, and present the rationale, tools, and techniques for a schema-focused approach for chronic patients. A case presentation at the end of the chapter illustrates how to conceptualize and treat an individual with chronic depression using a schema-focused approach. Although major depressive disorder was discussed in chapter 2 (this volume), a separate chapter on chronic depression is essential because it is now well recognized that chronic depression is clearly distinguishable from other depressive disorders with regard to clinical, personality, and demographic characteristics (described more fully later).

The *Diagnostic and Statistical Manual of Mental Disorders* (4th ed., text revision; *DSM–IV–TR*; American Psychiatric Association, 2000) recognizes two major forms of chronic depression: dysthymic disorder and major depressive disorder, chronic type. Both require a duration of 2 years or longer with no more than 2 months without symptoms. The criteria for dysthymic disorder and chronic major depressive disorder overlap, although the symptoms for chronic major depressive disorder are more severe. Most individuals with dysthymic disorder experience symptomatic exacerbations meeting criteria for major depressive disorder and then return to their dysthymic baseline (known as *double depression*; Keller & Shapiro, 1982).

Several studies have compared the different subgroups of chronic depression on a number of clinical validators; however, few differences emerged. For instance, dysthymic disorder and double depression are similar in terms of a family history of mood and personality disorders (Donaldson, Klein, Riso, & Schwartz, 1997), childhood adversity (Lizardi et al., 1995), Axis I and Axis II comorbidity (Klein, Riso, & Anderson, 1993; Pepper et al., 1995), and course and outcome (Hayden & Klein, 2001; Klein, Schwartz, Rose, & Leader, 2000). Moreover, patients with double depression and chronic major depressive disorder are similar with respect to demographic variables, comorbidity, family history, and response to antidepressant medication (McCullough et al., 2000). Thus, for many purposes, using the broader rubric *chronic depression* seems more appropriate than emphasizing the finer-grained distinctions among the different *DSM–IV* subgroups.

What factors distinguish chronic from nonchronic depression? A number of potential factors have been examined including biological factors, temperament and personality, early adversity, chronic stressors, and cognitive factors. Studies of biological variables have yet to identify consistent differences between chronic and nonchronic groups. Studies of hypercortisolemia (Gasto et al., 1994; Miller, Norman, & Dow, 1986), growth hormone secretion (Maes, Vandewoude, Maes, Schott, & Cosyns, 1989), sleep physiology (Appelboom-Fondu, Kerkhofs, & Mendlewicz, 1988), and neurotransmitter functioning (Ravindran, Bialik, Brown, & Lapierre, 1994) revealed that the abnormalities in chronic depression are similar to or less pronounced than those found in nonchronic cases (see Riso, Miyatake, & Thase, 2002, for a review). Some evidence has been found for increased rates of subclinical hypothyroidism for subgroups of individuals with chronic depression (Scott, Barker, & Eccleston, 1988; Tappy, Randin, Schwed, Werthermimer, & Memarchand-Beraud, 1987). No genetic (twin or adoption) studies of chronic depression are available, although chronic depression does run in families (Klein et al., 1995) and a familial loading of chronic depression predicts a poorer course for depression (Hayden & Klein, 2001).

By contrast, highly consistent differences between chronic and non-chronic depression have been found for developmental factors, personality, and cognitive variables. Chronically depressed groups consistently exhibit higher rates of Axis II personality disorders (Pepper et al., 1995; Riso et al., 1996) and there is some evidence that neuroticism is important for its long-term course (Duggan, Lee, & Murray, 1990; Weissman, Prusoff, & Klerman, 1978). Consistent support has also been found for the role of developmental factors in chronic depression. Compared with nonchronic depression, individuals with chronic depression report poorer parental bonding (Lizardi et al., 1995) and more insecure attachment (Fonagy et al., 1996). Adverse early home environments also predict long-term outcome of chronic depression, even after clinical and demographic variables are controlled for at baseline (Brown & Moran, 1994; Durbin, Klein, & Schwartz, 2000).

Our group examined core beliefs[1] in individuals with chronic depression compared with those with nonchronic depression (Riso et al., 2003). The results revealed that chronically depressed individuals exhibit elevated rates of maladaptive core beliefs even after controlling for both severity of depression and personality disorder symptoms. Moreover, maladaptive core beliefs discriminated between chronic and nonchronic groups more strongly than did personality disorder symptoms. The core beliefs that best discriminated chronic from nonchronic depression were themes of impaired autonomy (belief in low self-efficacy and a demanding environment) and overvigilance (rigid expectations for performance and a fear of making mistakes). Other work reported high rates of dysfunctional attitudes in chronic versus nonchronic groups (Klein, Taylor, Dickstein, & Harding, 1988).

In summary, a number of potential determinants of chronic depression have been studied. Neuroendocrine and neurotransmitter studies have consistently failed to distinguish between chronically and nonchronically depressed groups. However, support has been found for the role of early adversity, personality disorders, and cognitive variables. In particular, a number of observations are consistent with the role of maladaptive schemas in the development and maintenance of chronic depression. First, the findings of poor parental bonding and insecure attachment in chronic depression are

---

[1] The terms *schema* and *core belief* both represent thematic cognitive material and are used interchangeably in this chapter. However, others use the term *schema* to refer to implicit cognitive structure or the interconnectedness among cognitive elements and the term *core belief* to refer to the consciously available content of a schema (Clark & Beck, 1999).

consistent with the theoretical origins of core beliefs in early relationships. Second, core beliefs are more prominent in chronic versus nonchronic depression. Third, core beliefs discriminate between chronic and nonchronic depression more strongly than do personality disorders. Fourth, maladaptive core beliefs appear to be stable trait-like belief structures (Riso et al., in press). It is interesting to note that depressed mood can lead to the activation and accessibility of maladaptive schemas (Higgins, King, & Mavin, 1982). Thus, chronic depression may involve the mutually reinforcing factors of chronically depressed mood and chronic schema activation.

TREATMENT OF CHRONIC PATIENTS

This section focuses on the treatment of chronic depression. We address the need for a focus on schemas and the contributions of early adversity and maladaptive coping behaviors to this clinical problem. We conclude the section with specific interventional strategies.

Why Focus on Schemas?

The available research points to an important role for maladaptive schemas in the development and maintenance of chronic depression. Moreover, chronic depression presents difficulties for traditional cognitive therapy. Thase et al. (1994) found that cognitive–behavioral therapy (CBT) for depression was slower acting and less efficacious for chronic cases and noted that patients with chronic depression had difficulty "grasping or embracing the collaborative–empirical or self-help aspects of CBT" (p. 212). Although traditional or short-term CBT often assumes patients have specific clear-cut problems to target (Young, 1995), this is rarely the case for patients with chronic depression. They may have years (or even decades) of depressed mood, widespread interpersonal problems, unfulfilled ambitions, and dissatisfaction with their work and current relationships. When asked for a specific list of target problems for therapy, patients with chronic depression often report a general malaise and dissatisfaction with life. Attempts to probe further may result in a litany of complaints including loneliness, unassertiveness, feelings of detachment from friends and romantic partners, poor motivation, job dissatisfaction, identity confusion, difficulty getting along with family members, and low self-esteem. The CBT therapist who attempts to design thought records, behavioral experiments, and homework for each problem area in a piecemeal fashion will quickly become overwhelmed. Thus, conceptualizing patients with chronic depression in terms of generalized maladaptive schemas helps organize a large number of complaints under a common theme. In the following case example, the patient seemingly has a number of difficulties in several areas of his life:

> Andrew described being depressed, having low self-esteem, and feeling lonely for as long as he could remember. A review of his background revealed that before his divorce he had endured his wife's multiple affairs over several years, which made him feel dejected and unwanted. He described being painfully shy around women and spoke of feelings of unrequited affection for women whom he had met over the years. At his worst moments, he even felt insecure about his relationship with his two sons.

In therapy, these difficulties were organized under one schema: unlovability, or the belief that he did not possess the qualities that would inspire others to love and care about him. The unlovability schema was in part related to numerous experiences of painful rejection by his parents at an early age. Identifying the unlovability schema helped the patient consolidate his seemingly disparate set of complaints and brought structure and focus to the therapy. The patient felt less overwhelmed and instead of believing that he had problems in virtually every area of his life, he now saw himself as possessing a more circumscribed problem of an unlovability schema that cropped up in a number of situations like an Achilles' heel. As a consequence, he felt more motivated for therapy and more hopeful about being able to make changes in his life. Many of his thought records, behavioral experiments, and other therapeutic exercises focused on shifting this schema to a more functional and accurate view of how important, desirable, and lovable he was to others.

Finally, along with a lack of clear-cut problems, patients with chronic depression often have patterns of thinking and behaving that are extremely resistant to change. They may report that they understand intellectually that their cognitions are distorted, but their emotional reactions remain unchanged. Techniques that address only dysfunctional cognition at a superficial level of cognition (e.g., automatic thoughts) may leave patients hopeless about being able to improve their mood.

Early Adversity

The Cognitive Conceptualization Diagram (J. Beck, 1995) is an excellent way to organize clinical data and begin treatment planning (Figure 3.1). In light of the evidence described earlier for adverse early environments in individuals with chronic depression, the "Relevant Childhood Data" section of the diagram deserves special attention in chronic cases. Many patients with chronic depression report traumatic experiences. Others report subtle and insidious early adverse experiences such as critical or invalidating

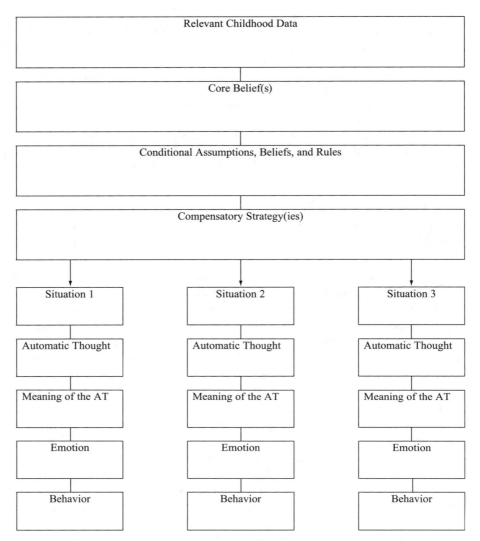

Figure 3.1. Case conceptualization diagram. Copyright 1993 by Judith Beck. Adapted with permission.

environments or environments with emotional coldness and low levels of warmth. These subtle adversities can actually have a greater impact on schema development than traumas because of the constant bombardment of negative messages. Moreover, criticism from caretakers, in particular, directly supplies the negative content for the development of a schema (e.g., "Stop acting like an idiot!" "You are a total scatterbrain"; Gibb et al., 2001). Along with the responses of caretakers, it is also essential to consider criticism and rejection from peers (Gibb, Abramson, & Alloy, 2004). Often physical development will play an important role in the responses of peers. One patient's severe acne as an adolescent elicited rejection from peers and contributed to a defectiveness schema. Another patient described being small and underdeveloped. His peers treated him as helpless and weak, which contributed to his vulnerability schema.

Coping Behaviors

The "Compensatory Strategies" section of the Cognitive Conceptualization Diagram includes behavioral strategies that patients use in an attempt to cope with or compensate for painful schemas (J. Beck, 1995). Coping or compensatory strategies for schemas may involve schema avoidance, schema surrender, and schema compensation (Young, Klosko, & Weishaar, 2003). *Schema avoidance* refers to an attempt to arrange one's life so that the painful schema is never activated. For instance, patients with an abandonment schema may avoid close relationships. They may also avoid thoughts, emotions, and images that trigger the schema by abusing substances, binge eating, or overworking. *Schema surrender* refers to a process whereby perceptions and behaviors are altered so that they conform to the schema. Thus, patients may choose partners who treat them in ways that are consistent with their negative self-views. *Schema compensation* refers to an attempt to counteract or neutralize the schema by acting in a way that is opposite to the content of the schema. Thus, patients with an underlying failure schema may become extremely perfectionistic or push themselves relentlessly at work. These extreme or forced attempts usually overshoot the mark and end up perpetuating the schema (Young, 1995).

Interventional Strategies

Years of unrelenting depression can render chronic patients hopeless about their future and their prospects for improving during therapy. Therefore, along with a focus on schemas, early symptom reduction is extremely important. The lack of any tangible sign of improvement in the first few weeks of therapy can reinforce the patient's hopelessness and defectiveness schemas. Thus, early on, behavioral activation strategies such as activity scheduling and assertiveness training along with targeted sleep interventions should be considered.

Once a schema has been identified, the therapist can assist the patient in examining the validity and usefulness of the schema, as well as arriving at alternative or more realistic beliefs. The Core Belief Worksheet (CBW; Beck, 1995; see Appendix 2.10) is a useful format for weighing the evidence for and against a schema and its related core belief. The CBW helps patients to articulate the core belief (or schema), rate the extent to which they agree with it, and systematically evaluate the data that support or refute it. The level of confidence in the belief is rerated after the data is examined, and the process is often continued over many sessions. The CBW helps patients discover how they exaggerate the "truthfulness" of the belief and establish some distance from inaccurate and destructive ideas. Over time, the CBW will help patients develop more accurate and functional alternative beliefs.

Another useful technique in addressing negative schemas is guided imagery. We have found the descriptions of guided imagery provided by Beck (1995); Edwards (1990); Layden, Newman, Freeman, and Morse (1993); and Waller, Kennerley, and Ohanian (see chap. 7, this volume) to be particularly helpful. Imagery exercises can be emotionally evocative and powerful vehicles for corrective experiences, although they must be handled with the utmost sensitivity. Patients who believe they are defective and unlovable because of the sexual abuse they once experienced may need to reprocess the trauma via imagery, actively and rationally responding to the faulty conclusions they had drawn about themselves. Of course, great care and caution needs to be exercised in such a situation to ensure that the patient understands the nature of and rationale for the procedure, and that he or she agrees to it in a collaborative discussion. In addition, care must be taken to ensure sufficient time is allotted in the session for the debriefing that follows. The imagery and reprocessing may be repeated over many sessions, until the patient is better equipped to rationally respond to the negative beliefs and connotations that the sexual abuse once engendered.

Guided imagery may be used in other ways. For example, patients can deliberately manipulate their images to "rewrite" a distressing outcome. One patient's image involved being helplessly berated by his intensely critical father when he was 9 years old (described later in the case illustration). By walking into the image as an adult, he could explain to the boy (i.e., himself at age 9) that his father was an extremely volatile person in the midst of an outburst, possibly related to his alcoholism. His criticisms and rantings at that moment, or any other for that matter, could hardly be construed as an accurate appraisal of anyone's character or abilities.

Role playing is another useful method of undermining problematic core beliefs and schemas. Therapist and patient can take turns playing the role of the schema, versus that of the healthy alternative viewpoint. This point–counterpoint technique (Young, 1995) allows for the brainstorming of many rational responses to the schema, under conditions of high affect and high sensory involvement. In a similar way, therapist and patient can role play important interpersonal situations in the patient's life that typically evoke schematic reactions (e.g., arguments with a parent; being criticized by a colleague). Such an exercise affords patients the chance to practice more adaptive cognitive and behavioral responses while validating the emotions that have been evoked by the high-risk situation. Through repetitions and constructive corrections, the patient learns to counteract even well established schemas and their concomitant emotions and behaviors, thus providing vital new interpersonal skills.

Patients with chronic depression often have schemas of helplessness, weakness, and inadequacy that lead to passivity during treatment. Thus, therapists must guard against a tendency to become overly directive and dominant during sessions, which will only breed more passivity. According to the interpersonal theory of Donald Kiesler (1983, 1996), dominance and submission are reciprocal tendencies. That is, patients who are submissive in session present an interpersonal pull for therapists to become more dominant (see also McCullough, 2000). However, this is an interpersonal trap in therapy because becoming more directive brings on the reciprocal tendency for patients to be even more passive and submissive. Consider this example:

> *Patient:* There's really nowhere to turn. You know, nobody who really cares. I just don't know how to climb out of this. I'm totally at a loss.
>
> *Therapist:* I'm sure your wife still cares. You really need to talk to her.
>
> *Patient:* You think so?
>
> *Therapist:* Yes. You need to be really honest and straightforward. This is no time to mince words.
>
> *Patient:* So the direct approach, huh? I guess you're right. But what should I say? I'd probably screw it up.

In this example, the therapist is getting deeper and deeper into telling the patient how to solve problems and is setting the stage for more and more passivity from the patient.

Other patients exhibit hostility toward therapists, which pulls for more hostility from the therapist. This dynamic occurs because friendliness and hostility are *corresponding* interpersonal tendencies (friendliness pulls for friendliness and hostility pulls for hostility). Remaining cognizant of the reciprocal and corresponding dynamics will help therapists recognize and respond to these challenging interpersonal pulls. At times, the therapist can even strategically vary his or her interpersonal stance. For instance, a therapist can actually take a passive stance (e.g., "I feel a little stumped myself") to pull for a more active and problem-solving approach from patients (e.g., "Well, I guess one thing I can do is talk to my wife").

RETAINING THE BASIC PRINCIPLES OF COGNITIVE THERAPY

A focus on schemas in the treatment of chronic depression differs from traditional cognitive therapy by placing a greater emphasis on early childhood experiences, making greater use of emotive techniques such as guided imagery, using the therapeutic relationship as a vehicle of change, and conducting a lengthier course of therapy because of the resistance to change of underlying schemas. Despite the somewhat different emphasis, it is essential to maintain the basic elements of traditional cognitive therapy including keeping the therapy active and directive, using cognitive therapy techniques, emphasizing self-help homework, and conducting structured sessions (Young, 1995). Most of all, it is essential to develop a list of clear therapeutic goals. Vague and global ideas are in need of specifics to decrease the chronic patient's confusion, hopelessness, and feelings of being overwhelmed with problems.

CASE ILLUSTRATION

The following is an actual case example of an individual with chronic depression. The cognitive therapy used during treatment was augmented with a schema-focuses approach. The basic demographic and clinical characteristics of the case were altered to preserve confidentiality.

Diagnostic Information and Background

Harold was a 52-year-old man who lived with his wife and two daughters (ages 10 and 13). He was employed as an insurance adjuster for a large insurance company. His chief complaints included chronic depression and marital discord. He met *DSM–IV* criteria for dysthymic disorder, which had been present for over 20 years. His level of depression had fluctuated over the years and he had experienced a number of superimposed major depressive episodes. He described feeling anxious much of the time but had no history of a frank anxiety disorder. He exhibited a number of avoidant personality disorder features including a fear of being criticized or ridiculed, being shy and reserved around others, and being unwilling to take interpersonal risks, although he did not meet full criteria for avoidant personality disorder. Harold had difficulty identifying determinants of his depression, although he mentioned not getting along with his wife and experiencing minor financial pressures as contributing factors. Although he described treatment with his previous therapist as "helpful," he still felt depressed much of the time and said that he felt there was "more to do."

As a child, Harold was well behaved although early in life he struggled in school. In the fifth grade, his extreme nearsightedness was discovered. His parents had failed to take him for regular checkups and his nearsightedness went undiagnosed for years. His difficulties in school apparently were a result of his poor vision. When he received corrective lenses, his school performance improved dramatically. Nonetheless, years of struggling in classes had left him feeling "incompetent" and like a "screw-up."

Harold's parents were described as neglectful and highly critical. Both abused substances and their behavior toward Harold was extremely erratic. His father in particular would yell and scream at Harold with little or no provocation. A particularly traumatic event occurred when Harold was 10 years old. Harold was taken to his grandparents' house, apparently for a visit. Without Harold noticing, his parents got back into their car and drove away, abandoning him; he lived at his grandparents' house for several years.

Conceptualization in Terms of Core Beliefs

Although Harold came across as likeable, competent, and intelligent, his days were filled with distorted thinking and beliefs that he was an incompetent screw-up with little to offer anyone. Because Harold had recently been in cognitive therapy with a different therapist, he was already quite skilled at identifying automatic negative thoughts and coming up with more balanced alternative thinking. However, despite his diligence and proficiency with thought records, he continued to feel depressed and dissatisfied with his life.

Treatment quickly focused on assessing Harold's more generalized negative core beliefs. Through a careful developmental history and an examination of underlying themes among his negative automatic thoughts, the therapist conceptualized many of Harold's difficulties as being related to the core beliefs of incompetence and vulnerability. His core belief of incompetence had its roots in the incessant berating and criticism from his father and his early difficulties in school. His core belief of vulnerability (to random events) began with the erratic and unpredictable behavior of his parents and the traumatic abandonment he experienced when he was left behind at his grandparents' house. Both core beliefs were actually elaborated on and reinforced by the choices Harold made during his life (i.e., schema surrender). He had very low expectations for himself and was consumed with the possibility of a sudden unexpected disaster in his life. Thus, he never tried to advance in his career because he believed that with the added responsibility, he would make a terrible mistake and lose his job. He kept the same job for 10 years even though he found it painfully boring and had grown to hate it. In Harold's mind, at least it was safe.

Harold conducted his life as though a disaster would strike at any moment and compensated by being compulsive, perfectionistic, regimented, and overly vigilant about the family's finances. His perfectionism kept him in the office until the evening hours as he labored to produce flawless reports. His anxiety about the family's finances prevented him from going on vacations or on outings with his wife and children. He avoided challenging situations for fear that he would fail, and rarely initiated interactions with others for fear they would quickly discover that he was a total screw-up. For instance, Harold described carpooling with the same coworker for more than 3 years and having never once started a conversation with her during their ride to work. He was unassertive, particularly with his wife, and reluctant to self-disclose personal thoughts and feelings because he felt it would make him appear "weak." Not only was he reluctant to express his affection for her, but he also tended to harbor resentments.

Interventions

One of the primary interventions during therapy was activity scheduling. Activity scheduling provided early symptom reduction and helped to counteract Harold's hopelessness and keep him engaged in treatment. At first, Harold had difficulty identifying potentially pleasurable activities. Rather than coming up with activities that he would like to do (e.g., go bowling, watch a movie with his wife), he tended to generate activities that he needed to do (e.g., paperwork, pay bills). The therapist helped Harold to distinguish between these two types of activities. Over time, he discovered which activities were linked to positive mood shifts and which were simply obligatory tasks that did not necessarily provide a lift for him. Throughout therapy he was also able to discover how his perfectionism at work and his overvigilance with money prevented him from engaging in more enjoyable and potentially mood-lifting activities.

The Core Belief Worksheet (see Appendix 2.10) was used to examine Harold's negative core beliefs and to search for more functional alternative beliefs. However, during this exercise, Harold often pointed out that although he was able to "intellectually" recognize that his beliefs were inaccurate, he continued to "feel" their impact. The therapist noticed that when Harold went through the worksheet, it appeared to be an intellectual exercise in which he remained emotionally disengaged. He was not accessing emotionally charged material. Therefore, with Harold's permission, a series of guided imagery exercises were used in therapy to reveal thoughts and memories that were more emotionally connected to his core beliefs. Some of the images involved actual memories of Harold's father's harsh criticism. He related one image in which his father made him enter a crawl space under their house to retrieve a piece of piping. Harold was terrified and then heard his father screaming over and over to hurry up and calling him an idiot for taking so long. Over time, guided imagery helped Harold to better understand the origins of his negative beliefs and to dismantle the erroneous evidence that supported them (e.g., "My father was a very troubled man with a severe alcohol problem. I guess he was in no position to judge my intelligence").

A series of behavioral experiments also helped to dispute Harold's negative core beliefs and sharpen his poorly developed social skills. On one occasion he tested the negative prediction that his wife would see him as weak if he self-disclosed something personal to her. On another occasion, he tested out negative predictions of what would happen if he initiated casual conversations with coworkers (e.g., with the woman with whom he carpooled). In each instance, Harold participated in role plays in session first to help counteract distorted and interfering cognitions and to hone his skills before he attempted the new behavior. When Harold actually engaged in these new behaviors, he was pleasantly surprised by the positive interactions that resulted with his wife and coworkers, and these experiences in turn helped to dismantle his negative core beliefs.

Harold's core belief of incompetence often required special attention to the therapeutic relationship. In one session, Harold was confronted by the therapist about the increasingly long list of agenda items he was bringing to therapy sessions. They were far too lengthy to be addressed in a single session. After some probing, Harold revealed that he often felt incompetent during therapy sessions and that his long list of agenda items would make the therapist see him as a cooperative and competent person, even if they were distracting and cumbersome for the therapy. The therapist invited Harold to check out his assumption against the therapist's actual opinion of him, which resulted in a highly productive exchange. The therapist was able to disclose feelings of respect, caring, and affection for Harold that directly contradicted Harold's earlier perceptions.

In summary, the therapy primarily focused on activity scheduling, negative core beliefs of incompetence and vulnerability, and behavioral experiments related to these core beliefs. Considerable therapeutic effort was expended on managing the therapeutic relationship to keep Harold from feeling subjugated by the therapist and to keep him engaged in treatment. The therapeutic relationship was also instrumental in helping Harold counteract his core belief of incompetence. Treatment lasted approximately 1 year and Harold met most of his stated goals. At the end of therapy, Harold's depression had improved considerably, with only mild dysphoria remaining. He attributed his enhanced outlook, improved skills, and new behavioral strategies primarily to the exploration of his core beliefs. At the end of treatment, Harold was able to warmly shake hands and thank the therapist, demonstrating his newfound ability to take interpersonal risks, self-disclose, and connect with others.

CONCLUSIONS AND UNRESOLVED ISSUES

There is accumulating evidence for the role of maladaptive schemas in the development and maintenance of chronic depression. We outlined strategies for eliciting and remediating schema-level problems. In light of the tendency toward global thinking in this group, it is essential that the focus on schemas does not deteriorate into an abstract, unfocused, and poorly structured course of therapy. Our case example illustrates how working on a patient's schemas can be incorporated into treatment while retaining structured sessions and a focus on the core skill-building elements of cognitive therapy.

Despite the promise of schema-level interventions with individuals with chronic depression, several questions and areas for future work remain. For instance, the concept of maladaptive schemas and core beliefs is in need of additional theoretical development. Maladaptive schemas are purportedly related to early experience, but there is little theory to account for this process or to understand how different types of developmental experiences lead to particular types of schemas. Future work may profit by incorporating attachment theory, which attempts to relate specific attachment schemas to specific developmental experiences. In this regard, the still-in-development two-dimensional model of attachment consisting of avoidant and anxious attachment dimensions (Brennan, Clark, & Shaver, 1998; Fraley & Shaver, 2000) warrants additional research attention within the clinical–cognitive literature.

A related issue is the measurement of maladaptive schemas. The most widely used measure is Young's (1995) Schema Questionnaire. However, this measure of maladaptive schemas needs additional validation, including an examination of how it may be affected by current mood state and the problem of the extensive overlap among the 16 schemas.

Finally, additional treatment outcome research is needed. There is now strong support for the efficacy of the cognitive–behavioral analysis system of psychotherapy (CBASP), a therapy designed specifically for chronic depression (Keller et al., 2000; McCullough, 2000). It is interesting to note, however, that CBASP does not focus on maladaptive schemas. Thus, future work is needed to examine whether or not a schema approach is needed to alleviate the symptoms of chronic depression and whether there are any advantages of a schema-focused approach over CBASP. It is also possible that certain subgroups of patients with chronic depression are better suited to either CBASP or schema-focused therapy and additional research may help identify patient characteristics to help match patients with chronic depression to the psychotherapeutic approaches available.

REFERENCES

Akiskal, H. S., & Cassano, G. B. (Eds.). (1997). *Dysthymia and the spectrum of chronic depressions.* New York: Guilford Press.

Alpert, J., & Fava, M. (Eds.). (2004). *Handbook of chronic depression: Diagnosis and therapeutic management.* New York: Marcel Dekker.

American Psychiatric Association. (2000). *Diagnostic and statistical manual of mental disorders* (4th ed., text rev.). Washington, DC: Author.

Appelboom-Fondu, J., Kerkhofs, M., & Mendlewicz, J. (1988). Depression in adolescents and young adults—polysomnographic and neuroendocrine aspects. *Journal of Affective Disorders, 14,* 35–40.

Beck, J. S. (1995). *Cognitive therapy: Basics and beyond.* New York: Guilford Press.

Brennan, K. A., Clark, C. L., & Shaver, P. R. (1998). Self-report measurement of adult romantic attachment: An integrative overview. In J. A. Simpson & W. S. Rholes (Eds.), *Attachment theory and close relationships* (pp. 46–76). New York: Guilford Press.

Brown, G. W., & Moran, P. (1994). Clinical and psychosocial origins of chronic depressive episodes I: A community survey. *British Journal of Psychiatry, 165,* 447–456.

Clark, D. A., & Beck, A. T. (1999). *Scientific foundations of cognitive theory and therapy of depression.* New York: Wiley.

Donaldson, S. K., Klein, D. N., Riso, L. P., & Schwartz, J. E. (1997). Comorbidity between dysthymic and major depressive disorders: A family study. *Journal of Affective Disorders, 42,* 103–111.

Duggan, C. F., Lee, A. S., & Murray, R. M. (1990). Does personality predict long-term outcome in depression? *British Journal of Psychiatry, 157,* 19–24.

Durbin, C. E., Klein, D. N., & Schwartz, J. E. (2000). Predicting the 2 1/2 year outcome of dysthymia disorder: The roles of childhood adversity and family history of psychopathology. *Journal of Consulting and Clinical Psychology, 68,* 57–63.

Edwards, D. J. A. (1990). Cognitive therapy and the restructuring of early memories through guided imagery. *Journal of Cognitive Psychotherapy: An International Quarterly, 4,* 33–50.

Fonagy, P., Leigh, T., Steel, M., Steele, H., Kennedy, R., Mattoon, G., et al. (1996). The relation of attachment status, psychiatric classification and response to psychotherapy. *Journal of Consulting and Clinical Psychology, 64,* 22–31.

Fraley, R. C., & Shaver, P. R. (2000). Adult romantic attachment: Theoretical developments, emerging controversies, and unanswered questions. *Review of General Psychology, 4*, 132–154.

Gasto, C., Vallejo, J., Menchon, J. M., Catalian, R., Otero, A., Martinez de Osaba, M. J., et al. (1994). Platelet serotonin-binding and dexamethosone suppression test in melancholia and dysthymia. *European Psychiatry, 9*, 281–287.

Gibb, B. E., Abramson, L. Y., & Alloy, L. B. (2004). Emotional maltreatment from parents, verbal peer victimization, and cognitive vulnerability to depression. *Cognitive Therapy and Research, 28*, 1–21.

Gibb, B. E., Alloy, L. B., Abramson, L. Y., Rose, D. T., Whitehouse, W. G., Donovan, P., et al. (2001). History of childhood maltreatment, negative cognitive styles, and episodes of depression in adulthood. *Cognitive Therapy and Research, 25*, 425–446.

Hayden, E. P., & Klein, D. N. (2001). Predicting the outcome of dysthymic disorder at 5-year follow-up: The impact of familial psychopathology, early adversity, personality, comorbidity, and chronic stress. *American Journal of Psychiatry, 158*, 1864–1870.

Higgins, E. T., King, G. A., & Mavin, G. H. (1982). Individual construct accessibility and subjective impressions and recall. *Journal of Personality and Social Psychology, 43*, 35–47.

Howland, R. H. (1993). Health status, health care utilization, and medical comorbidity in dysthymia. *International Journal of Psychiatry Medicine, 23*, 211–238.

Howland, R. H. (2004). Psychopharmacology of dysthymia. In J. Alpert & M. Fava (Eds.), *Handbook of chronic depression: Diagnosis and therapeutic management* (pp. 139–158). New York: Marcel Dekker.

Keitner, G. I., & Cardemil, E. V. (2004). Psychotherapy for chronic depressive disorders. In J. Alpert & M. Fava (Eds.), *Handbook of chronic depression: Diagnosis and therapeutic management* (pp. 159–182). New York: Marcel Dekker.

Keller, M. B., & Hanks, D. L. (1995). Course and natural history of chronic depression. In J. H. Kocsis and D. N. Klein (Eds.), *Diagnosis and treatment of chronic depression* (pp. 58–72). New York: Guilford Press.

Keller, M. B., McCullough, J. P., Klein, D. N., Arnow, B., Dunner, D. L., Gelenberg, A. J., et al. (2000). A comparison of nefazodone, the cognitive behavioral-analysis system of psychotherapy, and their combination for the treatment of chronic depression. *The New England Journal of Medicine, 342*, 1462–1470.

Keller, M. B., & Shapiro, R. W. (1982). "Double depression": Superimposition of acute depressive episodes on chronic depressive disorders. *American Journal of Psychiatry, 139*, 438–442.

Kiesler, D. J. (1983). The 1982 Interpersonal Circle: A taxonomy for complementarity in human transactions. *Psychological Review, 90*, 185–214.

Kiesler, D. J. (1996). *Contemporary interpersonal theory and research: Personality, psychopathology, and psychotherapy.* New York: Wiley.

Klein, D. N., Riso, L. P., & Anderson, R. L. (1993). DSM–III–R dysthymia: Antecedents and underlying assumptions. In L. J. Chapman, J. P. Chapman, & D. C. Fowles (Eds.), *Progress in experimental personality and psychopathology research* (Vol. 16, pp. 222–253). New York: Springer Publishing Company.

Klein, D. N., Riso, L. P., Donaldson, S. K., Schwartz, J. E., Anderson, R. L., Ouimette, P. C., et al. (1995). Family study of early-onset dysthymia: Mood and personality disorders in relatives of outpatients with dysthymia and episodic major depression, and normal controls. *Archives of General Psychiatry, 52,* 487–496.

Klein, D. N., Schwartz, J. E., Rose, S., & Leader, J. B. (2000). Five-year course and outcome of dysthymic disorder: A prospective, naturalistic follow-up study. *American Journal of Psychiatry, 157,* 931–939.

Klein, D. N., Taylor, E. B., Dickstein, S., & Harding, K. (1988). Primary early-onset dysthymia: Comparison with primary nonbipolar nonchronic major depression on demographic, clinical, familial, personality, and socio-environmental characteristics and short-term outcome. *Journal of Abnormal Psychology, 97,* 387–398.

Kocsis, J. H., & Klein, D. N. (Eds.). (1995). *Diagnosis and treatment of chronic depression.* New York: Guilford Press.

Layden, M. A., Newman, C. F., Freeman, A., & Morse, S. B. (1993). *Cognitive therapy of borderline personality disorder.* Needham Heights, MA: Allyn & Bacon.

Lizardi, H., Klein, D. N., Ouimette, P. C., Riso, L. P., Anderson, R. L., & Donaldson, S. K. (1995). Reports of the childhood home environment in early-onset dysthymia and episodic major depression. *Journal of Abnormal Psychology, 104,* 132–149.

Maes, M., Vandewoude, M., Maes, L., Schott, C., & Cosyns, P. (1989). A revised interpretation of the TRW test results in female depressed patients: Part I. *Journal of Affective Disorders, 16,* 203–213.

McCullough, J. P. (2000). *Treatment for chronic depression: Cognitive behavioral analysis system of psychotherapy.* New York: Guilford Press.

McCullough, J. P., Klein, D. N., Keller, M. B., Holzer, C. E., Davis, S. M., Kornstein, S. G., et al. (2000). Comparison of DSM–III–R chronic major depression superimposed on dysthymia (double depression): Validity of the distinction. *Journal of Abnormal Psychology, 109,* 419–427.

Miller, I. W., Norman, W. H., & Dow, M. G. (1986). Psychosocial characteristics of "double depression." *American Journal of Psychiatry, 143,* 1042–1044.

Pepper, C. M, Klein, D. N., Anderson, R. L., Riso, L. P., Ouimette, P. C., & Lizardi, H. (1995). Axis II comorbidity in dysthymia and major depression. *American Journal of Psychiatry, 152,* 239–247.

Ravindran, A. V., Bialik, R. J., Brown, G. M., & Lapierre, Y. D. (1994). Primary early onset dysthymia, biochemical correlates of the therapeutic response to fluoxetine: II. Urinary metabolites of serotonin, norepinephrine, epinephrine and melatonin. *Journal of Affective Disorders, 31,* 119–123.

Riso, L. P., du Toit, P. L., Blandino, J. A., Penna, S., Dacey, S., Duin, J. S., et al. (2003). Cognitive aspects of chronic depression. *Journal of Abnormal Psychology, 112*, 72–80.

Riso, L. P., Froman, S. E., Raouf, M., Gable, P., Maddux, R. E., Turini-Santorelli, N., et al. (in press). The long-term stability of early maladaptive schemas. *Cognitive Therapy and Research.*

Riso, L. P., Klein, D. N., Ferro, T., Kasch, K. L., Pepper, C. M., Schwartz, J. E., et al. (1996). Understanding the comorbidity between early-onset dysthymia and unstable personality disorders: A family study. *American Journal of Psychiatry, 153*, 900–906.

Riso, L. P., Miyatake, R., & Thase, M. E. (2002). The determinants of chronic depression: A review of six factors. *Journal of Affective Disorders, 70*, 103–115.

Scott, J., Barker, W. A., & Eccleston, D. (1988). The Newcastle chronic depression study: Patient characteristics and factors associated with chronicity. *British Journal of Psychiatry, 153*, 28–33.

Tappy, L., Randin, J. P., Schwed, P., Werthermimer, J., & Memarchand-Beraud, T. (1987). Prevalence of thyroid disorders in psychogeriatric inpatients. *Journal of Gerontological Society, 35*, 526–531.

Thase, M. E., Reynolds, C. F., III., Frank, E., Simons, A. D., Garamoni, G. G., McGeary, J., et al. (1994). Response to cognitive behavior therapy in chronic depression. *Journal of Psychotherapy Practice and Research, 3*, 204–214.

Weissman, M. M., Prusoff, B. A., & Klerman, G. L. (1978). Personality and the prediction of long-term outcome of depression. *American Journal of Psychiatry, 135*, 797–800.

Young, J. E. (1995). *Cognitive therapy for personality disorders: A schema-focused approach.* Sarasota, FL: Professional Resource Exchange.

Young, J. E., Klosko, J. S., & Weishaar, M. E. (2003). *Schema therapy: A practitioner's guide.* New York: Guilford Press.

4

SCHEMA CONSTRUCTS AND COGNITIVE MODELS OF POSTTRAUMATIC STRESS DISORDER

MATT J. GRAY, SHIRA MAGUEN, AND BRETT T. LITZ

Since the inception of posttraumatic stress disorder (PTSD) in the nosology (*Diagnostic and Statistical Manual of Mental Disorders, Third Edition* [*DSM–III*]; American Psychiatric Association, 1980), etiological models have grown in sophistication and explanatory power by using modern cognitive and social–cognitive terminology, concepts, and measures. In addition to the formal symptoms of PTSD represented by the subclusters of reexperiencing, avoidance and numbing, and hyperarousal (*Diagnostic and Statistical Manual of Mental Disorders, Fourth Edition, Text Revision* [*DSM–IV–TR*]; American Psychiatric Association, 2000), PTSD is associated with a pervasive change in an individual's view of him- or herself, others, and the world (e.g., Ali, Dunmore, Clark, & Ehlers, 2002; Janoff-Bulman, 1989, 1992, 1995; Janoff-Bulman & Frantz, 1997; Magwaza, 1999; Owens & Chard, 2001).

In the first section we discuss the important role that the schema construct has played in cognitive models of PTSD that attempt to account for findings relating to the role of cognitive factors in the pathogenesis and treatment of PTSD. Then we present studies of schema-related processing in PTSD followed by a description of schema-focused cognitive approaches to the treatment of PTSD. The chapter concludes with a discussion of future directions for schema-focused theories and therapeutic approaches to PTSD.

THE SCHEMA CONCEPT IN COGNITIVE THEORIES OF POSTTRAUMATIC STRESS DISORDER

Dalgleish (1999) argued that most cognitive theories of PTSD share the following core conceptualization: Individuals have preexisting cognitive representations (schemas, beliefs, etc.) of themselves, the world, and others that they have to somehow reconcile with the highly discrepant realities of trauma (annihilation, degradation, betrayal, shame, etc.). Such theories generally hypothesize that the difficulties in reconciling such discrepant information with preexisting mental representations underlie the avoidance and reexperiencing symptoms of PTSD. The following sections delineate theoretical models of PTSD that are primarily informed by schematic processes (i.e., molar schema theories) or that include schema-relevant themes among other explanatory constructs in accounting for PTSD (i.e., multi-representational cognitive theories of PTSD).

Molar Schema Theories of Posttraumatic Stress Disorder

Dalgleish (2004) identified two main types of unirepresentational models of PTSD: schema-focused models (e.g., Horowitz, 1973, 1976, 1979; Janoff-Bulman, 1989, 1992; Janoff-Bulman & Frantz, 1997; Janoff-Bulman & Frieze, 1983) and associative network models (Chemtob, Roitblat, Hamada, Carlson, & Twentyman, 1988; Creamer, Burgess, & Pattison, 1992; Foa, Steketee, & Rothbaum, 1989).

In Janoff-Bulman's cognitive appraisal model (Janoff-Bulman, 1989, 1992; Janoff-Bulman & Frantz, 1997; Janoff-Bulman & Frieze, 1983), three clusters of pretrauma assumptions are assumed to be shattered by the traumatic experience. As a result, coping involves rebuilding the assumptive world in a fashion that is more consonant with the recent trauma experience. The three basic assumptions assumed to be of relevance to PTSD are that the world is benevolent; that the world is meaningful—that is, a comprehensible place, in which outcomes are fairly distributed and "good and worthy people" who display cautious behaviors can prevent misfortune (Janoff-Bulman, 1989; Janoff-Bulman & Frieze, 1983); and that the self is worthy, which influences each of the other assumptions. For example, if self-perception includes the belief that one is moral and makes the right choices, then being a victim becomes more difficult to integrate into existing schemas. It is not uncommon for sexual assault victims to blame themselves as they struggle to assimilate the assault and assault-related cognitions into pretraumatic schemas of benevolence and meaningfulness. Schema-focused therapy necessarily involves an accommodation process whereby victims alter these pretraumatic schemas in recognition of the fact that bad things can happen to good people and outcomes are not necessarily distributed fairly.

Dalgleish (1999) pointed out that Janoff-Bulman's (e.g., 1989) theory does not provide an account of how these assumptions are represented or what processes are involved when these assumptions are shattered. In addition, the model does not provide an adequate rationale for selecting the three hypothesized assumptions, and pretrauma assumptions may well be more nuanced, individualized, and idiosyncratic. Finally, past trauma history, adverse childhood experiences, and past psychiatric history are risk factors for PTSD; presumably these risk factors are associated with assumptions about the self, the world, and others that are more likely to be confirmed than disconfirmed by traumatic experiences.

Horowitz's (Horowitz, 1973, 1976, 1979, 1986, 1997) formulation provides a more complex model of schematic processes and content involved in PTSD. Drawing on the work of Festinger (1957), Horowitz proposed that the *completion tendency* is the main driving force behind the processing of trauma-related information. This completion tendency involves the repeated matching of new, trauma-related information to preexisting cognitive beliefs, until the discrepancy between these two sets of representations is reduced. According to Horowitz (1986), immediately after the trauma, trauma-related information (e.g., thoughts, images, etc.) and preexisting mental beliefs cannot be reconciled. Moreover, despite the operation of defense mechanisms (e.g., numbing and denial) that strive to keep trauma-related information out of consciousness, trauma-related information is kept in active memory because of the completion tendency, causing trauma-related content (e.g., flashbacks and intrusive thoughts) to break into conscious awareness. The gradual process of integrating trauma-related information with preexisting meanings is characterized by the conflict between defense mechanisms and the completion tendency, leading to the repeated oscillation between phases of intrusion and denial and numbing.

Horowitz's model has provided a valuable heuristic to explain acute posttraumatic adaptation. However, accounts of its application in the study of chronic forms of PTSD are few. Furthermore, there is no evidence that emotional numbing symptoms (or denial and avoidance) occur generally as a phasic response following a period predominated by intrusions (e.g., Joseph, Yule, & Williams, 1995).

Multirepresentational Cognitive Theories of Posttraumatic Stress Disorder

Multirepresentational models of PTSD are information-processing based and considerably more molecular (Brewin, 2001a, 2001b; Brewin, Dalgleish, & Joseph, 1996; Ehlers & Clark, 2000). Although some multirepresentational theories of PTSD invoke the schema construct (Dalgleish, 1999; Foa & McNally, 1996; Foa & Rothbaum, 1998), others fail to provide an explicit account of generic representations of abstract, higher order models or assumptions and therefore fail to account for the role of pretrauma assumptions and the transformation of meaning in the course of the disorder. Excellent expositions of these theories are available elsewhere (e.g., Dalgleish, 1999) and therefore, we focus mostly on the role of the schema construct within these theories.

Edna Foa and colleagues argued that the extreme emotions experienced during a trauma lead to biased information processing of traumatic events, thereby producing disorganized, incoherent memory records of the traumatic experience (Foa, Molnar, & Cashman, 1995; Foa & Riggs, 1994). Trauma memories are furthermore characterized by a large number of stimulus–danger associations that give rise to a generalized perception of threat (Foa & Rothbaum, 1998). Trauma memories also encode a wide range of responses, physiological as well as behavioral, that may become linked to the appraisal of personal ineffectiveness in the face of threat, thus giving rise to a generalized representation of the self as totally inept. Such schematic representations are seen as playing an important role in the onset and maintenance of PTSD. If, for instance, a sexual assault survivor deems herself to be excessively vulnerable to future assaults, her safety-seeking responses may become overgeneralized. She may avoid objectively safe outings in an extreme effort to stave off dangerous encounters. Although such a strategy ensures safety, it comes at an unacceptable cost—that is, the confirmation of the self as vulnerable and inept and adoption of a coping strategy (i.e., avoidance) that is known to exacerbate symptoms of traumatic stress.

In concurrence with previous schema-based theories of PTSD (e.g., Janoff-Bulman, 1989, 1992), Foa and colleagues postulated that traumatic events may indeed violate preexisting self–world schemas. In addition, though, Foa and colleagues suggested that in individuals who have faced prior psychological adversity, traumas may actually prime pretrauma representations of the self as incompetent and the world as dangerous, thereby accommodating findings relating to the role of previous trauma, psychiatric history, and childhood adversity.

Power and Dalgleish (1997) originally developed the schematic, propositional, analogue, and associative representational systems (SPAARS) model of general emotional experience in an attempt to account for a wide range of psychopathology. Briefly stated, the general SPAARS model proposes four explicit systems of mental representation: The analogical representational system stores episodic (i.e., relating to specific events of an individual's life) or semantic (i.e., relating to the properties of an individual's experience of the world) information as nonverbal images (i.e., visual, olfactory, auditory, gustatory, body-state, and proprioceptive; Dalgleish, 1999; Power & Dalgleish, 1997). In the propositional representational system, semantic or episodic information is stored in the form of thoughts and beliefs that can be expressed in natural language (i.e., in verbal form) without any loss of meaning or content. In contrast, the higher order schematic representations system encodes abstract, generic information that cannot readily be expressed in natural language; for instance, the concept of personal ineptness invoked by Foa and Rothbaum (1998) is more complex and has a greater influence on schema-based processing than is suggested by a propositional-system statement such as "I am inept." The full representation of ineptness cannot be adequately captured by natural language because it represents visceral and nonverbal experience in addition to explicit and verbal meaning. The interplay between these three representational systems is used to account for the appraisal-driven generation of emotion (i.e., events and the appraisal of events are hypothesized to occur at the schematic model level, where the implication of incoming information for an individual's goals is represented; Dalgleish, 1999; Power & Dalgleish, 1997). In contrast, associative system representations (i.e., networks of event–emotion pairings) are involved in the automatic (i.e., non-appraisal-driven) generation of emotion.

Applied to PTSD, the SPAARS model proposes that threat-related appraisal of trauma information produces an intense experience of fear (Dalgleish, 1999). Analogical, propositional, and schematic-level trauma representations of the trauma are highly discrepant to an individual's preexisting schematic representations of the world and are therefore not integrated into these models. Dalgleish (1999) argued that trauma victims engage in the continual reappraisal of such schema-incompatible information in an effort to integrate such information. However, the appraisal of such information as threatening and schema-incompatible invariably produces a sense of current and imminent threat. The chronic activation of the emotion of fear is believed to configure the cognitive system in such a way that trauma-related cues are selectively processed and in turn reinforce the sense of current and constant threat.

COGNITIVE SCHEMAS AND INFORMATION-PROCESSING STUDIES ON PTSD

In this section, a distinction is made between the role of schema-related information processing and schema-related content in guiding theorizing about empirical findings in PTSD research.

Assumptions About Justice, Fairness, and the World or Others

Schema-based theories have generally posited that pretrauma schematic content may be a risk factor in PTSD. Although there is agreement that individuals who experience trauma are likely to have more posttrauma negative assumptions about the world or others, there is considerable debate about whether individuals with more positive or more negative preassault beliefs fare worse in the aftermath of trauma. As pointed out in the previous section, Janoff-Bulman and Frieze (1983) argued that individuals with more positive beliefs about the world are more at risk for psychopathology, whereas Foa and Riggs (1993) argued that individuals with more negative pretrauma beliefs are more likely to develop PTSD as a result of the confirmation of these beliefs. Because of the retrospective nature of research examining this question, it is difficult to draw reliable conclusions about this question.

Changes in worldview have been demonstrated for a variety of traumas. For example, witnessing the violent death of a close relative and surviving captivity and torture were both associated with changes in worldview (Magwaza, 1999). Several studies have demonstrated that after experiencing a traumatic event, individuals report more negative beliefs about others and the world. For example, Schwartzberg and Janoff-Bulman (1991) reported that individuals who experienced traumatic bereavement had more negative beliefs about fairness, justice, and predictability when compared with a control group. Frazier, Conlon, and Glaser (2001) found that following sexual assault, beliefs about the goodness of others and the fairness of the world continued to be negatively affected after 1 year. In this regard, Norris et al. (2002) suggested that long-term mental health consequences can be minimized if the trauma does not take on more symbolic meanings of human neglect or maliciousness.

It is not surprising that research has documented significant associations between posttraumatic changes in worldview and psychological distress. Owens and Chard (2001) examined the relationship between PTSD severity and cognitive distortions and found significant correlations between PTSD severity and decreased perceptions of self-worth. It should be noted that maladaptive cognitive schemas may differ by type of trauma. Wickie and Marwit (2000–2001) compared parents who lost children to homicide with parents bereaved by accidents, and found that those who lost a child to homicide demonstrated more negative views concerning the benevolence of the world. Furthermore, for both groups, meaningfulness of the world and benevolence of the world were more affected by the trauma than by worthiness of the self. Further research is needed to clarify the types of traumas that result in changes of worldview. In seeking to better understand whether there is a change of worldview following trauma, it is important to consider multiple issues, including severity of symptoms (and whether there has been a formal diagnosis or simply exposure to a traumatic event), severity of event, chronicity of event, and whether the trauma was inflicted on the individual or that person was a witness of suffering.

Ali et al. (2002) examined pre-and postassault beliefs of victims with and without PTSD, as well as of a control group. The authors used a 63-item Trauma-Sensitive Beliefs Questionnaire that assessed beliefs that may be influenced by the experience of assault. The measure included a wide range of beliefs, including being unable to trust others (e.g., "I cannot rely on other people"), beliefs about the safety and fairness of the world (e.g., "The world is a dangerous place" and "There is no justice in the world"), and beliefs about being invulnerable to assault (e.g., "No one will ever harm me"). The authors found that victims who did not develop PTSD following an assault reported more positive preassault beliefs (obtained retrospectively) in comparison with a no-assault control group. In contrast, the persistent PTSD group reported more negative preassault beliefs overall. They reported more negative appraisals of victims before the assault and they were more likely to endorse beliefs regarding a lack of trust in others, beliefs that the world is unsafe, and beliefs regarding invulnerability to harm to a greater extent than did the control group. Furthermore, those with more negative beliefs after the trauma were more likely to develop PTSD. Ali, Dunmore, Clark, and Ehlers (2002) speculated that positive preassault beliefs protect against the development of PTSD.

Meaning and Perceived Benefits

It is not the case that only maladaptive beliefs have implications for posttraumatic adjustment; many researchers believe that meaning making can be instrumental in helping victims cope with trauma. Schema-based conceptualizations of PTSD can certainly accommodate more adaptive schema-level meanings. In the stress literature, meaning and benefit-finding are fairly new research areas. Park and Folkman (1997) have distinguished two types of meanings that serve a heuristic function in conceptualizing how individuals reconcile trauma: *global meaning* and *situational meaning*. Global meaning is defined as an individual's enduring beliefs and goals, whereas situational meaning encompasses the interaction between global meaning and the circumstances and significance surrounding a particular event. In the case of trauma, one's preexisting beliefs (e.g., invincibility) typically are at odds with the significance and meaning of the trauma. In this context, *meaning-making* is defined as an individual's ability to integrate situational and global meaning. Integration includes an amalgam of the appraised meaning of a situation and an individual's more global beliefs and goals. In the process of meaning-making, individuals strive to reduce dissonance between the apprised meaning of an event and preexisting global meaning (Park & Folkman, 1997). For instance, a client seeking services after a life-threatening accident is forced to reconsider pretraumatic perceptions of invulnerability in light of an event that conflicts with this erroneous belief. He or she may view the accident as a wake-up call and reconsider life priorities. In this manner, the recognition that life could end quickly and prematurely does not have to result in unadulterated despair. Rather, it can be the impetus for living a more thoughtful, deliberate life, and the accident can stimulate a new belief system: recognition of the preciousness of life and the importance of living a fuller, more meaningful life.

After enduring a traumatic event, individuals question preexisting worldviews, most often because the traumatic experience counteracts notions of a just or fair world (see Lerner, 1980, for a discussion of the *just world theory*). As a result, following trauma, pronounced cognitive dissonance ensues and may result in adverse consequences such as rumination, intrusive memories, depression, and a host of other negative symptoms. Indeed, Silver, Boon, and Stones (1983) found that incest survivors who were able to make sense of their trauma were better socially adjusted and less psychologically distressed than were those who were unable to make sense of the event. The latter group also reported a higher incidence of intrusive thoughts, which arguably suggests that successful meaning-making had not occurred. Successful meaning-making, then, involves either assimilating the trauma into an individual's preexisting global meaning, which may also be viewed as a preexisting schema, or changing these preexisting global meanings to accommodate the trauma (Park & Folkman, 1997).

There is evidence that assimilation or accommodation may facilitate the creation of meaning following traumatic events. For example, in support of accommodation, a study by Schwartzberg and Janoff-Bulman (1991) found that 75% of participants changed their global beliefs, including those about the world, self, and others, in the aftermath of a traumatic event. There is also some evidence that certain tasks can reduce the discrepancy between situational and global meaning. Park and Blumberg (2002) found that individuals who had experienced a trauma and engaged in trauma disclosure through writing were able to change their appraisals to reflect less aversive situational meaning of their trauma as well as reduce symptoms of intrusion and avoidance.

Other meaning-making strategies identified in the literature include striving to understand causality (including both "Why did this happen?" and "Why did this happen to me?"), modifying discrepancies through constant reattributions (of the trauma, the self, the world, etc.), changing goals to promote consonance with new global meaning (e.g., focusing more on family after tragedies such as 9/11), finding some purpose in the event, and focusing on perceived benefits (or posttraumatic growth) that result from the situation (e.g., it made me a stronger person, a more understanding person, a more empathetic person). The meaning-making process is typically seen as deriving from an interaction of life history, personality variables, details of the traumatic event, and the broader sociocultural context in which the individual was traumatized (Lebowitz & Roth, 1994).

Meaning-making may also promote improvements in mental health and coping following traumatic events. Frommberger and colleagues (1999) found that following a motor vehicle accident, participants who were able to give meaning to the traumatic event were able to better comprehend, cope with, and manage the trauma. Individuals were assessed a few days following the trauma as well as after 6 months. Among several measures, individuals were asked to fill out a 29-item Sense of Coherence Scale designed by the authors. Individuals scoring higher on this scale demonstrated less psychopathology, including lower rates of PTSD and less anxious cognitions.

Ehlers and Steil (1995) proposed a model by which preventing a change in meaning inhibits improvement. They speculated that idiosyncratic meanings of intrusive thoughts experienced by those with PTSD will predict an individual's level of distress and will result in strategies to control these intrusive thoughts. If an individual perceives the intrusive thoughts as an indicator that he or she is losing control or going crazy, motivation to suppress such thoughts is heightened. This suppression keeps a vicious cycle in place; the control strategies result in maintenance of these intrusive thoughts and thus prevent change in the meaning of the trauma. Ehlers and Steil suggest a comprehensive assessment of the processes that prevents change in meaning, including safety behaviors, suppression of memories and thoughts related to the trauma, and selective information processing, including attentional and memory biases.

A related construct that can be used to better understand meaning in PTSD is the notion of perceived benefits or posttraumatic growth (PTG). PTG refers to potential positive outcomes resulting from trauma (Tedeschi & Calhoun, 1996; Tedeschi, Park, & Calhoun, 1998). The authors suggest that PTG is an umbrella term for a series of processes and outcomes that result when individuals who have experienced unfavorable events yet are able to thrive in the aftermath of adversity. Tedeschi and Calhoun (1996) proposed three categories of perceived benefits that have been identified by traumatized individuals, including changes in self-perception, changes in interpersonal relationships, and a changed philosophy of life. Adaptive change in these domains may promote faster or more complete recovery following trauma. In one study comparing breast cancer survivors with matched control participants, survivors of breast cancer showed a pattern of greater PTG, particularly in relating to others, appreciation of life, and spiritual change (Cordova, Cunningham, Carlson, & Andrykowski, 2001). There is also evidence that the degree of PTG may vary with type of trauma, gender, and time lapse since the traumatic event (Polatinsky & Esprey, 2000).

Attributions and Posttraumatic Pathology

Attribution theorists hold that when unexpected or unwanted events occur, people are motivated to generate causal explanations to account for those events, and that these attributions may influence the severity of subsequent psychopathology. Attributional tendencies may be associated with PTSD (Joseph, Yule, & Williams, 1993; Williams, Evans, Needham, & Wilson, 2002). For instance, in the case of sexual assault victims, self-blame (i.e., an internal attribution) has been shown to be associated with PTSD and generally poorer postassault adjustment (Wenninger & Ehlers, 1998). It is also reasonable to posit that greater posttraumatic pathology would be associated with more global and stable attributions for traumatic events. Attributing trauma to pervasive and enduring (i.e., global and stable) factors would represent a bleak, fatalistic outlook. Such global and stable trauma-related attributions could be seen as reflecting the trauma-related change in an individual's supraordinate schemas, with these attributional processes biasing causal attributions in a schema-consistent manner. These attributional responses to a traumatic event could lead to greater or more persistent anxiety relative to the opposite strategy: dismissing the event as an isolated occurrence. If victims believe that the circumstances that gave rise to their harrowing experience are pervasive and likely to be present in the future, heightened arousal and anxiety would be expected.

Some studies have focused on causal explanations offered by participants for their traumas. For instance, Falsetti and Resick (1995) examined the relationship between PTSD symptoms and causal explanations offered by crime victims for their victimizations. In their study, internal and stable attributions for victimizations were significant predictors of PTSD severity. The explanations offered by participants for their actual traumatic events were more strongly associated with PTSD symptoms than were indices of dispositional attributional style, suggesting that relative to attributions for negative events generally, trauma-specific attributions may have greater implications for posttraumatic distress. This possibility does not necessarily indicate that event-specific interpretations are more important than overriding schemas in determining posttraumatic adjustment. Rather, these findings may be consistent with the previously discussed notion that trauma represents a violation of pretraumatic schemas. If the trauma victim has not yet reconciled interpretations of the traumatic event with preexisting schemas, greater distress would be expected. Individuals with minimal distress in this study might have already reconciled trauma-specific information with pretraumatic schemas.

A more recent study also compared the usefulness of attributions that participants offer for actual traumatic experiences with the usefulness of attributions for more general negative events in predicting PTSD symptoms (Gray, Pumphrey, & Lombardo, 2003). In this study, participants were asked to write narrative accounts of their most traumatic events and to cite possible causes. Trauma-specific attributions were then evaluated with the content analysis of verbatim explanations (CAVE) technique (Schulman, Castellon, & Seligman, 1989). This technique involves the extraction of causal attributions from narrative accounts of life events and the subsequent rating of those attributions by trained judges who are blind to participants' symptom status. Gray et al. (2003) found that both dispositional attributional style and trauma-specific attributions were associated with PTSD symptoms. However, trauma-specific attributions were more consistently associated with PTSD symptoms. These findings were replicated in a subsequent investigation (Gray & Lombardo, 2004).

In conceptual terms, it makes sense that individuals who view their experiences as being caused by relatively immutable and enduring factors would experience more distress. To the extent that an event (good or bad) is attributed to alterable factors, one may perceive a greater degree of control over the environment and personal experiences. With such a viewpoint, a past trauma may be perceived as an isolated event or a fluke occurrence, and as having little bearing on whether or not a similar event will occur in the future.

Longitudinal, prospective research is needed to determine whether observed differences in attributions for life events between PTSD and non-PTSD populations exist prior to traumatic exposure, or whether traumatic exposure and development of PTSD symptoms subsequently alter the nature of explanations offered for life events. If attributional differences are found to exist prior to traumatic exposure and development of PTSD, knowledge of attributional tendencies could be predictive of pathology following a traumatic event. As a source of PTSD vulnerability, pessimistic attributions could be targeted in preventative efforts, particularly in high-risk populations. If future studies find that more pessimistic attributional differences in PTSD populations are not preexisting but rather evolve over time following a traumatic event, they could be an important focus of treatment. If individuals with PTSD come to believe that life events are caused by global and persistent factors, they may be less likely to take the necessary precautions to prevent similar events from occurring in the future, as some authors have theorized (e.g., Gold, Sinclair, & Balge, 1999; Peterson & Seligman, 1984). In addition, this cognitive set may exacerbate other symptoms of PTSD (e.g., symptoms of hypervigilance or increased arousal).

Risk and Threat Appraisal

Individuals with PTSD have been shown to interpret ambiguous social and emotional information as threatening. Furthermore, they have difficulty inhibiting the activation or priming of threat information, which is in part caused by selective allocation of attentional resources to threatening information (Kaspi, McNally, & Amir, 1995; Litz et al., 1996; McNally, 1998) and preferential encoding and recall of threatening information (McNally, Metzger, Lasko, Clancy, & Pitman, 1998). In terms of memory bias, Zeitlin and McNally (1991) found that when veterans with PTSD were compared with veterans without PTSD on a cued recall (explicit) and word completion (implicit) memory task, those with PTSD exhibited poorer memory for all but the combat words on the explicit memory task and biased priming of combat words in the implicit memory task. Amir, Coles, and Foa (2002) used a homograph paradigm to study the degree to which people with PTSD may interpret ambiguous information as threatening and have difficulties suppressing threat-related interpretations. It was hypothesized that PTSD would be associated with poorer inhibition of the threat-related meanings of homographs (words with double meanings such as *mug*). Individuals viewed sentences followed by a cue word and were asked whether the cue word was related to the meaning of the sentence. Researchers found that individuals with PTSD were more likely to construe the sentence as consistent with cue words that had threat meaning.

Schema-Focused Assessment

For researchers and clinicians interested in paper-and-pencil measures of beliefs germane to the development and maintenance of PTSD, a number of cognitive measures are available. Foa, Ehlers, et al. (1999) developed the Posttraumatic Cognitions Inventory, a 33-item measure with good psychometric properties containing three factors: Negative Cognitions About Self, Negative Cognitions About the World, and Self-Blame for the Trauma. The negative cognitions about the world subscale contain seven items and include measurement of assumptions concerning safety and threat (e.g., "I have to be especially careful because you never know what can happen next," "The world is a dangerous place," and "I have to be on guard all of the time").

The Personal Beliefs and Reactions Scale (PBRS; Resick, Schnicke, & Markway, 1991) is a 55-item self-report measure specifically designed to assess distortions in cognitive schemas that result from sexual assault. The PBRS contains eight subscales with items rated on a 6-point Likert scale, with higher scores representing less distorted beliefs. The subscales of the PBRS include safety, trust, control, esteem, intimacy, negative rape beliefs, self-blame, and undoing. Although the PBRS was designed for sexual assault survivors, it has been modified in several studies and used in a variety of trauma contexts (e.g., Foa, Ehlers, et al., 1999). The PBRS has been found to have good validity (Wenninger & Ehlers, 1998) and reliability (.81; Mechanic & Resick, 1993). The safety subscale of the PBRS measures an individual's perceived vulnerability to future harm as well as perceived effectiveness of self-protective efforts.

Janoff-Bulman (1989) developed the World Assumptions Scale, a 32-item scale that is an amalgamation of eight fundamental schemas: benevolence of the world, benevolence of people, justice, controllability, randomness, self-worth, self-controllability, and luck. When comparing individuals reporting trauma (including death of a loved one, incest, rape, destructive fire, and accident resulting in serious disability) with those who did not, Janoff-Bulman (1989) found that those experiencing trauma viewed themselves more negatively and the world as more malevolent. Men experiencing trauma saw the world as more random and women experiencing trauma saw it as less random. There were significant differences between those with and without a trauma history in each assumptive category proposed.

In terms of measuring cognitions that may be adaptive following trauma or may reflect positive adaptation, Tedeschi and Calhoun (1996) developed the Posttraumatic Growth Inventory (PTGI). The PTGI is a 21-item scale that taps five factors of posttraumatic growth including Relating to Others (e.g., a sense of closeness with others, putting effort into my relationships), New Possibilities (e.g., new opportunities are available that wouldn't have been otherwise), Personal Strength (e.g., a feeling of self-reliance, being able to accept the way things work out), Spiritual Change (e.g., a better understanding of spiritual matters), and Appreciation of Life (e.g., my priorities about what is important in life). The PTGI exhibits sound psychometric properties; accordingly, it is the most widely used instrument for measuring posttraumatic growth.

Dispositional attributional tendencies can be assessed with the Attributional Style Questionnaire (ASQ; Peterson, 1982). The inventory consists of six hypothetical positive life events (e.g., getting a raise) and six hypothetical negative events (e.g., a date going poorly). For each event, respondents are asked to vividly imagine the event happening to them and to generate a causal explanation for why the event occurred. The respondents then rate each attribution along three dimensions (internal–external, stable–unstable, global–specific) using a 7-point Likert-type scale. Higher scores reflect more internal, global, and stable attributions. The ASQ has demonstrated good reliability (Peterson, 1982) and validity (Burns & Seligman, 1989).

In terms of assessing attributions for specific life events such as traumas, coding schemes have been developed and could be adapted to meet the needs of the particular situation. For instance, the CAVE (Schulman et al., 1989) allows causal statements to be extracted from spontaneously offered verbal material (e.g., therapy transcripts); trained raters who are blind to symptom status rate the attributions along the three primary dimensions. This method can be an excellent way of assessing attributional changes over the course of cognitive therapy in research contexts. This coding system may be too cumbersome for routine clinical purposes, however. At a minimum, clinicians should attend to the extent to which victims attribute their traumas to internal, global, and stable factors even if these statements are not formally coded.

Schema-Focused Approaches and Cognitive Interventions for Posttraumatic Stress Disorder

In light of the prominence of schema-related representations in cognitive theories of PTSD, it is not surprising that there has been a growing interest in augmenting existing exposure-based interventions with more cognitive- or schema-focused therapeutic approaches (e.g., Meichenbaum, 1994).

Resick and Schnicke's (1992) cognitive processing therapy (CPT) is one of the first comprehensive treatments for PTSD that focuses systematically on modifying maladaptive beliefs related to trauma. Designed for the treatment of sexual assault victims, the intervention uses exposure based-techniques and cognitive restructuring. The treatment is designed to be administered over the course of 12 sessions, although the length can be modified depending on the needs of the individual. The first two sessions are largely psychoeducational as clients are informed about PTSD, the nature of the treatment, and the relationship between events, thoughts, and emotions. During this period, clients write an impact statement about the personal meaning of their assault. The purpose of this statement is not to begin exposure therapy per se, but to facilitate the exploration of rape-related cognitions and to identify maladaptive beliefs. More intensive exposure-based efforts begin following the next session; clients are encouraged to write a detailed account of the assault with as many sensory details as possible. They are encouraged to allow themselves to experience their emotional reactions fully while writing and then reading the account. Clients read their account aloud to the therapist during session 4. Exposure-based writing assignments continue as needed in subsequent sessions, but the focus of therapy is on cognitive restructuring. Beginning with session 4, the therapist uses standard cognitive therapy Socratic questioning regarding self-blame and other maladaptive beliefs that emerged during written accounts of the assault and its meaning. Additional homework assignments are given to facilitate the identification and modification of maladaptive beliefs. For instance, clients complete Challenging Beliefs Worksheets that require them to identify situations that elicit unpleasant thoughts, to identify attendant automatic thoughts and beliefs, and to generate disconfirming evidence. Later sessions focus on identifying and correcting overgeneralized beliefs related to specific themes known to be associated with greater postrape distress (safety, trust, power and control, esteem, and intimacy). At the end of therapy, clients write another impact statement reflecting current beliefs about the assault and the implications it has for one's life, which is used to underscore gains made in treatment.

Controlled trials of CPT have been encouraging. In one investigation, 171 female rape victims were randomly assigned to one of three conditions: CPT, prolonged exposure, or a minimal attention group (Resick, Nishith, Weaver, Astin, & Feuer, 2002). Active treatment conditions dramatically reduced PTSD and depression symptoms, and gains were maintained over the 9-month follow-up period. Although CPT and prolonged exposure resulted in generally equivalent treatment gains, CPT was superior to prolonged exposure in reducing maladaptive guilt cognitions. Thus, CPT's explicit cognitive focus appears to promote not only symptomatic change but schematic-processing improvement as well.

Owens, Pike, and Chard (2001) also documented adaptive changes in cognitions as well as significant alleviation of posttraumatic distress in individuals receiving CPT. In their study, 53 adult women with a history of childhood sexual assault were randomly assigned to either CPT or a minimal-attention waitlist control condition. At the end of treatment, only 2 of the 28 participants assigned to CPT continued to meet criteria for PTSD. In terms of CPT's impact on specific cognitive distortions, improvements in beliefs relating to safety, trust, power, esteem, and intimacy were associated with symptom reductions at 3-month and 1-year follow-up periods.

Foa and colleagues have also developed an intervention for rape and sexual assault survivors that incorporates exposure-based techniques and cognitive restructuring (Foa & Rothbaum, 1998; Jaycox, Zoellner, & Foa, 2002). Like CPT, the treatment begins with an educational component designed to provide clients with information about trauma and reactions as well as a rationale for the course of treatment. Unlike CPT, clients also begin relaxation training in the form of breathing retraining. Thus, in the first session victims begin to develop skills to help them manage their own anxiety. Clients begin mild exposure-based exercises following the second session, as they are encouraged to resume objectively safe trauma-reminiscent situations that they have been avoiding. Cognitive restructuring begins during session 3 and continues through the remainder of therapy (along with imaginal and in vivo exposure and deep breathing). Cognitive restructuring is intended to facilitate the identification, evaluation, and modification of negative thoughts. In particular, the intervention targets self-blame, self-worth, perceptions of control, and beliefs about the trustworthiness of others. Like CPT, prolonged exposure (PE) also uses homework assignments and Socratic questioning to challenge maladaptive schemas. This intervention is also designed to last approximately 12 sessions but may be modified to meet the individual needs of clients. In a controlled study comparing PE with two other active treatment conditions and a wait-list control group, PE resulted in the best end-state functioning, although all three interventions resulted in a significant improvement in posttraumatic distress (Foa, Dancu, et al., 1999).

Although PE is not schema-focused per se, exposure provides the optimal context for activating and modifying threat-related schemas. Furthermore, it is not clear how any schema-focused intervention to target PTSD could occur without an element of exposure because, in the broadest terms, exposure simply involves sustained engagement with thoughts or stimuli that one would otherwise attempt to avoid. Any intervention that attempts to activate and modify trauma- or threat-related schematic material necessarily entails sustained engagement with material that the client would otherwise seek to avoid.

Kubany, Hill, and Owens (2003) have developed a form of cognitive therapy that includes many of the same elements as Foa's comprehensive model. Cognitive trauma therapy for battered women emphasizes assessing and modifying dysfunctional beliefs and reducing negative self-talk, especially beliefs and self-talk related to shame and guilt. The Kubany et al. model also includes psychoeducation about PTSD, stress management and relaxation training, self-monitoring of maladaptive cognitions, and exposure-based techniques. Given that Kubany et al.'s model includes largely the same components as most cognitive–behavioral packages (e.g., the Foa model), it is not surprising that it has been found to be effective in reducing symptoms of PTSD and depression and altering maladaptive trauma-related cognitions such as guilt, shame, and self-blame (Kubany et al., 2003).

Cognitive therapy development and evaluation efforts historically have focused primarily on sexual and physical assault survivors. Interpersonal victimization may be especially likely to result in shattered assumptions of safety, control, and self-worth and thus require more systematic attention to maladaptive beliefs and schemas. However, because all forms of trauma create schematic biases and skewed meta-knowledge, cognitive interventions should be considered, especially because several investigators have targeted diverse traumas with cognitive therapy and found promising initial results (Marks, Lovell, Noshirvani, Livanou, & Thrasher, 1998; Tarrier et al., 1999). In the future, it is likely that there will be more systematic controlled research on cognitive interventions for diverse traumas.

PRACTICE GUIDELINES FOR SCHEMA-FOCUSED ASSESSMENT AND TREATMENT OF POSTTRAUMATIC STRESS DISORDER

A thorough ideographic assessment of maladaptive beliefs resulting from trauma is a necessary precursor to effective schema-focused therapy. This information can and should be obtained informally during initial sessions by engaging clients in discussions about belief systems that are typically disrupted following trauma (e.g., perceptions of safety). However, routine and continuing assessment with psychometrically sound measures of posttraumatic beliefs and cognitions such as the Posttraumatic Cognitions Inventory (Foa, Ehlers, et al., 1999) or the Personal Beliefs and Reactions Scale (Resick et al., 1991) will reveal the severity of maladaptive schemata and allow for regular feedback regarding therapeutic impact. Because these inventories provide information about distinct categories of beliefs that are often disrupted by trauma, clinicians can provide more efficient and effective treatment by quickly identifying maladaptive beliefs unique to each client. In this manner, clinicians can move from assessment to individually tailored intervention more quickly.

In general, the goal of therapy is to have trauma victims acknowledge and experience emotions associated with the trauma (instead of avoiding trauma-reminiscent cues and situations) while simultaneously identifying overgeneralizations and other maladaptive schemata and explicitly challenging these understandable but nevertheless erroneous cognitions. As discussed next, challenging maladaptive beliefs need not rely exclusively on cognitive-restructuring techniques such as Socratic questioning, but can and should include experiential exercises designed to provide ecologically valid disconfirmation of maladaptive beliefs. Exposure-based interventions (i.e., systematically exposing victims to objectively safe trauma-relevant thoughts and situations) can provide a context for activating and identifying maladaptive beliefs that may then be targeted with schema-focused therapy techniques. In schema-focused therapy, clients learn that simply having a particular interpretation of a traumatic experience does not necessarily mean that the interpretation is valid. Over the course of therapy, they should become increasingly adept at recognizing their interpretations as possibilities as opposed to truisms.

Anxiety disorders require interventions that are often counterintuitive to clients as they necessarily involve purposeful engagement with material that the clients would very much like to avoid. To achieve reductions in anxiety and cognitively process the trauma, clients will need to confront trauma-relevant thoughts and cues that, prior to therapy, they had been desperately trying to avoid. Proper psychoeducation about the role that avoidance plays in maintaining anxiety and the importance of exposure to trauma-relevant thoughts and contexts is thus a crucial component of any form of trauma-focused therapy.

Schema-focused therapists may use this period of psychoeducation to describe common but maladaptive belief alterations that may ensue following a particular type of trauma. Not only does this explanation help to normalize the client's reactions and thought processes, but it introduces the notion that some deeply held posttraumatic thoughts may not be accurate. This psychoeducation must be done with considerable tact and sensitivity. It is important that the therapist acknowledge that the shift in belief system is understandable and that alterations in beliefs resulting from personal experience are normal and often adaptive. In the context of extreme trauma, however, overcorrection or overaccommodation is associated with chronic impairments. Therapists can describe how these overcorrections serve to protect but at an unacceptable cost. If, for example, the person now views the world as pervasively dangerous, he or she may go to extreme lengths to avoid any and all situations in which harm may come. The following sexual assault case example is illuminating:

> *Client:* I know it sounds weird, but I can't help thinking that it was my fault.
>
> *Therapist:* How so?
>
> *Client:* I keep thinking of all the things that I could have done differently that would have changed how things went that day.
>
> *Therapist:* What sorts of things do you believe you should have done differently?
>
> *Client:* Well, I could have left the party earlier when my friends left or I could have just stayed home in bed that night.

Unfortunately, the trauma survivor not only identifies appropriate steps toward harm reduction (e.g., leaving a party with friends instead of by herself), but also begins to identify overly restrictive safety strategies. Such strategies can result in a very restricted existence in which the victim begins to avoid situations that are objectively safe and the probability of danger is vanishingly small. Therapists can normalize such alterations in belief systems but also begin to point out that these overcorrections can create new problems such as limited social contact and an impaired quality of life. These types of therapist explanations do not produce change, but they begin to orient the client to the goals of therapy and the implicit assumption in schema-focused therapy that some beliefs may be erroneous and may compromise one's quality of life.

Furthermore, with respect to psychoeducation, it is important for the therapist to validate the client's experience by noting that many of his or her beliefs are probably accurate and that the inaccurate beliefs may not be altogether wrong; they may simply be a bit too extreme or overgeneralized. In the case example introduced earlier, the therapist was later able to use the client's own beliefs and experiences to illustrate that although people often assume their beliefs to be absolute truths, they are often in error.

> *Therapist:* Tell me more about how the rape has affected the way you think about things.
>
> *Client:* Everything's different—everything. Before he raped me, it seemed like that would never happen to me—it couldn't possibly happen to me. I knew other girls who had guys take advantage of them, but I couldn't imagine it happening to me. It seemed like there was always something they did that I could point to and know that I would have handled the situation differently. They got really drunk or stayed at a party after their friends left. I guess I thought that I was invincible—strong enough and smart enough to keep it from happening to me.
>
> *Therapist:* How have your beliefs changed?
>
> *Client:* Well, I guess since I was raped, I must not be strong enough or smart enough to keep from getting assaulted.
>
> *Therapist:* So you still believe that being assaulted depends fully on one's smarts and strength?
>
> *Client:* I'm not sure I know what you mean.
>
> *Therapist:* Well, it seems like there might be a couple of ways of reconciling your prior beliefs about assault and the fact that you were assaulted. For one—and this is what we have been discussing—your beliefs about rape prior to your assault were entirely accurate. Only certain kinds of people—weak, naïve, etc.—get assaulted. If that's true, then when you get assaulted you must be one of those kinds of people. But I wonder if there's another possibility that is being over-looked.
>
> *Client:* Like what?

Therapist:	Well, is it possible that your prior belief was wrong? I mean, instead of your assault proving that you're a different sort of person than you thought you were, is it possible—possible— that your assault says something about the accuracy of your prior beliefs about rape?
Client:	I don't know. I guess I'd have to think about it.
Therapist:	(Strategic silence.)
Client:	I think I see what you're getting at—that maybe you could get raped even if you are very careful. I still think that lots of times people do put themselves in bad situations.
Therapist:	That might be true, but it sounded to me like before you were assaulted you believed that one could be raped *only* if she wasn't smart enough or strong enough. Is that right?
Client:	I suppose so.
Therapist:	So I guess I'm wondering whether that belief might be a bit too extreme or a bit too absolutist. Maybe there are times when bad judgment increases the likelihood that an assault could occur, but maybe assaults can sometimes occur to people who are bright and strong and who usually exercise good judgment.
Client:	I never really thought about it like that before. I guess at some level I had always thought that only certain kinds of women or women doing dumb things could get raped. Maybe that isn't always right. Maybe I believed that because it let me think that something like that could never happen to me.
Therapist:	So that belief might have been a bit strong, but before your assault, it served you well—it made you feel invincible.
Client:	I think so.
Therapist:	And, if you hadn't been raped, it wouldn't matter that that belief wasn't altogether accurate. But because you did get assaulted, it seems possible that the same belief that sort of helped you in a way before actually hurt you or made you feel worse about yourself after the assault. Is that right or am I off-base?
Client:	No, I think that is right. If rape happens only to people doing dumb things, then I guess by thinking that I sort of set myself up: I must be weak or dumb because I got assaulted.

The client noted that prior to the sexual assault, she never felt vulnerable and she felt that sexual assault was something that happened to "other people." The therapist was subsequently able to draw from the client's experience to suggest that just as the preassault belief was erroneous in its extreme form (i.e., assault cannot happen to me or assault happens only to people making bad decisions), her new belief system might also be erroneous in its extreme form (i.e., I will be assaulted again)—despite the fact that immediately after the assault, the victim perceived this belief to be a "truth." The therapist could not promise that another assault would not occur, but began to work with the client to challenge the perceived likelihood of a subsequent assault by examining her life history and the singularity of this event. The therapist was also able to enlist the client in identifying factors that would make assault more likely or less likely in similar contexts in the future to restore the client's sense of mastery and control.

Early in therapy, victims may be asked to provide a detailed, written, or oral account of the trauma, including information about what the event means to them and how it has impacted their beliefs about themselves and the world. For example, Resick and Schnicke's (1993) CPT commences with a written homework assignment that asks sexual assault survivors to describe the impact of the assault, particularly considering issues such as competency, power, safety, and trust. In this manner, therapists can begin the process of exposure therapy while explicitly probing for maladaptive beliefs. Clients may also be asked to engage in thought-monitoring homework exercises. When clients notice themselves thinking about the trauma or the way their life has been impacted by the trauma, they may be asked to write down their thoughts verbatim. These assignments may take any number of forms, from entirely unstructured narratives produced by the client to very structured and detailed thought-monitoring sheets. As an example of the latter, clients may be asked to document any activating event (a) that gave rise to thoughts about trauma, the resulting thoughts or beliefs (b) about the event, and the emotional and behavioral consequences (c) that resulted from these beliefs (e.g., Resick & Calhoun, 1996). In this manner, clients can begin to see the intimate connection between their belief systems and adverse emotional and behavioral experiences. During these initial sessions, the therapist is only gathering information about schemas that may be maintaining or exacerbating the client's distress. Working collaboratively with the client to challenge these thoughts and providing disconfirming behavioral experiments can be done only when both parties have a fairly good understanding of the beliefs that are contributing to the client's ongoing distress.

Once the client and clinician both have an appreciation of distressing schemas, the therapist can introduce exercises designed to target these belief systems. Orally and in writing, clients may be asked to provide evidence for and against these overgeneralized beliefs. If only disconfirming evidence is sought, it may be invalidating and may paradoxically result in the client becoming more resolute in his or her beliefs. By obtaining consistent and inconsistent evidence, the therapist engenders less reactance and also allows the client to see that the beliefs are not altogether wrong but are perhaps too extreme or too broadly applied. He or she can begin to identify tendencies to engage in dichotomous or catastrophic thinking, can begin to discern that some extreme thoughts may result from emotion (e.g., severe anxiety or fear) rather than reasoned appraisal, and can begin to consider the likelihood of similar events occurring in different situations. These schema-focused exercises will be optimally beneficial if the therapist couples them with objectively safe behavioral experiments designed to provide experiences that disconfirm unrealistic perceptions of threat or danger. For instance, an individual who was physically assaulted at a nightclub may begin avoiding numerous public places throughout the day. The therapist and client may design an outing that is objectively safe but that the client has been avoiding (e.g., going to the supermarket in the middle of the afternoon). Engaging in such activities will likely activate unrealistic fears and worries that the client can attend to and take note of and can provide powerful examples of how people can hold frankly erroneous beliefs with great certitude on the basis of strong emotion as opposed to objective reality. Exclusive use of dialogue and in-session challenging of cognitive distortions will be less than optimally effective—clients need real-world disconfirmation of errone-ous beliefs. In sum, schema-focused therapy consists of provision of psycho-education about PTSD and the role that cognitions play in maintaining distress, assessment and identification of maladaptive beliefs resulting from trauma, and in-session dialogue focused on critically evaluating trauma-relevant beliefs coupled with in vivo exercises and activities designed to disconfirm erroneous schemata.

Perhaps the most common posttraumatic belief system alteration, re-gardless of the type or nature of the traumatic event, pertains to victims' perceptions of safety. It is beyond the scope of this chapter to depict interven-tions for multiple maladaptive schemas. Because of the ubiquity of safety concerns following trauma, we describe schema-focused treatment for this particular maladaptive belief system for illustrative purposes.

It is not simply the case that individuals are fully accurate in their beliefs pretraumatically and that trauma invariably results in a shift from accurate appraisals of personal safety to inaccurate appraisals of safety. In-stead, following trauma, pretraumatic schemas of invulnerability are often overcorrected. Prior to trauma, individuals may perceive themselves to be invulnerable, thereby underestimating the very real possibility of personal danger. Although the statistical likelihood of victimization is low for most individuals, it is not nonexistent. Therefore, pretraumatic beliefs regarding personal safety are not necessarily entirely accurate, but they do not result in impaired functioning or a restricted lifestyle. Although misperceptions of invincibility may prevent an individual from taking necessary precautions and may increase the likelihood of accident, injury, or victimization, they are not associated with debilitating emotional distress that often results from commonly held but inaccurate posttraumatic beliefs. Trauma can result in overgeneralization of threat and unrealistically heightened perceptions of personal danger. Victims may overcorrect prior perceptions of invulnerability and may, posttraumatically, deem danger to be lurking everywhere. Unlike inaccurate pretrauma schemata, these belief disturbances are associated with a host of difficulties including pervasive anxiety and fear, curtailed activities outside the home, and increased isolation. Clinicians should thus routinely assess appraisals of safety following trauma as this particular belief alteration is especially likely to occur.

Through cognitive-monitoring forms and exercises described earlier, well-entrenched safety concerns are easily identified. Directly challenging the veracity of these thoughts is unlikely to be fruitful. When the evidence against these beliefs consists of population-based statistics and one's pretraumatic history, and the evidence for these beliefs consists of a recent harrowing personal experience, it is inordinately difficult for clients to dismiss erroneous beliefs as wrong no matter how skilled the therapist is. The schema-challenging ideas that the therapist is trying to instill are not likely to be directly adopted by the client. Trauma-related anxiety must be activated and the provision of schema-challenging experiences is typically required to facilitate alterations in maladaptive schemas. This is not to suggest that purely cognitive or verbal techniques cannot begin to chip away at maladaptive beliefs spawned by trauma. Having clients develop hierarchies of increasingly anxiety-provoking avoided situations results in tacit acknowledgement that a repeat incident of personal harm is not inevitable; instead, different activities and contexts are associated with varying probabilities of risk. Identification of a low-threat situation (even if the client is still overestimating risk inherent in that situation) is more readily accomplished when it is juxtaposed with a number of riskier situations and contexts.

Given the array of possible in vivo exposure situations, a client is more likely to engage in an objectively safe situation low on his or her anxiety hierarchy when all gradations of the hierarchy have been made explicit than if that situation had been posed in isolation. Mild resistance is still to be expected given that the client has actively avoided this situation. In session, therapeutic dialogue to evaluate the true likelihood of risk to motivate compliance with this particular behavioral exercise is likely to be helpful. For instance, the highly avoidant client who begins to avoid going to the supermarket unless absolutely necessary may be asked to estimate the number of times he or she has gone to the supermarket before and to estimate the number of occasions resulting in personal harm. The client need not believe that the situation is completely safe, nor is the goal of such dialogue to eradicate anxiety altogether. All that is required is that the client not experience immobilizing anxiety and that he or she consider the possibility that his or her appraisals of threat are inaccurate and unduly influenced by a single event. If the client can identify no history of personal harm despite hundreds of trips to the supermarket, he or she may still be anxious about going but may be more willing to engage in this exercise. The following case material illustrates this point.

> *Therapist:* Since the assault, are there other situations that make you really scared or anxious that didn't used to bother you?
>
> *Client:* Pretty much every time that I leave the house I'm more anxious than I used to be. Even just walking to my car is an ordeal now—I find myself looking over my shoulder a lot more and wondering if someone is around. I know it's crazy but I can't keep from worrying that someone might be around.
>
> *Therapist:* Does your anxiety in these situations cause you to live your life differently?
>
> *Client:* What do you mean?
>
> *Therapist:* Well, do you still do everything you used to but just feel more anxious, or have you started to avoid going places and doing things because you're a lot more worried now?
>
> *Client:* I do hang around the house a lot more now. I don't go out at night at all anymore—but lately, I've noticed that I'm also sticking around the house more during the day. Sometimes I don't go out unless I really have to.
>
> *Therapist:* Can you give me an example?
>
> *Client:* Well, I know this sounds crazy, but I don't go to the grocery store as often as I used to. Before the assault, if I ran out of something, like an ingredient for something I'm cooking, I'd jump in the car and go to the store to get it. Now, I just make something else to eat. I still have to go to the store—I mean I have to eat. But now it's kind of a last-resort thing. I see if there's a way to get by without going.
>
> *Therapist:* Can you recall what kinds of things go through your mind when you're thinking about going to the store but decide not to?
>
> *Client:* That's kind of hard to say. It's not like I think "If I go get more milk, I'm going to get jumped in the parking lot." I mean, it's not something that direct. It's just a real uneasy feeling I get—the thought of going out just makes me anxious. It's kind of a gut thing.

Therapist: It sounds like when you do stop and think about that uneasy feeling, your head and your gut are telling you different things?

Client: Yeah, I know it doesn't make sense to be worried about being in the grocery store parking lot in broad daylight, but it's hard to shake that gut feeling.

Therapist: I wonder how we might go about getting your head and your gut in sync.

Client: I don't know.

Therapist: Do you think that gut feeling is on target or do you think it's a false alarm?

Client: I'm not sure—all I know is it's a pretty strong reaction.

Therapist: Well, we can't say for sure what might happen in the future, but we can get some information about the likelihood of something bad happening by looking at your history. How many times would you guess you've been in the grocery store parking lot in broad daylight?

Client: I don't know—probably a couple hundred times anyway.

Therapist: Can you recall a time when something bad happened? When you were harmed or when something bad happened?

Client: Never—not once. I know in my head that probably nothing bad will happen—but again, my gut tells me something else and it's hard to shake.

Therapist: Do you think that it would be helpful to think about your history in grocery store parking lots when you go to the store? I mean, could that help take some of the edge off that scary gut feeling so that you could actually get out of the house?

Client: I don't know—I'm not sure.

Therapist: Well, when you've been deliberating about whether to go to the store or not the past few weeks, do you think about your experiences in that setting or do you think about something else?

Client: No, I usually don't think about that kind of stuff—I guess I just stay focused on the possibility of something bad happening.

Therapist: Well, I wonder if it's worth a shot. Maybe it wouldn't calm you down completely—but maybe when you're thinking about going to the store and get that nervous feeling, maybe slowing the process down a bit and thinking about things like all the times you've been in that parking lot without incident might make it more manageable—still kind of scary, sure—but doable. Is that possible?

Client: I don't know. Maybe.

Therapist: I wonder if it could help get your mind and gut in sync. At a minimum, maybe we can get a better idea of the kinds of things that go through your head that are keeping you cooped up in the house. What do you think—is it worth trying?

Client: I guess I don't have much to lose. I don't want to stay inside my house forever.

The point of such dialogue at the beginning of therapy then is to begin to motivate compliance and reduce avoidance, not to alleviate all anxiety or fully disabuse the client of perceptions of threat. If schema-challenging dialogue can promote these conditions, then the client can engage in activities outside of session that will provide continuing disconfirmation of erroneous beliefs. In the case of PTSD, exposure to actual feared situations is not simply an adjunct to in-session schema-focused dialogue. These therapeutic experiences are the most effective ways to modify maladaptive belief systems. Because erroneous posttraumatic beliefs are the result of personal experience, exposure is a powerful tool in directly challenging maladaptive schemas. Overgeneralizations, dichotomous thinking, and catastrophic thinking are likely to abate to the extent that the clinician and client can evaluate the veracity of these thoughts in light of the client's ongoing real-world experience.

Over the course of schema-focused therapy, client and clinician work collaboratively together to evaluate the accuracy of threat and harm appraisals in light of personal experience. Together, they work successively through increasingly anxiety-provoking but objectively safe avoided contexts, situations, and experiences. In advance of these behavioral exercises, schema-focused therapeutic dialogue is not designed to eliminate maladaptive thoughts or fully reduce irrational anxiety; it is designed to reduce both modestly such that the client is willing to consider engaging in these activities. Furthermore, the client is being encouraged to experience negative emotions of fear and anxiety so that he or she may learn that although these feelings are aversive, they are not dangerous in their own right.

Once the client engages in an exercise designed to challenge erroneous cognitions, therapeutic dialogue allows the client to attempt to reconcile previous beliefs with consistently incompatible personal experiences. Therapeutic dialogue from a later session of the case presented earlier illustrates this point.

Therapist:	Have you continued to have difficulties getting out of the house because of a fear that something bad would happen, or has that gotten better?
Client:	Both! [Laughs.] What I mean is, I'd be lying if I said that I wasn't nervous at all anymore when I'm by myself in a parking lot or something. I don't know if that will ever go away—I'm on my toes a lot more and I still look over my shoulder a lot more on the way to my car than I used to. But it's not so bad that I can't leave the house. I'm still not as active as I was before the assault but I get out of the house a lot more. I don't look for excuses to stay home.
Therapist:	What made the difference, do you think?
Client:	I don't know—practice, I guess.
Therapist:	Tell me more about that.
Client:	Well, each time I go out it's a little easier and I'm a little less scared. Again, I'm still pretty wary when I'm by myself—but not to the level that I won't go out. At the beginning (of therapy) it was a big struggle—I had to psych myself up, give myself a pep talk. But each time it got just a little easier. I don't have to think about it so much before going out—it's not until I'm in the situation that I find myself thinking about the possibility of someone lurking around. So it's still kind of there—but not as strong, and not in a way that keeps me from doing things.
Therapist:	It sounds like your experience of going out without anything bad happening started to chip away a little at that gut feeling you had after the assault that something bad was going to happen.
Client:	Yeah, I think that's it. If I didn't force myself to start getting out there again I'd probably be just as scared or nervous as I ever was.

It is important to note that the active agent in disputing the erroneous beliefs is not the therapist but the client's own personal experience. The client is compelled to modify extreme beliefs in the face of consistently disconfirming personal experience. The therapist need not continually be the dissenting voice—he or she can lead clients to call on their own experiences to evaluate the truth of their assumptions. It is also important to note that fully accurate appraisals and cognitions are not the sine qua non of successful therapy. As a result of experiencing a traumatic event, the client may always have unrealistically high appraisals of threat or harm and may be more vigilant than would a nontraumatized individual. Following therapy, if the client does not experience such debilitating levels of anxiety that he or she continues to avoid safe situations and the experience of negative emotionality, and if the anxiety experienced does not prevent the client from fully engaging in life, then therapy may be deemed successful. Therapists cannot promise their clients that their anxiety will be fully eradicated, nor can therapists ensure them that therapy will result in a return to pretraumatic levels of functioning. What therapists can do, however, is to work with clients to challenge erroneous beliefs that render them incapable of living a full, meaningful life.

FUTURE DIRECTIONS

At the end of the day, schema-based conceptualizations of posttraumatic adjustment problems are valid only if they inform methods of helping people recover from trauma. Much more research is needed to extend schema-focused interventions to varied trauma contexts and samples. Although many of the specific beliefs targeted in schema-based approaches are applicable to all forms of trauma (e.g., safety), certain maladaptive cognitions are unique to or more prominent in specific trauma contexts. For instance, cognitive interventions for combat veterans might be designed to address hostility and survivor guilt in contrast to interventions for sexual assault victims, which emphasize intimacy and self-blame.

Research to date has documented unequivocally that the severity of posttraumatic difficulties is related to the frequency and pervasiveness of negative, self-defeating beliefs. Research has also affirmed that cognitive interventions reduce posttraumatic anxiety and depression and effect positive changes in core schemas and metacognition. However, it is not clear whether belief change promotes symptom reduction or whether symptom reduction brings about more adaptive cognitive sets. The assumption of cognitive restructuring is that maladaptive beliefs maintain or exacerbate distress and that altering these beliefs is necessary for symptom alleviation. This assumption may be true, but most treatment-outcome studies assess only cognitive change and symptom change prior to treatment and upon completion of treatment. Repeated assessments of beliefs and symptoms over the course of treatment are required to ascertain whether cognitive change causes symptom reduction. At least one study documented that symptoms lessened prior to improvement in several key beliefs, suggesting that reducing distress allows for alteration of maladaptive beliefs (Livanou et al., 2002).

It is also unclear whether cognitive techniques are required to promote cognitive change. In studies comparing exposure therapy without an explicit emphasis on cognitive restructuring with cognitive therapy, exposure therapy alone promoted significant changes in maladaptive beliefs—sometimes to the same degree as did interventions explicitly targeting cognitions (Livanou et al., 2002; Marks et al., 1998; Tarrier et al., 1999). It may be that exposure-based interventions include cognitive restructuring components but that these are not explicitly emphasized in the description or rationale. Indeed, Resick et al. (2002) found that CPT promoted greater cognitive change than did exposure therapy when clinicians went to great lengths to ensure that the exposure therapy condition did not include cognitive techniques. Although the exposure condition in CPT is arguably artificial in that it deviates from how exposure-based interventions are typically delivered, Resick et al. were able to isolate the unique impact of cognitive restructuring. It is also possible that belief change is necessary for optimal improvement but that there are multiple paths to belief change. Explicit evaluation and modification of negative thoughts certainly can bring about cognitive change. However, as originally proposed by Foa and Kozak (1986), exposure therapy affects cognition because the experience of extinction disconfirms overgeneralized beliefs about threat and reduces exaggerated perceptions of danger. Future dismantling studies will help to elucidate these issues.

In sum, the past 2 decades have witnessed increasing attention to beliefs and cognitions that are associated with sustained posttraumatic difficulties. Comprehensive treatment packages have been designed to target belief systems that are thought to maintain and exacerbate distress. These interventions have consistently been proven to be efficacious and have expanded the repertoire of techniques and interventions available to clinicians. Although certain conceptual issues remain to be resolved empirically and although cognitive interventions for diverse trauma populations remain underdeveloped, there is every reason to believe that cognitive approaches will be increasingly prominent in the conceptualization and treatment of PTSD.

REFERENCES

Alba, J. W., & Hasher, L. (1983). Is memory schematic? *Psychological Bulletin, 93,* 203–231.

Ali, T., Dunmore, E., Clark, D., & Ehlers, A. (2002). The role of negative beliefs in posttraumatic stress disorder: A comparison of assault victims and non victims. *Behavioural and Cognitive Psychotherapy, 30,* 249–257.

American Psychiatric Association. (1980). *Diagnostic and statistical manual of mental disorders* (3rd ed.). Washington, DC: Author.

American Psychiatric Association. (2000). *Diagnostic and statistical manual of mental disorders* (4th ed., text revision). Washington, DC: Author.

Amir, N., Coles, M. E., & Foa, E. B. (2002). Automatic and strategic activation and inhibition of threat-relevant information in posttraumatic stress disorder. *Cognitive Therapy and Research, 26,* 645–655.

Brewin, C. R. (2001a). A cognitive neuroscience account of posttraumatic stress disorder and its treatment. *Behaviour Research and Therapy, 39*, 373–393.

Brewin, C. R. (2001b). Memory processes in post-traumatic stress disorder. *International Review of Psychiatry, 13*, 159–163.

Brewin, C. R., Dalgleish, T., & Joseph, S. (1996). A dual representation theory of posttraumatic stress disorder. *Psychological Review, 103*, 670–686.

Burns, M., & Seligman, M. (1989). Explanatory style across the lifespan: Evidence for stability over 52 years. *Journal of Personality and Social Psychology, 56*, 471–477.

Chemtob, C. M., Roitblat, H. L., Hamada, R. S., Carlson, J. G., & Twentyman, C. T. (1988). A cognitive action theory of posttraumatic stress disorder. *Journal of Anxiety Disorders, 2*, 253–275.

Cordova, M. J., Cunningham, L., Carlson, C. R., & Andrykowski, M. A. (2001). Posttraumatic growth following breast cancer: A controlled comparison study. *Health Psychology, 20*, 176–185.

Creamer, M., Burgess, P., & Pattison, P. (1992). Reaction to trauma: A cognitive processing model. *Journal of Abnormal Psychology, 101*, 452–459.

Dalgleish, T. (1999). Cognitive theories of post-traumatic stress disorder. In W. Yule (Ed.), *Post traumatic stress disorders: Concepts and therapy* (pp. 193–220). New York: Wiley.

Dalgleish, T. (2004). Cognitive approaches to posttraumatic stress disorder: The evolution of multirepresentational theorizing. *Psychological Bulletin, 130*, 228–260.

Ehlers, A., & Clark, D. M. (2000). A cognitive model of posttraumatic stress disorder. *Behaviour Research and Therapy, 38*, 319–345.

Ehlers, A., & Steil, R. (1995). Maintenance of intrusive memories in posttraumatic stress disorder: A cognitive approach. *Behavioural and Cognitive Psychotherapy, 23*, 217–249.

Falsetti, S. A., & Resick, P. A. (1995). Causal attributions, depression, and post-traumatic stress disorder in victims of crime. *Journal of Applied Social Psychology, 25*, 1027–1042.

Festinger, L. (1957). *A theory of cognitive dissonance.* Oxford, England: Row.

Foa, E. B., Dancu, C. V., Hembree, E. A., Jaycox, L. H., Meadows, E. A., & Street, G. P. (1999). A comparison of exposure therapy, stress inoculation training, and their combination for reducing posttraumatic stress disorder in female assault victims. *Journal of Consulting and Clinical Psychology, 67*, 194–200.

Foa, E. B., Ehlers, A., Clark, D. M., Tolin, D. F., & Orsillo, S. M. (1999). The Posttraumatic Cognitions Inventory (PTCI): Development and validation. *Psychological Assessment, 11*, 303–314.

Foa, E. B., & Kozak, M. J. (1986). Emotional processing of fear: Exposure to corrective information. *Psychological Bulletin, 99*, 20–35.

Foa, E. B., & McNally, R. J. (1996). Mechanisms of change in exposure therapy. In R. M. Rapee (Ed.), *Current controversies in the anxiety disorders* (pp. 329–343). New York: Guilford Press.

Foa, E. B., Molnar, C., & Cashman, L. (1995). Change in rape narratives during exposure therapy for posttraumatic stress disorder. *Journal of Traumatic Stress, 8,* 675–690.

Foa, E. B., & Riggs, D. S. (1993). Post-traumatic stress disorder in rape victims. In J. Oldham, M. B. Riba, & A. Tasman (Eds.), *American Psychiatric Press Review of Psychiatry* (Vol. 12, pp. 273–303). Washington, DC: American Psychiatric Press.

Foa, E. B., & Riggs, D. S. (1994). Posttraumatic stress disorder and rape. In R. S. Pynoos (Ed.), *Posttraumatic stress disorder: A clinical review* (pp. 133–163). Baltimore, MD: The Sidran Foundation & Press.

Foa, E. B., & Rothbaum, B. O. (1998). *Treating the trauma of rape: Cognitive-behavioral therapy for PTSD.* New York: Guilford Press.

Foa, E. B., Steketee, G., & Rothbaum, B. O. (1989). Behavioral/cognitive conceptualizations of post-traumatic stress disorder. *Behavior Therapy, 20,* 155–176.

Frazier, P. A., Conlon, A., & Glaser, T. (2001). Positive and negative life changes following sexual assault. *Journal of Consulting and Clinical Psychology, 69,* 1048–1055.

Frommberger, U., Stieglitz, R. D., Straub, S., Nyberg, E., Schlickewei, W., Kuner, E., et al. (1999). The concept of "sense of coherence" and the development of posttraumatic stress disorder in traffic accident victims. *Journal of Psychosomatic Research, 46,* 343–348.

Gold, S., Sinclair, B., & Balge, K. (1999). Risk of sexual revictimization: A theoretical model. *Aggression and Violent Behavior, 4,* 457–470.

Gray, M. J., & Lombardo, T. W. (2004). Life event attributions as a potential source of vulnerability following exposure to a traumatic event. *Journal of Loss & Trauma, 9,* 59–72.

Gray, M. J., Pumphrey, J. E., & Lombardo, T. W. (2003). The relationship between dispositional pessimistic attributional style versus trauma-specific attributions and PTSD symptoms. *Journal of Anxiety Disorders, 17,* 289–303.

Horowitz, M. J. (1973). Phase-oriented treatment of stress response syndromes. *American Journal of Psychotherapy, 27,* 506–515.

Horowitz, M. J. (1976). *Stress response syndromes.* New York: Jason Aronson.

Horowitz, M. J. (1979). Psychological response to serious life events. In V. Hamilton & D. M. Warburton (Eds.), *Human stress and cognition* (pp. 235–263). New York: Wiley.

Horowitz, M. J. (1986). *Stress response syndromes* (2nd ed.). Northvale, NJ: Jason Aronson.

Horowitz, M. J. (1997). *Stress response syndromes: PTSD, grief, and adjustment disorders* (3rd ed.). Northvale, NJ: Jason Aronson.

Janoff-Bulman, R. (1989). Assumptive worlds and the stress of traumatic events: Applications of the schema construct. *Social Cognition, 7,* 113–136.

Janoff-Bulman, R. (1992). *Shattered asumptions: Towards a new psychology of trauma.* New York: Free Press.

Janoff-Bulman, R. (1995). Victims of violence. In G. S. Everly, Jr. (Ed.), *Psychotraumatology: Key papers and core concepts in post traumatic stress* (pp. 73–86). New York: Plenum Press.

Janoff-Bulman, R., & Frantz, C. M. (1997). The impact of trauma on meaning: From meaningless world to meaningful life. In M. J. Power & C. R. Brewin (Eds.), *The transformation of meaning in psychological therapies: Integrating theory and practice* (pp. 91–106). Chichester, England: Wiley.

Janoff-Bulman, R., & Frieze, I. H. (1983). A theoretical perspective for understanding reactions to victimization. *Journal of Social Issues, 39,* 1–17.

Jaycox, L. H., Zoellner, L., & Foa, E. B. (2002). Cognitive-behavior therapy for PTSD in rape survivors. *Journal of Clinical Psychology, 58,* 891–906.

Joseph, S., Yule, W., & Williams, R. (1993). Post-traumatic stress: Attributional aspects. *Journal of Traumatic Stress, 6,* 501–513.

Joseph, S., Yule, W., & Williams, R. (1995). Psychosocial perspectives on post-traumatic stress. *Clinical Psychology Review, 15,* 515–544.

Kaspi, S. P., McNally, R. J., & Amir, N. (1995). Cognitive processing of emotional information in posttraumatic stress disorder. *Cognitive Therapy and Research, 19,* 433–444.

Kubany, E. S., Hill, E. E., & Owens, J. A. (2003). Cognitive trauma therapy for battered women with PTSD: Preliminary findings. *Journal of Traumatic Stress, 16,* 81–91.

Lebowitz, L., & Roth, S. (1994). "I felt like a slut": The cultural context and women's response to being raped. *Journal of Traumatic Stress, 7,* 363–390.

Lerner, M. J. (1980). *The belief in a just world: A fundamental delusion.* New York: Plenum Press.

Litz, B. T., Weathers, F. W., Monaco, V., Herman, D. S., Wulfsohn, M., Marx, B., et al. (1996). Attention, arousal, and memory in posttraumatic stress disorder. *Journal of Traumatic Stress, 9,* 497–520.

Livanou, M., Basoglu, M., Marks, I. M., De Silva, P., Noshirvani, H., Lovell, K., et al. (2002). Beliefs, sense of control and treatment outcome in post-traumatic stress disorder. *Psychological Medicine, 32,* 157–165.

Magwaza, A. S. (1999). Assumptive world of traumatized South African adults. *Journal of Social Psychology, 139,* 622–630.

Marks, I., Lovell, K., Noshirvani, H., Livanou, M., & Thrasher, S. (1998). Treatment of posttraumatic stress disorder by exposure and/or cognitive restructuring: A controlled study. *Archives of General Psychiatry, 55,* 317–325.

McNally, R. J. (1998). Experimental approaches to cognitive abnormality in posttraumatic stress disorder. *Clinical Psychology Review, 18,* 971–982.

McNally, R. J., Metzger, L. J., Lasko, N. B., Clancy, S. A., & Pitman, R. K. (1998). Directed forgetting of trauma cues in adult survivors of childhood sexual abuse with and without posttraumatic stress disorder. *Journal of Abnormal Psychology, 107*, 596–601.

Mechanic, M. B., & Resick, P. A. (1993, November). *The Personal Beliefs and Reactions Scale: Assessing rape-related cognitive schemata.* Paper presented at the 9th annual meeting of The International Society for Traumatic Stress Studies, San Antonio, TX.

Meichenbaum, D. (1994). *A clinical handbook/practical therapist manual for assessing and treating adults with posttraumatic stress disorder.* Waterloo, ON: Institute Press.

Norris, F. H., Friedman, M. J., Watson, P. J., Byrne, C. M., Diaz, E., & Kaniasty, K. (2002). 60,000 disaster victims speak: Part I. An empirical review of the empirical literature, 1981-2001. *Psychiatry: Interpersonal and Biological Processes, 65*, 207–239.

Owens, G. P., & Chard, K. M. (2001). Cognitive distortions among women reporting childhood sexual abuse. *Journal of Interpersonal Violence, 16*, 178–191.

Owens, G. P., Pike, J. L., & Chard, K. M. (2001). Treatment effects of cognitive processing therapy on cognitive distortions of female child sexual abuse survivors. *Behavior Therapy, 32*, 413–424.

Park, C. L., & Blumberg, C. J. (2002). Disclosing trauma through writing: Testing the meaning-making hypothesis. *Cognitive Therapy and Research, 26*, 597–616.

Park, C. L., & Folkman, S. (1997). Meaning in the context of stress and coping. *Review of General Psychology, 1*, 115–144.

Peterson, C. (1982). The attributional style questionnaire. *Cognitive Therapy and Research, 6*, 287–300.

Peterson, C., & Seligman, M. (1984). Causal explanations as a risk factor for depression: Theory and evidence. *Psychological Review, 91*, 347–374.

Peterson, C., & Seligman, M. (1993). Learned helplessness and victimization. *Journal of Social Issues, 39*, 103–116.

Polatinsky, S., & Esprey, Y. (2000). An assessment of gender differences in the perception of benefit resulting from the loss of a child. *Journal of Traumatic Stress, 13*, 709–718.

Power, M. J., & Dalgleish, T. (1997). *Cognition and emotion: From order to disorder.* Hove, England: Psychology Press.

Resick, P. A., & Calhoun, K. (1996). Posttraumatic stress disorder. In C. Lindemann (Ed.), *Handbook of the treatment of the anxiety disorders* (pp. 191–216). Lanham, MD: Aronson.

Resick, P. A., Nishith, P., Weaver, T. L., Astin, M. C., & Feuer, C. A. (2002). A comparison of cognitive-processing therapy with prolonged exposure and a waiting condition for the treatment of chronic posttraumatic stress disorder in female rape victims. *Journal of Consulting and Clinical Psychology, 70*, 867–879.

Resick, P. A., & Schnicke, M. K. (1992). Cognitive processing therapy for sexual assault victims. *Journal of Consulting and Clinical Psychology, 60,* 748–756.

Resick, P. A., & Schnicke, M. K. (1993). *Cognitive processing therapy for rape victims: A treatment manual.* Thousand Oaks, CA: Sage.

Resick, P. A., Schnicke, M. K., & Markway, B. G. (1991, November). *Personal Beliefs and Reactions Scale: The relation between cognitive content and posttraumatic stress disorder.* Paper presented at the 25th annual convention for the Association for Advancement of Behavior Therapy, New York.

Schulman, P., Castellon, C., & Seligman, M. E. P. (1989). Assessing explanatory style: The content analysis of verbatim explanations and the attributional style questionnaire. *Behaviour Research and Therapy, 27,* 505–512.

Schwartzberg, S. S., & Janoff-Bulman, R. (1991). Grief and the search for meaning: Exploring the assumptive worlds of bereaved college students. *Journal of Social and Clinical Psychology, 10,* 270–288.

Silver, R. C., Boon, C., & Stones, M. (1983). Searching for meaning in misfortune: Making sense of incest. *Journal of Social Issues, 39*(2), 81–102.

Tarrier, N., Pilgrim, H., Sommerfield, C., Faragher, B., Reynolds, M., Graham, E., et al. (1999). A randomized trial of cognitive therapy and imaginal exposure in the treatment of chronic posttraumatic stress disorder. *Journal of Consulting and Clinical Psychology, 67,* 13–18.

Tedeschi, R. G., & Calhoun, L. G. (1996). The Posttraumatic Growth Inventory: Measuring the positive legacy of trauma. *Journal of Traumatic Stress, 9,* 455–472.

Tedeschi, R. G., Park, C. L., & Calhoun, L. G. (1998). Posttraumatic growth: Conceptual issues. In R. G. Tedeschi & C. L. Park (Eds.), *Posttraumatic growth: Positive changes in the aftermath of crisis* (pp. 1–22). Mahwah, NJ: Erlbaum.

Wenninger, K., & Ehlers, A. (1998). Dysfunctional cognitions and adult psychological functioning in child sexual abuse survivors. *Journal of Traumatic Stress, 11,* 281–300.

Wickie, S. K., & Marwit, S. J. (2000–2001). Assumptive world views and grief reactions of parents of murdered children. *Omega, 42,* 101–113.

Williams, W. H., Evans, J. J., Needham, P., & Wilson, B. A. (2002). Neurological, cognitive and attributional predictors of posttraumatic stress symptoms after traumatic brain injury. *Journal of Traumatic Stress, 15,* 397–400.

Zeitlin, S. B., & McNally, R. J. (1991). Implicit and explicit memory bias for threat in post-traumatic stress disorder. *Behaviour Research and Therapy, 29,* 451–457.

5

SPECIALIZED COGNITIVE BEHAVIOR THERAPY FOR RESISTANT OBSESSIVE–COMPULSIVE DISORDER: ELABORATION OF A SCHEMA-BASED MODEL

DEBBIE SOOKMAN AND GILBERT PINARD

Obsessive–compulsive disorder (OCD) is a highly heterogeneous, often incapacitating, disorder that is distinct from other anxiety disorders in terms of psychopathology and treatment requirements (Frost & Steketee, 2002). Cognitive behavior therapy (CBT), with the essential procedures of exposure and response prevention (ERP), is the empirically established psychotherapy of choice (March, Frances, Carpenter, & Kahn, 1997). Several controlled studies found that combined CBT plus pharmacological treatment was no more effective than CBT alone for this disorder (Foa, Franklin, & Moser, 2002). Recently, there have been impressive advances in this field. Identification of procedural factors which impact efficacy of ERP, such as duration of exposure and thoroughness of response prevention, has suggested criteria for its "optimal" administration. Response rates reported seem best in specialized OCD clinics where clinical and research expertise and resources focus on this disorder (see Kozak & Coles, 2005, for a review). An international group of OCD researchers (Obsessive Compulsive Cognitions Working

Group [OCCWG], 1997, 2001, 2003, 2005) have identified domains of dysfunctional beliefs related to obsessions and behavioral rituals: over-importance and need to control intrusive thoughts, overestimation of threat, intolerance of uncertainty, responsibility, and perfectionism. Cognitive therapy (CT) specifically designed to address the beliefs in each of these domains has yielded promising results (Wilhelm et al., 2005), and may improve compliance with and learning during ERP. Given the heterogeneity of OCD, an important area of research has been the development of specialized CBT approaches to improve the response of OCD subtypes (see Sookman, Abramowitz, Calamari, Wilhelm, & McKay, 2005 for a review). However, research to date indicates that approximately 50% of patients still do not respond optimally to CBT, even when combined with pharmacotherapy (Baer & Minichiello, 1998; Stanley & Turner, 1995). Criteria for treatment resistance include: the patient does not participate fully in exposure, and some avoidance remains; the patient does not engage in complete response prevention during and/or between sessions; cognitive or behavioral rituals persist; and symptom-related pathology such as beliefs are not resolved. Residual symptoms persist in a substantial number of responders. A new generation of studies is needed that integrate recent theoretical/clinical advances, examine mechanisms of change, utilize more stringent criteria for improvement, and identify characteristics and degree of change in treatment responders versus nonresponders.

The purpose of this chapter is to elaborate and illustrate the specialized CBT approach developed by Sookman and colleagues (Sookman & Pinard, 1999; Sookman, Pinard, & Beauchemin, 1994) for resistant OCD of different subtypes. This approach was developed at the Obsessive Compulsive Disorder Clinic of the McGill University Health Centre, with patients who were considered resistant or refractory to previous trials of CBT. Patients with OCD of all ages are accepted for treatment, regardless of severity of illness or comorbidity. In this approach, schema-focused interventions are combined with "optimal" cognitive and behavioral strategies based on the empirical literature (e.g., see J. S. Abramowitz, 2006; Clark, 2004, for reviews). In the first section, we present the theoretical model that forms the basis for individualized case conceptualization, formulation of interventions, and assessment of change. Next, we summarize our CBT approach, and describe several CBT schema focused interventions. Finally, the efficacy of this approach and indications for further research are discussed.

A SCHEMA-BASED THEORETICAL MODEL

The cognitive behavior model of OCD proposed by Sookman et al. (1994) was intended to be theoretically broad and schema based. The

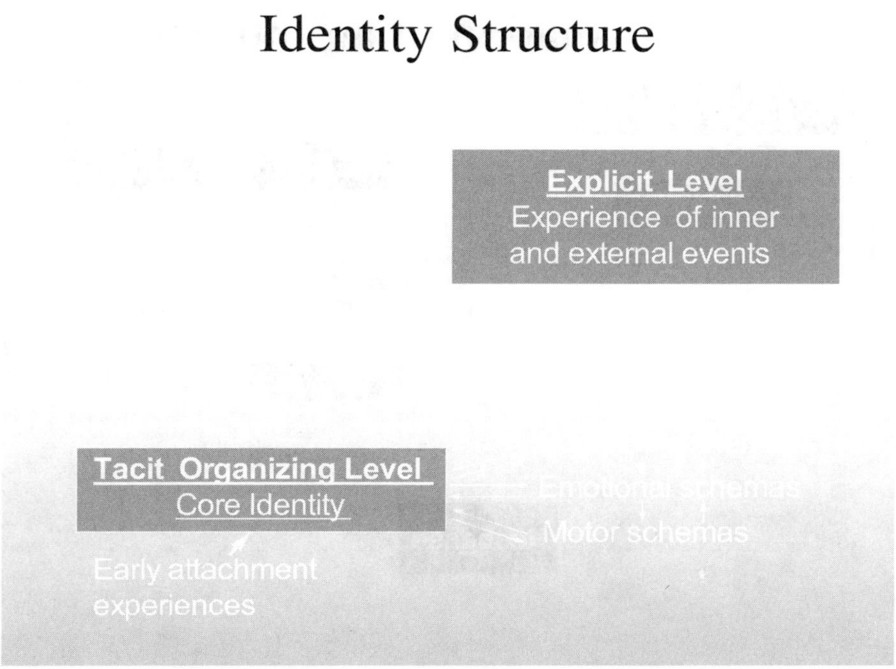

Identity Structure

Figure 5.1. Representation of identity structure. From "Multidimensional Schematic Restructuring Treatment for Obsessions: Theory and Practice," by D. Sookman, G. Pinard, and N. Beauchemin, 1994, *Journal of Cognitive Psychotherapy, 8,* p. 178. Copyright 1994 by Springer Publishing Company. Reprinted with permission.

following were proposed as relevant to OCD symptoms, based on available literature: (a) metacognitive and appraisal theory (Salkovskis, 1985, 1989; Wells & Mathews, 1994); (b) notion of schemas (A. T. Beck, Freeman, & Davis, 2004; Young, 1990); (c) developmental theory (e.g., Piaget, 1960); (d) role of attachment experiences (Bowlby, 1985; Liotti, 1988); and (e) constructivist model of identity structure (Guidano & Liotti, 1985).

Figure 5.1 shows that aspect of the model pertaining to identity structure. In this conceptualization, cognitive, emotional, and motor schemas interact at a core, tacit level (beyond accessibility to awareness) and influence ongoing information processing, cognitive content, emotional experience, and behavioral responses. Some core beliefs are hypothesized to be less readily accessible to awareness, hence the concept of tacit which refers to Piagetian schemas, which are structured and transformed throughout development. Core schemas are hypothesized to develop in the context of early attachment and learning experiences (e.g., Bowlby, 1985). Sookman et al. (1994) proposed that multiple schemas are relevant in OCD; in

Transformation of an Intrusion

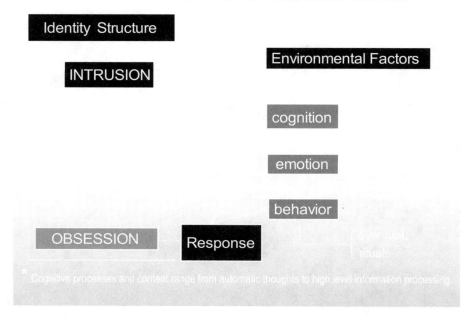

Figure 5.2. Factors relevant to the development of an obsession. From "Multidimensional Schematic Restructuring Treatment for Obsessions: Theory and Practice," by D. Sookman, G. Pinard, and N. Beauchemin, 1994, *Journal of Cognitive Psychotherapy, 8,* p. 179. Copyright 1994 by Springer Publishing Company. Reprinted with permission.

particular those related to perceived vulnerability to danger (core beliefs and emotional memories about danger); difficulty with unpredictability, newness and change; difficulty with strong feelings; and excessive need for control. The multidimensionality of schematic underpinnings of psychopathology, and centrality of emotional schemas as a factor in resistance to change, has been emphasized in recent conceptual models (A. T. Beck, 1996; Leahy, 2002). Figure 5.2 illustrates the interaction among core schemas and other factors proposed to be relevant to symptoms. Dysfunctional cognitive processes include emotional reasoning ("I feel scared so I must be in danger," Arntz, Rauner, & van den Hout, 1995) and thought–action fusion ("If I think of a bad event, it is more likely to happen"; Shafran, Thordarson, & Rachman, 1996). Cognitive process and content we refer to in Figure 5.2 range from automatic thoughts and appraisals (A. T. Beck, 1976; Salkovskis, 1985) to high-level strategic processes such as reflection upon one's own thought content and process (metacognition). Autonomic (e.g., increased heart rate) and strategic processing of events are considered to be products of activated schemas (A. T. Beck, 1996).

Sookman, Pinard, and Beck (2001) elaborated on the concept of vulnerability schemas proposed in the above model. A *Vulnerability Self-Concept schema* was defined as "an excessive sense of personal susceptibility to danger from internal as well as from external (illness, accidents, interpersonal) sources. Internal events or stimuli which may be perceived as dangerous include sensations, thoughts, images, impulses, and feelings" (p. 11). This is associated with a *Concept of World as Dangerous schema*. Dysfunctional vulnerability schemas were hypothesized to be a central underlying mechanism of excessive threat appraisals in response to stimuli that are objectively "innocuous." It was hypothesized that patients with OCD experience as particularly threatening situations involving unpredictability, newness, or change that require flexible coping. In some cases, there may also be an associated *Concept of Self as Dangerous*. This seems characteristic of patients whose checking or neutralizing are intended to avoid misfortune, washers who fear spreading contamination or illness to others, and patients with horrific temptations. These patients seem to view *others as vulnerable* to their own thoughts or actions, and feel excessively responsible (Salkovskis, 1985) for being the cause of danger. Thus they engage in protective behaviors. A study carried out to validate a scale developed to measure core beliefs related to perceived vulnerability (Vulnerability Schemata Scale) found that OCD patients more strongly endorsed these beliefs compared with other anxiety disorder patients, those with mood disorders, and normal control participants (Sookman et al., 2001).

Theoretical models that have been particularly important in the development of CBT strategies for OCD have been described by Salkovskis (1985, 1989; Salkovskis, Shafran, Rachman, & Freeston, 1999), Rachman (1997, 1998a, 1998b, 2003), and the OCCWG (1997, 2001, 2003, 2005). These models have been invaluable in elucidating specific aspects of psychopathology in this disorder that have been empirically examined (see Clark, 2004 for a review). As stated above, beliefs characteristic of the disorder have been identified in multisite studies carried out by the OCCWG. Theorists have recently focused on proposed schema aspects related to symptoms. For example, Salkovskis et al. (1999) proposed several pathways that may lead to the development of dysfunctional responsibility beliefs in OCD, including childhood experiences of too much or too little responsibility, rigid codes of behavior, and incidents in which inaction or action contributed to misfortune to self or others. Rachman (1998a, 1998b) hypothesized that specific intrusions can develop into obsessions only if appraised as personally significant, as well as signifying a threat. Intrusions that are catastrophically misinterpreted as threatening are those "important in the patient's system of values" (p. 390). In his cognitive control theory of obsessions, Clark (2004) proposed a "vulnerability level" that includes "ambivalent self-evaluation" (p. 135):

> If obsession prone individuals have a preexisting ambivalent or fragile self view, then unwanted thoughts that are completely contrary to core elements of this self-view are more likely to be interpreted as highly significant and threatening. That is, vulnerable persons are more likely to appraise their unwanted intrusive thoughts as alien to their fragile self-identities. (Clark, 2004, p. 141)

However, there has been very little empirical research on schemas that may be related to the myriad of symptoms in OCD.

Given the heterogeneity of the disorder, the model presented above offers an adaptable frame for individualized case conceptualization and treatment planning based on presenting symptom subtype(s), the meaning and function of symptoms, related beliefs and feelings, and schemas at a more core level. In our view, a flexible breadth and depth of conceptualization are clinically useful for several reasons. Similar OCD symptoms have different functions for different patients (e.g., washing to prevent feared illness as opposed to reduce feelings of disgust). Symptom-related beliefs differ across symptom subtypes. For example, responsibility appraisals (Salkovskis, 1985) are characteristic of checkers with harm-related obsessions, but are not characteristic of washers who describe "feeling" contaminated (OCCWG, 2003). Catastrophic misappraisal of thoughts as dangerous, specifically those viewed as contrary to one's value system (Rachman, 1998a, 1998b), with efforts at thought control (Clark, 2004), are central for many patients with obsessions. However, this aspect of psychopathology is not reported by other subtypes (e.g., some washers, hoarders). Thought–action fusion is experienced by some checkers (e.g., "If I have the thought death, a family member will die") but not by others (e.g., "If I don't check my stove properly, my house will burn down"). Individuals concerned with symmetry, order, or exactness may report feeling a need for perfection, or rather, that their symptoms are associated with a sense of incompleteness (Summerfeldt, 2004) or "not just right" experiences (Coles, Frost, Heimberg, & Rheaume, 2003). Contemporary CBT theory posits that (a) dysfunctional cognitive, emotional, and behavioral responses to inner/external events are manifestations of dysfunction at the core schema level, and (b) modification of the structure and content of dysfunctional schemas is necessary in order to forestall the recurrence of symptoms (A. T. Beck, 1996). Cognitive behavior treatment to modify these would seem to necessitate an integrative, schema based approach. The treatment approach used by Sookman and colleagues for resistant OCD will be summarized next.

THE MODEL IN PRACTICE

Schema based interventions for OCD are used on an individualized basis to broaden the scope of CT, to improve collaboration with intensive ERP, to improve generalization and maintenance of improvement, and to reduce susceptibility to relapse. These are combined with Beckian cognitive therapy for characteristic appraisals/beliefs, intensive ERP, behavioral experiments, and skills techniques. The rationale is that some dysfunctional schemas may interfere with basic CBT because they do not accommodate well to disconfirmatory experience, including treatment, i.e., they interfere with learning (Rosen, 1989). Core beliefs such as *"I am a vulnerable or dangerous person"* can influence ongoing strategic processing of intrusions and other experience. Dysfunctional schemas may underlie intransigent emotional beliefs about threat (Sookman & Pinard, 2002), and risk aversion (Steketee & Frost 1994), in patients who are unable to engage fully in ERP. Case illustrations of our approach are also presented in Sookman, Pinard, and Beauchemin (1994), Sookman and Pinard (1999), and Sookman and Steketee (in press).

SUMMARY OF CBT FOR RESISTANT OCD

1. Subtype characteristics are assessed and targeted, and a multidimensional profile is conceptualized with each patient. Treatment strategies are tailored to each patient's idiosyncratic experiences, especially those hypothesized to interfere with collaboration and learning in CT and ERP.

2. Symptoms, and different levels of belief (appraisals, assumptions, core beliefs), are assessed ideographically and on validated scales. Ideographic measures include self-report of emotional aspect of specific symptom-related appraisals and beliefs, with the following instruction: "Please rate on this 1 to 100 scale for each of the following beliefs how much you (a) *believe* this idea is true, and (b) *feel* this idea is true." Appraisals and beliefs are assessed on the Interpretation of Intrusions Inventory and Obsessive Beliefs Questionnaire—87 or 44 (OCCWG, 2001, 2003, 2005). Core beliefs are assessed on the Vulnerability Schemata Scale (Sookman et al., 2001). Other measures are administered on an individualized basis: (a) the *Personal Significance Scale* (Rachman, 2003), which assesses the personalized meanings patients assign to their intrusions; (b) *Thought–Action Fusion Scale* (Shafran et al.,

1996), and/or (c) Thought–Fusion Instrument (Wells, Gwilliam, & Cartwright-Hatton, 2001), which assesses three domains of metacognitive beliefs about thoughts; (d) Not Just Right Experience Questionnaire—Revised (Coles et al., 2003); and (e) Homework Compliance Form (Pimakoff, Epstein, & Covi, 1986).

3. Beckian (e.g., A. T. Beck, Emery, & Greenberg, 1985; J. S. Beck, 1995) cognitive therapy is carried out with virtually all patients prior to and during ERP, behavioral experiments, and other homework assignments. Specific dysfunctional belief domains targeted in each case are based on those most strongly endorsed on rating scales, as well as during ERP/behavioral experiments. Strategies to tolerate, decenter, and reappraise strong feelings as well as thoughts are integral.

4. Beckian CT strategies are used to address core cognitive and emotional schemas, including a focus on relevant attachment and developmental experiences (see below). Schema based CBT is not considered appropriate, or necessary, for all OCD patients. These aspects are addressed in about 50% of cases: in general for those patients who are unable to collaborate fully in ERP or sustain response prevention, and/or whose dysfunctional beliefs do not adequately resolve.

5. Intensive in vivo ERP is administered for behavioral and cognitive rituals and, with the aim of remission in mind, is complete whenever possible (i.e., no areas of avoidance or rituals). ERP is therapist-assisted in patients' naturalistic environment (home, work) as needed. Severely ill patients may be hospitalized for intensive CBT, for up to three or four hour sessions, four times weekly.

6. Family members participate routinely, unless they are deemed unable to therapeutically participate and/or if this is not considered appropriate for the patient.

7. Relapse prevention and generalization strategies are essential. These include imaginal rehearsal of triggers using adaptive strategies, and fading of therapist involvement. Booster sessions are available as needed.

8. Treatment is not time limited. Duration of CBT ranges from 6 weeks to 2 years, based on clinical need. Length of treatment for severely ill patients who receive schema-based interventions may continue for up to 2 years, followed by booster sessions as needed. Psychiatric consultation and pharmacological intervention is available as required.

SUMMARY OF SCHEMA BASED ASSESSMENT/TREATMENT INTERVENTIONS[1]

1. Core aspects thought to be related to symptoms that are accessible to the patient's awareness are identified and reappraised. OCD patients often spontaneously report some links among their thoughts, feelings, and behavior. For example, "*I get thoughts I might molest my child. I feel this is the most abhorrent thought. I'm scared this might mean I want to actually do it, I have to check my underwear to make sure there's no semen, that I have no sexual feelings, there's no chance I did it.*" Patients' core beliefs about their intrusive thoughts, images, impulses, urges, or feelings are assessed (e.g., "*Good fathers don't have thoughts of harming their helpless babies*"); as well as perceived need for safety behaviors such as ritualization, reassurance seeking, and avoidance. Self-percept and interpersonal meanings of symptoms are explored ("*I am a bad father*"). Some of these may be core, but nonetheless readily accessible. For example, the patient who reports in the initial session: "*The fact that I have these thoughts means I am a bad/dangerous/immoral/weak person.*"

2. Core aspects that are less accessible to awareness are identified and reappraised. First, tacit aspects are made more explicit. Patients are typically less aware of (a) the role of their cognitive, emotional, and behavioral responses in perpetuating symptoms; (b) the influence of more core aspects, such as their personal value system, (Rachman, 1998a, 1998b), on their responses to specific thoughts or events; and (c) the influence of past experience on current functioning. Use of downward arrow technique (A. T. Beck et al., 1985; Burns, 1980) to identify core beliefs in OCD has been described (e.g., Freeston et al., 1997; Steketee, 1999). The aim of the downward arrow in this approach is to reach a level of belief that is relatively undissociated from emotion, that is, at the implicational level (Teasdale & Barnard, 1993). The therapist assesses and targets dysfunctional emotional beliefs such as "*I don't believe it's true, but I feel it's true.*" For example, "*I know I can't get HIV from passing a red spot on the wall, but I feel there's a threat so I have to wash.*" Theoretically, we would expect a closer association between symptoms and emotional versus intellectual aspects of belief. Core schemas are hypothesized to influence the strength, and accessibility to change, of emotional beliefs.

3. Core schemas are linked to current symptoms. Based on our conceptual model, here is an illustrative sequence of maladaptive information processing that would be communicated to the patient (inserting his/her specific content):

---

[1]From Sookman and Pinard (1999). Adapted with permission.

Preexisting dysfunctional cognitive and emotional schemas (e.g., vulnerability schemas) influence autonomic and strategic processing of events—specific inner and external events are experienced/appraised as dangerous—strong feelings of anxiety/discomfort, urge to act to restore predictable feelings of safety/comfort, fear of loss of control—hyperattention, vigilance, thoughts about thoughts, thought suppression, cognitive rituals, behavioral rituals, reassurance seeking, avoidance—appraisals and beliefs about (inevitable) failure of dysfunctional strategies—perceived confirmation of dysfunctional core schemas—escalating anxiety and symptoms.

4. Obsessions are reappraised, in part, as expressions of emotions. For example, "*My thoughts of harming my baby are related to my beliefs about myself as a caretaker of a helpless child; fatigue and loneliness, frustration with my wife that we're not having sex, though I don't ask for it; rather than relating to my belief that I am a bad, dangerous father.*"

5. Effects of past experiences on current responses are explored. The therapist addresses possible origins of difficulties to help the patient to decenter from entrenched patterns and promote healthier alternatives. Of central importance is learning to tolerate strong feelings during ERP and behavioral experiments. For example: "*I'm afraid if I participate in ERP I will feel overwhelmed like I was in previous experiences (i.e., in feared situations, including as a child). I will not be able to cope. I can't stand those feelings, my obsessions and anxiety will never stop.*" Sessions and homework assignments involve identifying and modifying responses that are currently being "colored" by past experiences. ERP is combined with strategies to tolerate, decenter, and reappraise these feelings.

6. Relevant attachment experiences are identified and reappraised. Reevaluation of beliefs and feelings about childhood experiences are used to develop more adaptive, contemporary schemas. For example,

> *If I make any mistakes at work I will feel like an incompetent failure. I may have developed the need to be perfect because as a child I was often criticized for little things I did wrong. I have a basic belief that nothing I do is good enough. Another way to see this is that my father was overly rigid. I have learned to try to avoid mistakes and painful feelings of rejection with excessive checking. No one's perfect, and my colleagues, unlike my father, don't expect me to be.*

7. Specific behavioral experiments are designed to disconfirm dysfunctional beliefs related to attachment experiences. For example, intentionally making a few harmless mistakes, observing "with new eyes" the responses of others and how these may differ from childhood experiences.

8. The therapist creates a therapeutic environment which fosters "*relational affective relearning.*"

This term denotes

the process by which *emotionally meaningful* change in the patient's dysfunctional/self-interpersonal schemas (Safran, 1990) occurs in the context of an interpersonal relationship. In therapy, the aim is to create experiences that allow for schema modification (accommodation), as described by Piaget (1960). Specific disconfirming strategies involve the use of a therapeutic style that differs from the patient's expectations, where these are considered to be maladaptive. (Sookman & Pinard, 1999, p. 355)

Several ingredients may facilitate change, such as modeling of normal "risk taking" and anxiety management, explicit disconfirmation of dysfunctional emotional beliefs when they occur during sessions, and practice of new skills.

9. Schema-based interventions are combined with ERP and behavioral experiments to optimize emotionally meaningful learning. ERP homework and behavioral experiments are designed to disconfirm a variety of core beliefs such as "*I am an immoral/dangerous person.*"

TREATMENT EFFICACY AND INDICATIONS FOR RESEARCH

Sookman and Pinard (1999) and Sookman, Dalfen, Annable, and Pinard (2003) examined change in symptoms and dysfunctional beliefs following the above approach with two samples (N = 39) of CBT-resistant OCD patients. All symptom subtypes were included in these trials. Duration of previous cognitive therapy and ERP, with poor response, was 2 years or greater. Outpatient, individual treatment (1 or 2 times weekly) was administered for an average of 9.7 months. Thirty-two out of 39 patients showed clinically significant improvement in OCD symptoms and depression (Jacobson & Truax, 1991). In the second study, mean Yale–Brown Obsessive Compulsive Scale (Y–BOCS) scores were reduced from 23.2 to 11.9 (n = 32). More importantly, 10 patients from this previously resistant sample were recovered at post treatment (Y–BOCS < 7). Symptoms of 10 patients had reduced to within mild range (Y–BOCS < 16). For five patients, although their symptoms had dropped > 33% these remained in the moderately severe range. Results indicated synchrony of change among beliefs and symptoms. In the second study (by which time the Obsessive Beliefs Questionnaire was available) dysfunctional beliefs assessed on the Obsessive Beliefs Questionnaire) and core beliefs on the Vulnerability Schemata Scale, improved reliably for the responders and were unchanged for the nonresponders. The improved response found for samples considered previously resistant might

EXHIBIT 5.1.
Assessment of Treatment Outcome

- Statistical comparisons
- Percentage symptom reduction on Y–BOCS (e.g., Goodman & Price, 1992)
- Clinically significant change: at least 6-point decrease on Y–BOCS and final posttreatment score of 12 or less (Jacobson & Truax, 1991)
- Post score of 7 or less on Y–BOCS

Note. Recommended criteria: improvement to within normal range of functioning in symptoms, *related pathology, and strategic processing of previously feared* events. Y–BOCS = Yale–Brown Obsessive Compulsive Scale.

be related to the specificity of this CBT approach, such as attention to subtype characteristics and to specific aspects hypothesized to be relevant to resistance to change. Some patients who were previously unable to participate in ERP were able to do so in these trials. A crucial question we are examining is maintenance of change at long-term follow-up.

We hypothesize that among the central aspects related to resistance to CBT for OCD, are schemas related to perceived vulnerability, overestimation of threat to (personally relevant) inner and external events, especially those experienced as unpredictable, and perceived or actual difficulty coping with strong feelings. Excessive need for control of thoughts and external events may be conceptualized in some cases as a secondary response to these schemas. Presence and activation of vulnerability schemas may be among the characteristics of individuals who are too frightened to risk perceived threat in ERP. These hypotheses require further empirical examination. Consistent with A.T. Beck's hypothesis that modification of the structure and content of dysfunctional schemas is necessary in order to forestall the recurrence of symptoms (A.T. Beck, 1996), the aim of this approach is to treat to remission.

Exhibit 5.1 shows some of the criteria that have been used to designate change in the treatment literature. Statistical significance of mean pre–post scores and effect sizes, though important, are of limited value alone. In our view, an essential question is for which patients can we achieve sustained improvement to within normal range of functioning in symptoms and associated pathology. Patients who continue to ritualize in response to feared events remain susceptible to relapse under stress. This may also be the case for patients whose dysfunctional beliefs are insufficiently changed. An important question that merits study is extent of change in patients' *strategic processing* of (previously) feared events. Susceptibility to maladaptive reactions to intrusions may recur under stress without instigating relapse if the patient's strategic processing is corrective. For example,

> I had a image of molesting my child. [intrusion] *What if that means I might do it?* [appraisal] *No, as I learned in therapy, this appraisal is inaccurate.*

EXHIBIT 5.2.
Specialized Cognitive Behavior Therapy for Resistant
Obsessive–Compulsive Disorder

Multidimensional Assessment
- Psychometric-dependent measures
- Idiographic recordkeeping
- Behavioral avoidance tasks
- Completion of ERP homework
- Therapist–patient relationship
- Reports of significant others
- Neurobiological indices

It's just a harmless thought. I feel scared. I have the urge to check my underwear to make sure there's no semen. But, as I learned in therapy, this feeling is not a reliable index of actual danger. I will not let it affect my behavior.

Assessment of change is a multidimensional endeavor. Exhibit 5.2 summarizes the methods we use in the above approach to evaluate improvement in resistant OCD samples. Among the most important that may emerge as a predictor of long-term maintenance of change are patients' responses to behavioral challenges (e.g., Steketee et al., 1996). In other words, what are the patient's cognitive, emotional, and behavioral responses not only at rest when completing scales but during in vivo ERP which involves facing events most feared or avoided at pretreatment? Neurobiological indices of resolution to within normal limits, under provocation, would be another interesting arena for further research to examine to what extent we can modify the structure and content of dysfunctional schemas in Obsessive Compulsive Disorder.

REFERENCES

Abramowitz, J. S. (2006). *Understanding and treating obsessive-compulsive disorder: A cognitive behavioral approach.* Mahwah, NJ: Erlbaum.

Abramowitz, S., & Houts, A. (Eds.). (in press). *Concepts and controversies in obsessive-compulsive disorder.* New York: Springer Publishing Company.

Arntz, A., Rauner, M., & van den Hout, M. (1995). "If I feel anxious, there must be danger": Ex-consequentia reasoning in inferring danger in anxiety disorders. *Behaviour Research and Therapy, 33,* 917–925.

Baer, L., & Minichiello, W. E. (1998). Behavior therapy for obsessive compulsive disorder. In M. A. Jenike, L. Baer, & W. E. Minichiello (Eds.), *Obsessive compulsive disorder: Practical management* (pp. 132–164). St. Louis, MO: Mosby.

Beck, A. T. (1976). *Cognitive therapy and the emotional disorders*. New York: International Universities Press.

Beck, A. T. (1996). In P. M. Salkovskis (Ed.), *Frontiers of cognitive therapy* (pp. 1–25). New York: Guilford Press.

Beck, A. T., Emery, G., & Greenberg, R. L. (1985). *Anxiety disorders and phobias: A cognitive perspective*. New York: Basic Books.

Beck, A. T., Freeman, A., & Davis, D. D. (2004). *Cognitive therapy of personality disorders* (2nd ed.). New York: Guilford Press.

Beck, A. T., & Young, J. E. (1985). Depression. In D. H. Barlow (Ed.), *Clinical handbook of psychological disorders: A step-by-step treatment manual* (pp. 206–244). New York: Guilford Press.

Beck, J. S. (1995). *Cognitive therapy: Basics and beyond*. New York: Guilford Press.

Bowlby, J. (1985). The role of childhood experience in cognitive disturbance. In M. J. Mahoney & Freeman, A. (Eds.), *Cognition and psychotherapy* (pp. 181–200). New York: Plenum Press.

Bowlby, J. (1988). *A secure base: Parent-child attachment and healthy human development*. New York: Basic Books.

Bowlby, J. (1989). *The role of attachment in personality development and psychopathology*. In S. Greenspan & G. Pollock (Eds.), *Course of life. Vol. 1: Infancy* (pp. 229–270). Madison, CT: International Universities Press.

Burns, D. D. (1980). *Feeling good*. New York: Morrow.

Clark, D. M. (2004). Developing new treatments: On the interplay between theories, experimental science and clinical innovation [Special issue]. *Behaviour Research and Therapy, 42*, 1089–1104.

Coles, M. E., Frost, R. O., Heimberg, R. G., & Rheaume, J. (2003). "Not just right experiences": Perfectionism, obsessive-compulsive features and general psychopathology. *Behaviour Research and Therapy, 41*, 681–700.

Foa, E. B., Franklin, M. E., & Moser, J. (2002). Context in the clinic: How well do cognitive-behavioral therapies and medications work in combination? *Biological Psychiatry, 52*, 989–997.

Freeston, M. H., Ladouceur, R., Gagnon, F., Thibodeau, N., Rheume, J., Letarte, H., & Bujold, A. (1997). Cognitive–behavioral treatment of obsessive thoughts: A controlled study. *Journal of Consulting and Clinical Psychology, 65*, 405–413.

Frost, R. O., & Steketee, G. (2002). *Cognitive approaches to obsessions and compulsions: Theory, assessment, and treatment*. Amsterdam: Pergamon Press/Elsevier Science.

Goodman, W. K., & Price, L. H. (1992). Assessment of severity and change in obsessive compulsive disorder. *The Psychiatric Clinics of North America, 15*, 861–869.

Guidano, V. F., & Liotto, G. (1985). A constructivist foundation for cognitive therapy. In M. J. Mahoney & A. Freeman (Eds.), *Cognition and psychotherapy* (pp. 101–142). New York: Plenum Press.

Jacobson, N. S., & Truax, P. (1991). Clinical significance: A statistical approach to defining meaningful change in psychotherapy research. *Journal of Consulting and Clinical Psychology, 59,* 12–19.

Kozak, M. J., & Coles, M. E. (2005). Treatment for obsessive compulsive disorder: Unleashing the power of exposure. In J. S. Abramowitz & A. C. Houts (Eds.), *Concepts and controversies in obsessive–compulsive disorder* (pp. 283–304). New York: Springer Publishing Company.

Leahy, R. L. (2002). A model of emotional schemas. *Cognitive and Behavioral Practice, 9,* 177–190.

Liotti, G. (1988). Attachment and cognition: A guideline for the reconstruction of early pathogenic experiences in cognitive psychotherapy. In C. Perris, I. M. Blackburn, & H. Perris (Eds.), *Cognitive therapy: Theory and practice* (pp. 62–79). London: Springer-Verlag.

March, J. S., Frances, A., Carpenter, D., & Kahn, D. A. (Eds.). (1997). The expert consensus guideline series: Treatment of obsessive–compulsive disorder. *Journal of Clinical Psychiatry, 58*(Suppl. 4).

Obsessive Compulsive Cognitions Working Group. (1997). Cognitive assessment of obsessive-compulsive disorder. *Behaviour Research and Therapy, 35,* 667–681.

Obsessive Compulsive Cognitions Working Group. (2001). Development and initial validation of the obsessive beliefs questionnaire and the interpretation of intrusions inventory. *Behaviour Research and Therapy, 39,* 987–1006.

Obsessive Compulsive Cognitions Working Group. (2003). Psychometric validation of the Obsessive Beliefs Questionnaire and the Interpretation of Intrusions Inventory: Part I. *Behaviour Research and Therapy, 41,* 863–878.

Obsessive Compulsive Cognitions Working Group. (2005). Psychometric validation of the Obsessive Beliefs Questionnaire and the Interpretation of Intrusions Inventory—Part 2: Factor analyses and testing of a brief version. *Behaviour Research and Therapy, 43,* 1527–1542.

Piaget, J. (1960). *The child's conception of the world.* Oxford, England: Littlefield, Adams.

Pimakoff, L., Epstein, N., & Covi, L. (1986). Homework compliance: An uncontrolled variable in cognitive therapy outcome research. *Behavior Therapy, 17,* 433–446.

Rachman, S. (1997). A cognitive theory of obsessions. *Behaviour Research and Therapy, 35,* 793–802.

Rachman, S. (1998a). A cognitive theory of obsessions. In E. Sanavio (Ed.), *Behavior and cognitive therapy today: Essays in honor of Hans J. Eysenck* (pp. 209–222). Oxford, England: Elsevier Science.

Rachman, S. (1998b). A cognitive theory of obsessions: Elaborations. *Behaviour Research and Therapy, 36,* 385–401.

Rachman, S. (2003). *The treatment of obsessions.* Oxford, England: Oxford University Press.

Rosen, H. (1989). Piagetian theory and cognitive therapy. In A. Freeman, K. M. Simon, L. E. Beutler, & H. Arkowitz (Eds.), *Comprehensive handbook of cognitive therapy* (pp. 189–212). New York: Plenum Press.

Safran, J. D. (1990). Towards a refinement of cognitive therapy in light of interpersonal theory: II. Practice. *Clinical Psychology Review, 10,* 107–121.

Salkovskis, P. M. (1985). Obsessional-compulsive problems: A cognitive-behavioural analysis. *Behaviour Research and Therapy, 23,* 571–583.

Salkovskis, P. M. (1989). Cognitive-behavioural factors and the persistence of intrusive thoughts in obsessional problems. *Behaviour Research and Therapy, 27,* 677–682.

Salkovskis, P., Shafran, R., Rachman, S., & Freeston, M. H. (1999). Multiple pathways to inflated responsibility beliefs in obsessional problems: Possible origins and implications for therapy and research. *Behaviour Research and Therapy, 37,* 1055–1072.

Shafran, R, Thordarson, D. S., & Rachman, S. (1996). Thought–action fusion in obsessive compulsive disorder. *Journal of Anxiety Disorders, 10,* 379–391.

Sookman, D., Abramowitz, J. S., Calamari, J. E., Wilhelm, S., & McKay, D. (2005). Subtypes of obsessive compulsive disorder: Implications for specialized cognitive behavior therapy. *Behavior Therapy, 36,* 393–400.

Sookman, D., Dalfen, S., Annable, L., & Pinard, G. (2003, March). *Change in dysfunctional beliefs and symptoms during CBT for resistant OCD.* Paper presented at the 23rd annual convention of the Anxiety Disorders Association of America, Toronto, Ontario, Canada.

Sookman, D., & Pinard, G. (1999). Integrative cognitive therapy for obsessive-compulsive disorder: A focus on multiple schemas. *Cognitive and Behavioral Practice, 6,* 351–362.

Sookman, D., & Pinard, G. (2002). Overestimation of threat and intolerance of uncertainty in obsessive compulsive disorder. In R. O. Frost & G. Steketee (Eds.), *Cognitive approaches to obsessions and compulsions: Theory, assessment, and treatment* (pp. 63–89). Amsterdam: Pergamon Press/Elsevier Science.

Sookman, D., Pinard, G., & Beauchemin, N. (1994). Multidimensional schematic restructuring treatment for obsessions: Theory and practice. *Journal of Cognitive Psychotherapy, 8,* 175–194.

Sookman, D., Pinard, G., & Beck, A. T. (2001). Vulnerability schemas in obsessive-compulsive disorder. *Journal of Cognitive Psychotherapy, 15,* 109–130.

Sookman, D., & Steketee, G. (in press). Directions in specialized cognitive behavior therapy for resistant obsessive compulsive disorder: Theory and practice of two approaches [Special issue]. *Cognitive Behavioral Practice.*

Stanley, M. A., & Turner, S. M. (1995). Current status of pharmacological and behavioral treatment of obsessive-compulsive disorder. *Behavior Therapy, 26,* 163–186.

Steketee, G. (1999). *Overcoming obsessive-compulsive disorder: A behavioral and cognitive protocol for the treatment of OCD.* Oakland, CA: New Harbinger.

Steketee, G., Chambless, D. L, Tran, G. Q., Worden, H., & Gillis, M. (1996). Behavioral Avoidance Test for obsessive compulsive disorder. *Behaviour Research and Therapy, 34,* 73–83.

Steketee, G., & Frost, R. O. (1994). Measurement of risk-taking in obsessive-compulsive disorder. *Behavioural and Cognitive Psychotherapy, 22,* 287–298.

Steketee, G., Wilhelm, S., & Fama, J. (2004, November). *Contribution of changes in schemas to the outcome of cognitive therapy for OCD.* Paper presented at the annual conference of the Association for Advancement of Behavior Therapy, New Orleans, LA.

Summerfeldt, L. J. (2004). Understanding and treating incompleteness in obsessive–compulsive disorder. *Journal of Clinical Psychology/In Session, 60,* 1155–1168.

Teasdale, J. D., & Barnard, P. J. (1993). *Affect, cognition, and change: Re-modelling depressive thought.* Hillsdale, NJ: Erlbaum.

Wells, A., Gwilliam, P., & Carthwright-Hatton, S. (2001). *The thought fusion instrument.* Unpublished instrument, University of Manchester, England.

Wells, A., & Matthews, G. (1994). *Attention and emotion: A clinical perspective.* Hove, England: Erlbaum.

Wilhelm, S., & Steketee, G. (2006). *Cognitive therapy of obsessive-compulsive disorder: A guide for professionals.* Oakland, CA: New Harbinger.

Wilhelm, S., Steketee, G., Reilly-Harrington, N. A., Deckersbach, T., Buhlmann, U., & Baer, L. (2005). Effectiveness of cognitive therapy for obsessive-compulsive disorder: An open trial. *Journal of Cognitive Psychotherapy, 19,* 173–179.

Young, J. E. (1990). *Cognitive therapy for personality disorders: A schema-focused approach.* Sarasota, FL: Professional Resource Exchange.

6

COGNITIVE–BEHAVIORAL AND SCHEMA-BASED MODELS FOR THE TREATMENT OF SUBSTANCE USE DISORDERS

SAMUEL A. BALL

This chapter summarizes four cognitive–behavioral theoretical and therapeutic models for substance use disorders: relapse-prevention coping skills, rational–emotive behavior therapy, cognitive therapy, and dual-focus schema therapy. All models view faulty cognition as a core component of addictive behavior. Although genetic vulnerability, biochemical processes, cultural factors, past events, unconscious processes, and environmental contingencies may be important factors, an individual's core beliefs, attitudes, and assumptions are viewed as important factors contributing to emotional

The author acknowledges the support of the National Institute on Drug Abuse (R01 DA10012-01; R01 14967). Portions of this paper have been appeared in other publications including Ball (1998), Ball and Cecero (2001), Ball and Young (2000), and Ball (2003) and are reprinted with permission from the Association for the Advancement of Behavior Therapy, Guilford Press, and Wiley. Correspondence concerning this article should be addressed to the author at Yale University School of Medicine, VA CT Healthcare (151D), 950 Campbell Avenue—Building 35, West Haven, CT 06516 or via e-mail at samuel.ball@yale.edu.

and behavioral problems and the most relevant foci for psychological intervention. These models view the initial decision to use alcohol and drugs as being related to reasons of social acceptance, pleasure, risk, and curiosity. A pattern of substance use emerges when it provides short-term pleasure or relief from dysphoria that increasingly serves as a stimulus for continued or resumed use. The transition to a more compulsive pattern of use is usually associated with a conclusion by the individual that his or her life seems better or less aversive with a substance that has become associated with maladaptive coping or maintenance of a particular relationship(s). Once compulsive use is established, the individual's functioning, self-efficacy, coping, and thinking deteriorate and a range of situations, events, and beliefs becomes capable of triggering substance use. Chronic use results in the accumulation of negative consequences that result in a voluntary or coerced decision to seek help.

The relapse-prevention coping skills model was developed specifically for the addictive disorders. In contrast, the other three models reviewed were developed for depression, anxiety, or personality disorders, and then extended to work with substance use disorders. Nonetheless, all models share a number of core constructs, especially negative, irrational, or maladaptive beliefs about addictive substances, craving, and (low) self-efficacy regarding abstinence. Cognitive events are viewed as important mediators between external triggering events (also called high-risk situations), internal experiences (e.g., negative mood, craving), and behaviors (resisting urges vs. initial use vs. relapse). Although differing somewhat in emphasis, the therapy approaches associated with these four models all seek to reduce negative emotional and behavior reactions by changing irrational, dysfunctional, or faulty thoughts, beliefs, and assumptions. All models build their somewhat differing interventions off a fundamental behavioral technique called *functional analysis of behavior*. As an example, the A-B-C-D-E approach of rational–emotive behavior therapy focuses on activating events, beliefs, consequences, disputes, and effects. Through a careful examination of the sequence of cognitive, emotional, and behavioral events, this technique helps patients understand the process of substance use and the role of cognitive events and decisions. Better self-control and enhanced self-efficacy may also be experienced if the therapist slows down the process and intervenes at various points.

In addition to functional analysis, therapists in all four models seek to improve the patient's understanding of the way that behavioral choices and dysfunctional thinking contribute to the maintenance of their addictive disorder. Daily life patterns are identified and then targeted for modification to help the patient understand the difference between real-life problems and perceived problems. Real-life problems require problem-solving efforts and behavioral coping skills whereas perceived problems require cognitive disputing or affect management techniques. Because it is impossible to eliminate, minimize, or avoid all triggering events in one's life, therapy focuses on patients developing active, alternative cognitive interpretations and behavioral choices for when they are faced with high-risk situations for substance use. Each model emphasizes to varying degrees the development of adaptive and pleasurable activities, coping skills, social supports, assertiveness, affect regulation or tolerance skills, and acceptance of the validity of more reality-based beliefs.

Although these four models have commonalities, there also are important differences, especially the relative emphasis placed on different theoretical constructs and primary intervention targets (e.g., behavioral vs. cognitive vs. affective). After briefly reviewing these models, I discuss research findings, paying particular attention to my work on a specialized schema-focused cognitive–behavioral model for substance abuse patients with personality disorders.

COGNITIVE–BEHAVIORAL THEORY AND THERAPIES FOR SUBSTANCE USE DISORDERS

Relapse-Prevention Coping Skills

One of the most widely studied and used cognitive–behavioral approaches for understanding and treating substance dependence is relapse-prevention coping skills. The relapse-prevention treatment model was first introduced to a wide range of clinicians and scientists through the publication of Marlatt and Gordon's (1985) seminal text. In the past 20 years, there has been a proliferation of texts and therapy manuals, and a body of treatment–outcome research now supports the efficacy of relapse-prevention coping skills in reducing substance abuse and improving psychosocial outcomes in a range of alcohol and drug abusers. Marlatt and Gordon's (1985) original model was a clinical extension of Albert Bandura's social learning theory. It described addictive behavior as a learning process in which environmental factors (e.g., drug availability, peer groups, family systems, life stressors) interacted with psychological factors (e.g., cognition, affect, coping, self-regulatory mechanisms) to increase risk for substance use, progression to abuse and dependence, and relapse following treatment. The pharmacological effects of drugs and the biological processes underlying addiction proneness are not ignored in this model, but greater emphasis is placed on the individual's beliefs and expectancies about the psychological effects of substances (e.g., affect regulation, stress reduction, reinforcement, sensation seeking, social enhancement). In more specific terms, the theory emphasizes the cognitive interpretations and behavioral reactions to environmental events both as relevant to the etiology and maintenance of addictive behavior and as important targets for treatment intervention.

The interaction between cognition and behavior within this model (Brownell, Marlatt, Lichtenstein, & Wilson, 1986; Marlatt & Gordon, 1985) can be summarized as follows: High-risk situations (most typically involving negative mood, interpersonal conflict, social pressure, cue exposure) are thought to threaten sobriety through their effects on self-efficacy. If coping resources exist and the person successfully abstains, then self-efficacy is enhanced. If substances are used, then self-efficacy decreases, heightening the probability of continued use. This process is most dramatically expressed in the abstinence violation effect, a phenomenon involving a combination of dichotomous and catastrophic thinking that turns an initial behavioral slip into full relapse. After an initial reexposure to substances, the person who has established an abstinence goal for him- or herself is hypothesized to engage in a sequence of automatic, self-defeating thoughts that increase the likelihood of continued use. Relapse also can be a sequence of automatic cognitions and behaviors as in the concept of apparently or seemingly irrelevant decisions in which the individual engages in thoughts and actions that bring him or her into closer contact with people and situations in which substance availability is likely.

Relapse-prevention and coping skills treatments (Kadden et al., 1992; Marlatt & Gordon, 1985; Monti, Abram, Kadden, & Cooney, 1989) have been evaluated in several well-controlled treatment outcome studies and have emerged as promising treatment approaches for substance abuse (see Beck, Wright, Newman, & Liese, 1993; Carroll, 1997b, for reviews). Although this treatment repeatedly has been shown to be efficacious, the interventions most emphasized in all clinical trials tend to focus on behaviors rather than dysfunctional thoughts, attitudes, beliefs, or schemas. The session topics focus on changing behaviors through avoidance of high-risk situations (drinking and drug use settings, geographic moves, changing phone numbers, ending relationships, direct deposit of paycheck), stimulus control (eliminating supply, destroying paraphernalia), contingency contracting, activity scheduling, job training, behavioral substitution, relaxation training, coping with affects, imagery or distraction techniques for craving control, refusal skills, receiving criticism, nonverbal communication, emergency planning, assertiveness skills, communication skills, problem-solving skills, and developing social supports.

The identification, testing, and disputing of cognitive distortions is deemphasized and rarely used as a core technique within the 12- to 16-week time limits of most clinical trial protocols. Some core techniques have a cognitive focus (e.g., preventive messages about catastrophic thinking involved in the abstinence violation effect; education about apparently irrelevant decisions that inadvertently result in exposure to increasingly risky substance use situations; completion of decision matrix exercises that consider the pros and cons of using vs. not using). However, these interventions are primarily behavioral, psychoeducational, or motivational in aim rather than used in conjunction with Socratic questions, downward arrow discussion of irrational beliefs, or rational disputes. Thus, in many ways, a more purely cognitive model of substance abuse therapy does not yet have much empirical support for its efficacy. A review of the alcoholism outcome literature for rational–emotive behavior therapy (REBT; see next section) does suggest some changes in the endorsement of irrational thinking but limited impact on changes in drinking behavior (Terjesen, DiGiuseppe, & Gruner, 2000) or in drug abuse outcomes.

Rational–Emotive Behavior Therapy

Rational–emotive behavior therapy was first described by Albert Ellis in the 1950s, and then 30 years later was applied to addictive behavior (Ellis, McInerney, DiGiuseppe, & Yeager, 1988). Ellis articulated three overarching constructs (pleasure seeking, discomfort anxiety, and low frustration tolerance) within his model of addictive beliefs. Pleasure seeking drives the anticipatory-oriented beliefs and is particularly relevant during the early phase of substance use. Drug and alcohol use is initially valued as a rapid, accessible source of positive reinforcement or gratification from either the chemical intoxication or the surrounding social context ("It will be fun to get high with my friends"). Even as substance use becomes more habitual, patients often persistently attempt to recapture the early pleasurable experience. Nonetheless, pleasure seeking traits or states and their related anticipatory-oriented beliefs lose their primacy as motivators once substance use becomes problematic (abuse) and are gradually supplanted by alcohol and drug use for negative reinforcement. Relief-oriented beliefs begin to dominate the cognitive–motivational landscape as substance dependence (i.e., addiction) develops. These beliefs are related to a goal of reducing negative experiences such as stress ("I need to use so I don't have to deal with this problem"), craving, withdrawal, or negative emotions ("I will feel sad, empty, and alone unless I go out and get high").

The activation of both anticipatory-oriented (for positive reinforcement) and relief-oriented (for negative reinforcement) beliefs is thought to be important in the stimulation or exacerbation of cravings for substances, but by themselves neither are sufficient to culminate in an episode of substance use. Ellis conceptualizes the actual seeking and use of substances as related to a separate category of beliefs called *facilitating–permissive beliefs*. These self-statements are driven primarily by two other core constructs that Ellis regards as central to addictive beliefs: (a) low frustration tolerance and (b) discomfort anxiety. Discomfort anxiety is an emotional state related to the anticipation of unpleasant experiences in life driven by the irrational belief that such human experiences are intolerable (Ellis et al., 1988). Low frustration tolerance is related to abstinence from substances, including the inability to resist urges ("I cannot stand avoiding drugs any longer") or inability to function or cope without using ("I cannot abstain because life is too painful"). Therapy is difficult because the chemical means of reducing discomfort and frustration are so easy and available whereas rational, emotional, and behavioral control techniques take time and effort to learn and implement consistently across a range of triggering events. The distinction between the anticipatory–relief-oriented and facilitating–permissive beliefs is important because it suggests different opportunities for rational disputes and behavioral assignments with the client.

A major goal within Ellis's model is to develop better (rational) control strategies and responses to the activation of these various addictive beliefs. Through the A-B-C-D-E model, patients learn that events do not cause emotions or behaviors but rather trigger a cognitive interpretation or decision that results in certain emotional or behavioral reactions. As with all forms of irrational thought, addictive beliefs are automatic, nonconscious, and reinforced through experience. At the core of many of the irrational beliefs is a sense of "demandingness" characterized by misguided, grandiose attempts to control what cannot be controlled through irrational rules containing the language of *must, needs, have to,* and *should* rather than the more reasonable *desire, prefer, want,* or *wish.* Therapy involves disputing these thoughts by bringing them to consciousness through the ABC part of the model and then changing them through D and E. Through this work, patients learn to have better self-acceptance for experiencing a fuller range of positive and negative emotions, while focusing attention on which behavior (rather than substance use) is most appropriate for a given thought or emotion. An important task in this regard is to understand how some negative emotions are helpful to indicate problems that need to be defined, solved, or simply accepted as a normal consequence of being human.

Cognitive Therapy

Aaron Beck developed cognitive therapy (CT) several years after Ellis developed rational therapy; initially, CT was a psychotherapeutic approach for depression (Beck, Rush, Shaw, & Emery, 1979). Since then, it has been adapted for other psychiatric disorders, including substance abuse (Beck et al., 1993). Beck makes the important distinction between dysfunctional beliefs that are the result of chronic substance use (addictive beliefs) versus those that may be antecedent (predispositional characteristics). Addictive beliefs are important for the maintenance of the disorder and are major factors involved in relapse. These beliefs center on themes of pleasure seeking, problem solving, relief, and escape and include the perceived need for a substance to (a) maintain psychological balance, (b) improve different areas of functioning, (c) provide pleasure or soothing, (d) enhance a sense of power and control, and (e) relieve boredom, negative mood, stress, or craving. These basic beliefs are then fueled by secondary permission-giving beliefs related to justifying use, taking risks, and feeling entitled to use.

Beck's *predispositional characteristics* are often closely connected with core beliefs or core schemas that together stimulate addictive beliefs in many high-risk situations. One set of core beliefs centers on an individual's sense of self (helpless, trapped, defeated, inferior, weak, inept, useless, or a failure) and the other is related to a sense of connection to others (unlovability, unacceptability). Predispositional characteristics center primarily on concepts of affect dysregulation and impulsivity: (a) sensitivity to unpleasant or changing mood (affect dysregulation); (b) poor motivation to control behavior (impulsivity); (c) poor skill at controlling behavior; (d) automatic, nonreflective yielding to impulses; (e) sensation seeking and boredom intolerance; (f) diminished future time perspective; and (g) low frustration tolerance. As in REBT, low frustration tolerance is heavily emphasized in CT as an important target for cognitive disputes, especially the dysfunctional beliefs that life should always go smoothly, that it is awful when goals get blocked, and that people should be blamed or punished when they block one's goals. Once an activity or expectation is impeded, substance abusers with low frustration tolerance often exaggerate the loss or consequences they are experiencing, blame others, and overlook alternative solutions to the problem. Unless the problem is solved or the tension is reduced appropriately, either retaliation occurs or substance use ensues as an alternative to reduce the tension. Either form of "relief" is temporary, and the individual fails to learn more effective methods of solving problems, which perpetuates the susceptibility to experiences of low frustration tolerance and helplessness.

Beck also describes a network of substance-related dysfunctional beliefs that center on the inability to resist urges ("Even if I stop using, the craving will never stop"), improved coping ("If I use, I can handle my life better"), social facilitation ("I need to use to control my social anxiety"), or beliefs in controlled use ("I can do this once and then stop"). The behavior of substance use is similar to the relative balance between urges and control in any given situation. Whereas urges are felt more viscerally, control must be exerted mentally through cognitive decision making, often initially through a weighing of the pros and cons of choosing to use (permission giving) or not use (refusal). The stronger the craving, the more difficult the internal debate, so any coping method that even temporarily delays action can reduce craving and provide more room for careful cognitive deliberation and decision making. Therapy attempts to increase this ratio of control relative to craving through techniques such as imagery, behavioral assignments, and cognitive disputing.

The cognitive therapist's overall task is to introduce and reinforce more adaptive, reality-based beliefs and behaviors to take the place of the addictive beliefs and to coach the patient to anticipate and solve problems and tolerate affect. This process typically occurs over several steps. The therapist initially examines the sequence of external and internal events preceding and following substance use through a functional analysis of behavior. Then, he or she facilitates the exploration of beliefs about the value of using substances through a detailed cost–benefit analysis of the short-term and long-term advantages and disadvantages of continued use. This exploration is facilitated through traditional cognitive techniques of Socratic questioning, guided discovery, and downward arrow. For example, guided discovery can facilitate an open discussion of the abstinence violation effect to provide concrete substance-related examples of both dichotomous ("I am either a totally sober, valuable person in recovery or a completely relapsed, worthless addict") and catastrophic ("One slip means I am a total personal failure") thinking. Work on these maladaptive cognitive and behavioral reactions often provides an opportunity to initiate work on cognitive distortions. The therapeutic goals with all cognitive distortions are to (a) identify and define them, (b) explore the evidence for and against their validity, (c) explore what is wrong or distorted through cognitive disputes, (d) examine alternatives or advantages or disadvantages of believing distortions, and (e) develop new statements or alternative beliefs.

Dual-Focus Schema Therapy

Beck, Freeman, and Davis (2004) and Young (1994) have defined maladaptive or dysfunctional schemas as enduring, unconditional, negative beliefs about oneself, others, and the world that organize one's experiences and subsequent behaviors. These schemas are very broad, pervasive themes that develop early in life most often through an interaction of biologically influenced temperament and parenting practices. They are then elaborated in adolescence, reinforced through repetitive experiences, and perpetuated into adulthood primarily through relational patterns. These dysfunctional, core themes are deeply entrenched, central to self, self-perpetuating, and difficult to change (Young, Klosko, & Weishaar, 2003). Because the experience of thoughts, feelings, and impulses associated with early maladaptive schemas is distressing to the individual or others, the individual typically develops behavioral strategies to cope. These long-standing, overlearned, usually unrecognized, cognitive, affective, interpersonal, and behavioral responses to the triggering of a schema are called maladaptive coping styles. Although these behaviors may effectively reduce the negative affect associated with schema activation, they are self-defeating and impede the meeting of basic needs and the change process (Young, 1994; Young et al., 2003).

The dual-focus schema therapy model (DFST; Ball, 1998, 2003; Ball & Rounsaville, 2006; Ball & Young, 2000) views addiction as a primary disorder, but also conceptualizes schema activation and maladaptive avoidance as heightening the ongoing risk for relapse among individuals with significant personality problems. The model hypothesizes that substance use can occur as a direct behavioral expression of the activation of impaired-limits schemas (entitlement, insufficient self-control) or when an other-directedness schema (subjugation, self-sacrifice, approval seeking) gets triggered within a substance abusing or otherwise dysfunctional relationship. Another potent relapse risk factor is the patient's overreliance on avoidance as a maladaptive means of coping with the affect or conflict associated with the activation of schemas (and associated memories) especially around themes of disconnection and rejection (schemas of abandonment, mistrust or abuse, emotional deprivation, defectiveness, social isolation) or impaired autonomy or performance (schemas of dependence or incompetence, vulnerability to harm, enmeshment, failure to achieve). Many methods of schema avoidance, including social withdrawal, psychological withdrawal, compulsive stimulation seeking, and addictive self-soothing, seem to be common among individuals with severe addictions (Young, 1994; Young et al., 2003).

Dual-focus schema therapy is a time-limited, manual-guided individual therapy consisting of a set of core topics, the specific content and delivery of which are determined by an assessment and conceptualization of the individual's early maladaptive schemas and coping styles. Dual-focus schema therapy includes traditional, symptom-focused relapse-prevention coping skill techniques for interpersonal, affective, and craving factors (Kadden et al., 1992; Marlatt & Gordon, 1985; Monti et al., 1989) and schema-focused techniques for the maladaptive schemas and coping styles (Young, 1994; Young et al., 2003). Therapeutic attention to current symptoms, conflicts, and issues attempts to reduce risk for Axis I relapse and promote the necessary cognitive, emotional, and interpersonal stability necessary for later work on personality and coping styles. Although work on initiating and maintaining abstinence from substances is continually integrated within the framework of the schema-focused approach, therapists may shift to a primary focus on relapse prevention when clinically indicated.

Dual-focus schema therapy interventions are focused on addictive behaviors and personality problems and are integrated by a common core of techniques. For example, functional analysis is used to understand recent episodes of substance use and craving as well as maladaptive schema and coping triggering events. Self-monitoring, problem solving, and coping skills training (e.g., for negative emotions and interpersonal conflicts) all occur for both the addiction and personality problems. Dysfunctional beliefs about substance use are conceptualized as a critically important component or expression of underlying core schemas. Dual-focus schema therapy hypothesizes that a broad range of the patient's difficulties can be subsumed by a single or few early maladaptive schemas and coping styles and that targeted change in substance use and core schemas can have a significant impact on a broader range of behaviors by disrupting the behavioral and interpersonal chain of events that perpetuate problems in adulthood. Cognitive, experiential, relational, and behavioral interventions are based on a detailed conceptualization that includes assessment and feedback on personality traits, schemas, coping styles, interpersonal conflict, substance abuse, and psychiatric symptoms (Ball, 1998, 2003).

Case Study

Bill, a 36-year-old divorced man who began using substances at the age of 14, had several prior substance abuse treatments before starting methadone maintenance 1 year before beginning individual therapy. His heroin dependence was in remission and his primary drug abuse problem at the beginning of therapy was cocaine with more sporadic use of a high-potency solvent to which his part-time job gave him ready access. Bill also met structured diagnostic interview criteria for obsessive–compulsive personality disorder and had two additional personality disorders (antisocial; depressive) that appeared secondary to his chronic substance abuse.

Bill's primary early maladaptive schema was unrelenting standards that appeared to originate from the seemingly contradictory combination of parental perfectionism (with physical or emotional abuse for Bill's "failures" as a child) and defeat secondary to both parents being torture survivors who escaped to the United States from another country. Bill put a great deal of pressure on himself, and any minor deviation in his striving for perfection triggered a massive substance relapse, irresponsible giving up, and antisocial acting out. Bill engaged in a number of maladaptive coping behaviors that perpetuated his schema including expecting too much of himself and others and being a perfectionistic workaholic. At other times, he sought relief from the pressures of these standards and would avoid occupational or social commitments, develop somatic symptoms, procrastinate, or give up in defeat and use drugs when he could not get things perfect. These avoidance strategies actually reinforced the unrelenting standards even more as he would subsequently have to redouble his efforts to get desired outcomes.

Bill began his course of DFST in a loud, challenging manner, wanting to know for sure that therapy was going to help him, and that he was going to get as much out of it as the research team got from him as a study participant. Because he continued to abuse cocaine and inhalants for the first 3 months, therapy necessarily remained more relapse-prevention focused while he struggled to grasp cognitively the schema-focused psychoeducational material. By the fourth month, he had achieved complete abstinence from solvents and was using cocaine much less frequently. However, little if any decrease in his unrelenting standards was noted.

Cognitively oriented interventions included cost–benefit analyses of his unrelenting standards and reduction of the perceived risks of imperfection in his relationships. A core cognitive distortion targeted for dispute was "When I don't accomplish the best or get what I want, I should get enraged, give up, use drugs, and be dejected." Experiential techniques involved imagery dialogues with his parents about how they always catastrophized mistakes. Behavioral techniques included learning to accept "good enough" work from himself and others, accepting directions from people he did not respect, and redeveloping old leisure interests. Therapeutic relationship interventions included the therapist modeling acceptance of his own mistakes, processing homework noncompliance resulting from self-imposed rigid standards, and confronting his dichotomous views of the therapist. Much of the work in his outside relationships and in the therapeutic relationship focused on helping him change his dichotomous view of other people as well as his own recovery (i.e., all good–sober vs. all bad–relapsed). Despite a rather turbulent course of treatment, Bill appeared genuinely interested in improving himself and made some significant changes over the course of the 24-week manual-guided DFST. In addition to his reduced substance abuse, he also experienced significant reductions in psychiatric symptoms and negative affect (adapted from Ball & Young, 2000).

SCHEMA-RELATED RESEARCH IN SUBSTANCE ABUSE

Substance Use and Core Beliefs

To date, there has been relatively limited research on negative thoughts, core beliefs, dysfunctional attitudes, and maladaptive schemas of substance abusers. A distinction is often made in the depression literature between automatic negative thoughts that exist only during periods of acute illness and dysfunctional attitudes and underlying assumptions that persist beyond acute states and into periods of depression recovery (Kovacs & Beck, 1978; Segal, 1988). Such enduring, core assumptions that persist in symptom-free states are usually called dysfunctional or negative self-schemas. Young (1994) further differentiated these constructs from early maladaptive schemas that he believed are a specific subclass and that have their origins in early development and incorporate not only cognitive beliefs or assumptions but also maladaptive emotional and relational processes and memory structures. According to this theory (Young et al., 2003), early maladaptive schemas are most relevant to the Axis II disorders and to treatment-refractory, chronically relapsing Axis I conditions. Many substance-dependent individuals fall into one or both of these categories.

When the assessment and treatment of substance abuse are being considered, the distinction between automatic thoughts, core beliefs, and early maladaptive schemas is important for several related reasons. First, many of the automatic negative thoughts experienced by substance-abusing individuals may be the direct result of acute or chronic substance use. Substance intoxication, dependence, and withdrawal are characterized by marked changes in cognitive, emotional, and social functioning that may mimic many of the symptoms of personality disorders and depression (Ball, Rounsaville, Tennen, & Kranzler, 2001). Furthermore, from the standpoint of a cognitive–behavioral therapy (CBT) of substance abuse, it may be reasonable to expect that one class of automatic negative thoughts (see earlier discussion about addictive beliefs related to anticipation or relief) will likely remit solely with achievement of short-term abstinence through standard behaviorally based relapse-prevention techniques. In contrast, other core distortions or beliefs may have developed through years of substance abuse (see earlier discussion about discomfort anxiety and low frustration intolerance) that may remit only with persistent cognitive disputes, behavioral task assignments, self-help meetings, and prolonged abstinence. Finally, early maladaptive schemas (see earlier discussion about disconnection–rejection themes rooted in repetitive early experiences) may never be eliminated entirely. Instead, realistic treatment goals may need to emphasize greater awareness of schema-triggering situations, decreased affect associated with schema activation, and substitution of more adaptive coping strategies for maladaptive interpersonal processes that perpetuate the schemas.

The Dysfunctional Attitudes Scale (DAS; Weissman & Beck, 1978) is a measure of negative (i.e., depressotypic) beliefs, assumptions, or self-evaluations that are hypothesized to heighten one's vulnerability to depression. Although research has found elevated levels of dysfunctional attitudes and negative automatic thoughts in depression, these appear to be mostly limited to the depressive episode (Whisman, 1993). An important exception to this rule is for patients with depression and co-occurring personality disorder. Just as the personality disorder persists when the depression remits, so too apparently do the dysfunctional attitudes and beliefs (Iliardi & Craighead, 1999; Iliardi, Craighead, & Evans, 1997). Because depression and personality disorders are the most common co-occurring psychiatric disorders in substance-abusing individuals, it is reasonable to assume that a substantial number of addicted individuals experience dysfunctional attitudes and beliefs that may persist even during prolonged periods of abstinence and that may be severely exacerbated by chronic use.

Supporting this assumption, Hill, Oei, and Hill (1989) found evidence of dysfunctional automatic thoughts and attitudes in patients with depression, personality disorder, and substance abuse. Calache, Martinez, Verhulst, Bourgeois, and Peyre (1994) compared 38 substance-abusing patients (half with depression, half without) and 30 healthy control participants using the DAS. Both depressed and nondepressed substance-abusing patients had higher DAS scores than did normal patients, and depressed substance-abusing patients scored higher than did nondepressed users. Chabrol, Massot, Chouicha, Montovany, and Roge (2001) found that the intensity of addictive beliefs (anticipatory, relief-oriented, permissive beliefs) was correlated with the frequency of cannabis use in a sample of 285 high school seniors in France. Ramsey, Brown, Stuart, Burgess, and Miller (2002) demonstrated that depressed alcohol-dependent patients treated with either CBT or relaxation therapy in the context of a partial hospitalization program showed decreased levels of dysfunctional attitudes. Although there were no differences between the conditions in terms of DAS changes, the CBT patients showed better improvements in self-efficacy, alcohol-related expectancies, and drinking outcomes. Denoff (1988) found that parental child rearing and a client's irrational beliefs were independent predictors of substance abuse among adolescents seeking residential treatment. Child-rearing practices related to achievement pressure, conditional approval, and avoidance of responsibility were particularly salient predictors.

With regard to Young's early maladaptive schemas and substance abuse, Decouvelaere, Graziani, Gackiere-Eraldi, Rusinek, and Hautekeete (2002) compared 46 alcohol-dependent patients with 50 nonalcoholic control participants using a French translation of the schema questionnaire. The alcohol-dependent group scored higher on almost all schemas, with insufficient self-control, mistrust or abuse, self-sacrifice, and abandonment being especially salient. Likewise, Brotchie, Meyer, Copello, Kidney, and Waller (2004) found that individuals who abused alcohol (either alone or in combination with opiates) scored higher on schemas of vulnerability to harm, subjugation, and emotional inhibition than did a nonclinical comparison group. Ball and Cecero (2001) evaluated the association of personality disorder severity with early maladaptive schemas and interpersonal problems in 41 methadone-maintained outpatients diagnosed with a personality disorder. A summary of these correlational analyses in Table 6.1 suggests that the severity of each personality disorder was associated with a somewhat different pattern of cognitive schemas and interpersonal problems.

Although Young emphasized the particular importance of early maladaptive schemas for personality disorders or patients with treatment-resistant Axis I disorders, others suggested that the schemas have relevance for a broader range of psychiatric patients. As Stopa, Thorne, Waters, and Preston (2001) has suggested, research in this area needs to evaluate whether

TABLE 6.1
Personality Disorder Symptom Correlates With Early Maladaptive Schemas and Interpersonal Problems

Personality disorder	Early maladaptive schemas	Interpersonal problems
Paranoid	Mistrust–abuse	Domineering Vindictive
Schizoid	Mistrust–abuse Social isolation	Socially avoidant
Schizotypal	Mistrust–abuse Social isolation	Domineering
Antisocial	Mistrust–abuse Vulnerability to harm Emotional inhibition	Domineering Vindictive Cold Exploitable (lower)
Borderline	Abandonment Mistrust–abuse	Socially avoidant
Histrionic	Mistrust–abuse Social isolation Dependence–incompetence Unrelenting standards	
Narcissistic		Overassertiveness
Avoidant	Subjugation	Exploitable
Dependent	Abandonment Dependence–incompetence Subjugation	Exploitable Overly nurturing
Obsessive–compulsive	Self-sacrifice (lower)	Exploitable (lower)

Axis I and II patients differ from each other (as well as from control groups) in the degree or type of dysfunctional schemas or the absence of more adaptive coping to counteract the schemas. Very little is currently known about the existence or relevance of early maladaptive schemas in different clinical groups or whether the targeting of schemas in treatment is as necessary for Axis I patients as it has been hypothesized to be by Beck and Young for patients with personality disorder.

Development of the Early Maladaptive Schema Questionnaire—Research Version

A schema-focused therapeutic approach should use a reliable and valid assessment of its core constructs: (a) early maladaptive schemas and (b) maladaptive coping styles. Self-report inventories developed by Young and colleagues are one of several ways to determine a patient's more salient schemas. Although no research to date has evaluated the reliability and validity of inventories of the maladaptive coping styles, a number of studies support the factor structure, internal consistency, test–retest reliability, and discriminant validity (Ball & Cecero, 2001; Brotchie et al., 2004; Lee, Taylor, & Dunn, 1999; Mihaescu et al., 1997; Petrocelli, Glaser, Calhoun, & Campbell, 2001; Schmidt, Joiner, Young, & Telch, 1995; Stopa et al., 2001; Waller, Meyer, & Ohanian, 2001; Welburn, Coristine, Dagg, Pontefract, & Jordan, 2002) of the Young Schema Questionnaire (YSQ) in both the long form (205 items) and short form (75 items) versions in both clinical and community samples.

Although these scale reliability and factorial validity results are encouraging, in the course of my DFST treatment development work with lower functioning patients with personality disorder (discussed later), I became concerned with three issues related to the integrity of the YSQ as a research instrument. First, its grouping of items for each schema, rather than mixing the item order, potentially artificially inflates factor loadings and scale coherence. Second, all items for 15 schemas are positively worded so that higher Likert ratings are indicative of a schema, rendering the scale more susceptible to biased responding, which again may affect scale reliability and validity. Third, the reading comprehension level required to answer many questions is too high for a severely impaired population with limited education. For this reason, I worked closely with Jeffrey Young who developed the YSQ short and long forms and made wording changes to increase simplicity and clarity of the 75-item short form and to allow at least one reverse-scored item for each schema. After an initial item tryout and analysis, the item order was then varied so that, for example, the spacing of items for emotional deprivation was changed from 1 to 5 (as on the YSQ short form) to 1, 16, 31, 46, and 61. In addition, for easier responding, the scale metric was changed from a 6-point scale (1 = *completely untrue of me*; 6 = *describes me perfectly*) to a 4-point scale (0 = *very false*, 1 = *part false*, 2 = *part true*, 3 = *very true*). The Early Maladaptive Schema Questionnaire—Research Version (EMSQ–R) and scoring key are provided in Appendix 6.1.

In an early study of the construct validity of the EMSQ–R, Cecero, Nelson, and Gillie (2004) evaluated its psychometric properties in 292 undergraduates and its relation to childhood traumatic experiences and adult attachment. Their factor solution identified 14 of the 15 factors (defectiveness–shame did not emerge). They found adequate levels of internal consistency (when three items with low item-total correlations were removed) with the exception of the Subjugation, Enmeshment, Entitlement, and Insufficient Limits scales that had low alphas. Several early maladaptive schemas (abandonment or instability, subjugation, social isolation, mistrust or abuse, vulnerability to harm, emotional inhibition) were associated with maladaptive attachment styles. Abandonment–

instability and dependence–incompetence were associated with childhood traumatic experiences.

Loper (2003) has also evaluated the validity of the EMSQ–R in 116 female prisoners with personality disorders, many of whom also had substance abuse problems. The impaired-limits domain (insufficient self-control; entitlement) was the highest endorsed grouping (domain) of schemas and was associated with several personality disorders, hostility symptoms, institutional misconduct, and violence perpetuation and victimization. The disconnection–rejection domain was the second highest endorsed grouping of schemas and was related to multiple psychiatric symptoms. Three of the schema domains showed adequate internal consistency and validity. The other-directedness and overvigilance–inhibition domains did not show acceptable internal consistency.

In ongoing data collection of more than 800 patients using the EMSQ–R in a therapeutic community program, the highest scoring schemas are self-sacrifice, unrelenting standards, entitlement, mistrust–abuse, and emotional inhibition. Lower scores are found for emotional deprivation and enmeshment. Although waiting for complete data collection before offering a conclusion, it is unclear what to make of the high scores on self-sacrifice and unrelenting standards given that this treatment population is highly antisocial (pathologically self-centered) and impulsive (careless, irresponsible). In randomized clinical trials treating homeless, substance-abusing individuals with personality disorders (Ball, Cobb-Richardson, Connolly, Bujosa, & O'Neall, 2005), early maladaptive schemas were evaluated using the EMSQ–R and interpersonal problems that bear some resemblance to maladaptive coping styles in the interpersonal domain. The most commonly reported maladaptive schemas in descending order of score were self-sacrifice, social isolation, unrelenting standards, entitlement, emotional inhibition, and mistrust–abuse. With regard to interpersonal problems, the most commonly reported interpersonal problems subscales were Cold, Overly Nurturant, Social Avoidance, Exploitative, Vindictive, and Nonassertive. In general, maladaptive avoidance was a severe problem that seemed to be a defining characteristic of this complex population.

Dual-Focus Schema Therapy: Model Development and Findings

In a behavioral therapy development study funded by the National Institute on Drug Abuse (NIDA), my fellow researchers and I recruited a total of 41 methadone-maintained patients with personality disorders (Ball & Cecero, 2001). I treated ten patients for 24 weeks (under Jeffrey Young's supervision) while developing the treatment manual and then training the additional therapists who subsequently treated 30 patients randomly assigned to receive either DFST or standard 12-step drug counseling. With regard to the initial 10 participants, trends in the data suggested that patients treated with DFST decreased their frequency of substance use and saw a decrease in the severity of their psychiatric symptoms and ratings of dysphoria as well. Subjective ratings of dysphoria (depression, anxiety, hostility) decreased by month 4 to the point of equaling positive affect ratings (which remained fairly stable across the study). Furthermore, although these data are subjective in nature, the eight patients evaluated at study termination reported that they found DFST one of the most useful therapeutic interventions they had received in their multiple-treatment histories (Ball & Young, 2000).

After the 10 initial participants were studied, the small randomized clinical trial found that patients assigned to DFST reduced substance use frequency more rapidly over the 24-week treatment than did patients assigned to a 12-step drug counseling condition. Evaluation of the data over time suggested a difference beginning to emerge at month 3 that corresponded to a point in the manual when the treatment was shifting from an assessment and education focus to an active change phase. Analyses of the dysphoria ratings showed that the 12-step therapy patients exhibited steady decreases in this summary measure of negative mood (as distinct from psychiatric symptoms) over time in comparison with DFST patients who showed no change in dysphoria. As it turned out, however, this sustained dysphoric mood was not related to relapse or dropout. In addition, DFST patients reported an increase from a good early therapeutic alliance to a very strong alliance over the months of treatment whereas 12-step therapy patients demonstrated no such increase. Likewise, from the therapist's perspective, DFST was associated with a stronger working alliance than was 12-step counseling (Ball, in press).

Dual-focus schema therapy has also been compared with a standard substance abuse counseling group for homeless drop-in center clients with substance abuse and personality disorders through funding provided by the Jacob and Valeria Langeloth Foundation in New York City (Ball et al., 2005). Fifty-two homeless clients meeting structured diagnostic interview criteria for substance abuse and personality disorder at the drop-in center were randomly assigned to one of the two onsite manual-guided 24-week treatment conditions; primary outcomes were therapy retention and utilization. Overall, these outcomes favored DFST over the standard substance abuse group offered. However, the data suggested that clients with more severe personality disorder symptoms had somewhat better utilization of the substance abuse group than the DFST individual therapy, which was regarded as a highly novel service offered in this setting.

Another, larger randomized clinical trial funded by NIDA is nearing completion in a residential therapeutic community (TC) for adolescents and adults with significant substance abuse and criminal justice problems.

Dual-focus schema therapy first focuses on improving engagement in the residential milieu through psychoeducation of the patient on the patient's personality and the suitability, relevance, and usefulness of a TC for addressing these individual differences and needs. This first stage of DFST treatment provides a form of psychological inoculation for why the TC may be a difficult form of treatment (because of the interaction of the patient's schemas with the program's confrontational atmosphere). In such a situation, the impulse to escape, avoid, or act out is accepted as normal but must be restrained for benefits to be achieved from the TC model. The behavior change techniques used in the second phase of DFST (at 2–6 months) are conceptualized as working synergistically with the TC methods, processes, or elements. For example, schemas and maladaptive coping are triggered through job (adult patients) or school (adolescent patients) responsibilities, community incidents, rules, consequences, and groups, and the TC is a specialized, safe, and therapeutic learning laboratory in which this can be worked through more adaptively. A total of 115 patients have been randomly assigned to receive either DFST or another manual-guided individual therapy (individual drug counseling) with primary outcomes including retention and changes in psychological indicators related to personality and substance use disorders.

CONCLUSIONS

Of the four models reviewed, currently only the relapse-prevention coping skills model has a robust empirical literature supporting its efficacy for substance abusers. This model is different from the other three in placing proportionately greater emphasis on behavioral techniques through coping skills training in comparison to the more traditional use of rational or cognitive therapy techniques that are central to Ellis's and Beck's models or the more experiential and relational focus of Young's schema therapy or its adaptation as DFST for personality-disordered substance abusers.

In light of the prominence of cognitive–behavioral theory and therapies for substance abuse, the paucity of studies on its core constructs (maladaptive beliefs and schemas) represents a significant gap in the literature. Substance abusers do seem to have elevations of certain types of dysfunctional beliefs, but it is unclear whether these problems are specific to substance abuse or are related to many forms of psychopathology. Likewise, it is unknown whether these beliefs, attitudes, or schemas should be considered relevant to the etiology of substance abuse or a consequence of the profound cognitive, emotional, behavioral, and relational effects of chronic use of mind-altering chemicals.

Nonetheless, it is important to recognize that a CBT model of addiction may have several advantages over other models. Such an approach for substance abuse has theoretical grounding (social learning and cognitive development theory), varying degrees of empirical support, and technical flexibility and compatibility. With regard to flexibility, CBT can be adapted to work with patients with different patterns of comorbidity and at different levels of recovery. It is the only empirically validated treatment for addiction that also has empirical support for its separate use with mood, anxiety, eating and personality disorders, and with an evolving literature for schizophrenia. CBT can work at the level of behavioral symptoms, conscious beliefs, and deeper core issues (schemas). With regard to compatibility, this approach has been integrated or sequenced with motivational interviewing, 12-step facilitation, and insight-oriented therapies. It has also been readily integrated into every addiction treatment modality, including detoxification, outpatient, methadone maintenance, partial hospital, inpatient, and residential therapeutic communities as well as with all available pharmacotherapies for addiction. In fact, preliminary evidence suggests that it may be a better psychosocial platform from which to add a medication strategy than other approaches would be (Carroll, 1997a). It also has models for both adolescent treatment and for family and couples therapy. Thus, CBT provides a reasonably comprehensive model for understanding addictive beliefs and behaviors and one of the more promising treatment approaches for these disorders alone and in combination with the other forms of psychopathology reviewed in this volume.

Early Maladaptive Schema Questionnaire—Research Version

INSTRUCTIONS: Listed below are statements that you might use to describe yourself. Please answer all items. Do not leave any blank. Circle one of the following choices for each statement:

Very False: Does not describe you or your situations at all; the opposite is more true.
Part False: Somewhat more false than true; does not describe you or your situation too well.
Part True: Somewhat more true than false; describes you fairly well in some but not all situations.
Very True: Describes you well; true in most situations and most of the time.

	0	1	2	3
1. I know people who really understand what I feel and need.	Very False	Part False	Part True	Very True
2. I fit in well with most people.	Very False	Part False	Part True	Very True
3. I hold on to people because I fear they will leave me.	Very False	Part False	Part True	Very True
4. People take advantage of me.	Very False	Part False	Part True	Very True
5. People won't like me once they see my weak points.	Very False	Part False	Part True	Very True
6. I do as well as other people at work (or school).	Very False	Part False	Part True	Very True
7. I can't get by doing things on my own.	Very False	Part False	Part True	Very True
8. I get into trouble when I do what I want.	Very False	Part False	Part True	Very True
9. I don't really worry about bad things happening.	Very False	Part False	Part True	Very True
10. I experience things differently from my parent(s) or partner.	Very False	Part False	Part True	Very True
11. I'm the one who takes care of others.	Very False	Part False	Part True	Very True
12. I must be the best at everything I do.	Very False	Part False	Part True	Very True
13. I enjoy showing my positive feelings toward people.	Very False	Part False	Part True	Very True

	0	1	2	3

14. It's hard for me to take "no" for an answer.
Very False / Part False / Part True / Very True

15. I like doing routine or even boring tasks.
Very False / Part False / Part True / Very True

16. I don't get much warmth and affection from others.
Very False / Part False / Part True / Very True

17. I feel different from other people.
Very False / Part False / Part True / Very True

18. I worry about losing people I need.
Very False / Part False / Part True / Very True

19. I trust that people who know me won't hurt me.
Very False / Part False / Part True / Very True

20. People won't get close if they know the real me.
Very False / Part False / Part True / Very True

21. I'm as good at getting things done as other people.
Very False / Part False / Part True / Very True

22. I need other people even for very simple things.
Very False / Part False / Part True / Very True

23. I let other people make many choices for me.
Very False / Part False / Part True / Very True

24. I think about really bad things happening suddenly.
Very False / Part False / Part True / Very True

25. My parent(s) and I are too involved in each other's lives.
Very False / Part False / Part True / Very True

26. I think of others more than of myself.
Very False / Part False / Part True / Very True

27. I can't accept second best.
Very False / Part False / Part True / Very True

28. It is hard for me to show my real feelings.
Very False / Part False / Part True / Very True

29. I think many rules shouldn't apply to me.
Very False / Part False / Part True / Very True

30. I give up quickly if I can't get what I want.
Very False / Part False / Part True / Very True

31. I don't feel special to anyone.
Very False / Part False / Part True / Very True

32. I feel like a loner.
Very False / Part False / Part True / Very True

33. People I feel close to will be with me for a long time.
Very False / Part False / Part True / Very True

34. Soon enough someone will betray me.
Very False / Part False / Part True / Very True

35. I deserve love and respect no matter what I do.
Very False / Part False / Part True / Very True

36. I'm not as successful as other workers (or students).
Very False / Part False / Part True / Very True

37. I have excellent common sense.
Very False / Part False / Part True / Very True

38. I let the other person control our relationship.
Very False / Part False / Part True / Very True

	0	1	2	3
	Very False	Part False	Part True	Very True

39. I worry about being hurt or robbed.

Very False / Part False / Part True / Very True

40. I feel like I have to let my parent(s) know everything.

Very False / Part False / Part True / Very True

41. I spend more time and energy on me than helping others.

Very False / Part False / Part True / Very True

42. I must meet all my responsibilities all the time.

Very False / Part False / Part True / Very True

43. I am a warm, positive, and emotional person.

Very False / Part False / Part True / Very True

44. I dislike being stopped from doing what I want.

Very False / Part False / Part True / Very True

45. It's easy to say "no" to things now to get better things later.

Very False / Part False / Part True / Very True

46. There are people who care deeply about me.

Very False / Part False / Part True / Very True

47. I feel cut off from people even when I am near them.

Very False / Part False / Part True / Very True

48. I get scared when people pull away from me.

Very False / Part False / Part True / Very True

49. I wonder a lot about if people might harm me.

Very False / Part False / Part True / Very True

50. I feel that I am not lovable.

Very False / Part False / Part True / Very True

51. Most people are more talented than I am.

Very False / Part False / Part True / Very True

52. I make good choices by myself.

Very False / Part False / Part True / Very True

53. People get back at me if I don't do what they want.

Very False / Part False / Part True / Very True

54. I worry that I'll lose everything I have.

Very False / Part False / Part True / Very True

55. My parent(s) live their lives through me.

Very False / Part False / Part True / Very True

56. I listen to everybody's problems.

Very False / Part False / Part True / Very True

57. I feel great pressure to get things done perfectly.

Very False / Part False / Part True / Very True

58. I try to control my feelings.

Very False / Part False / Part True / Very True

59. I like following the same rules that other people do.

Very False / Part False / Part True / Very True

60. It's easy doing things I don't like when it's for my own good.

Very False / Part False / Part True / Very True

61. I have people who help me with good advice.

Very False / Part False / Part True / Very True

62. I am on the outside of groups.

Very False / Part False / Part True / Very True

	0	1	2	3
63. I am so worried about people leaving that I push them away.	Very False	Part False	Part True	Very True
64. I watch for the hidden reasons why people do things.	Very False	Part False	Part True	Very True
65. I don't want people to know about my personal flaws.	Very False	Part False	Part True	Very True
66. I'm a failure in many ways.	Very False	Part False	Part True	Very True
67. It's easy for me to solve everyday problems on my own.	Very False	Part False	Part True	Very True
68. It's easy for me to stand up for myself.	Very False	Part False	Part True	Very True
69. I worry I'm very sick even when doctors say nothing's wrong.	Very False	Part False	Part True	Very True
70. I seem to lose myself when around people I feel close to.	Very False	Part False	Part True	Very True
71. I do too much for others and not enough for myself.	Very False	Part False	Part True	Very True
72. Mistakes are okay if I have a good reason.	Very False	Part False	Part True	Very True
73. People see me as uptight about my feelings.	Very False	Part False	Part True	Very True
74. What I have to offer is better than others can give.	Very False	Part False	Part True	Very True
75. I always stick to what I agree to do.	Very False	Part False	Part True	Very True

Early Maladaptive Schema Questionnaire—Research Version Scoring Sheet

Emotional deprivation	Social isolation	Abandonment	Mistrust–abuse	Defectiveness–shame	Failure to achieve	Dependence–Subjugation incompetence
1 ____ (R)	2 ____ (R)	3 ____	4 ____	5 ____	6 ____ (R)	7 ____
16 ____	17 ____	18 ____	19 ____ (R)	20 ____	21 ____ (R)	22 ____
31 ____	32 ____	33 ____ (R)	34 ____	35 ____ (R)	36 ____	37 ____ (R)
46 ____ (R)	47 ____	48 ____	49 ____	50 ____	51 ____	52 ____ (R)
61 ____ (R)	62 ____	63 ____	64 ____	65 ____	66 ____	67 ____ (R)
TOTAL: ____	____	____	____	____	____	____

Vulnerability to harm	Enmeshment	Self-sacrifice	Unrelenting standards	Emotional inhibition	Entitlement	Insufficient limits
9 ____ (R)	10 ____ (R)	11 ____	12 ____	13 ____ (R)	14 ____	15 ____ (R)
24 ____	25 ____	26 ____	27 ____	28 ____	29 ____	30 ____
39 ____	40 ____	41 ____ (R)	42 ____	43 ____ (R)	44 ____	45 ____ (R)
54 ____	55 ____	56 ____	57 ____	58 ____	59 ____ (R)	60 ____ (R)
69 ____	70 ____	71 ____	72 ____ (R)	73 ____	74 ____	75 ____ (R)
TOTAL: ____	____	____	____	____	____	____

Note. (R) indicates a reverse scored item: 3 = >0, 2 = >1, 1 = >2, and 0 = >3. Any scale summed to 10 to 12 suggests an elevated schema. Any scale summed to 13 to 15 suggests a very elevated schema. Any scale summed to 0 to 3 suggests high defensiveness.

Copyright 2001 by Samuel A. Ball. Printed with permission of the author.

REFERENCES

American Psychiatric Association. (1994). *Diagnostic and statistical manual of mental disorders* (4th ed.). Washington, DC: Author.

Ball, S. A. (1998). Manualized treatment for substance abusers with personality disorders: Dual Focus Schema Therapy. *Addictive Behaviors, 23,* 883–891.

Ball, S. A. (2004). Treatment of personality disorders with co-occurring substance dependence: Dual focus schema therapy. In J. J. Magnavita (Ed.), *Handbook of personality disorders: Theory and practice* (pp. 398–425). New York: Wiley.

Ball, S. A. (in press). Comparing individual therapies for personality disordered opioid dependent patients. *Journal of Personality Disorders.*

Ball, S. A., & Cecero, J. J. (2001). Addicted patients with personality disorders: Traits, schemas, and presenting problems. *Journal of Personality Disorders, 15,* 72–83.

Ball, S. A., Cobb-Richardson, P., Connolly, A. J., Bujosa, C. T., & O'Neall, T. W. (2005). Substance abuse and personality disorders in homeless drop-in center clients: Symptom severity and psychotherapy retention in a randomized clinical trial. *Comprehensive Psychiatry, 46,* 371–379.

Ball, S. A., & Rounsaville, B. J. (2006). Refinishing without rebuilding: Dual focus schema therapy for personality disorder and addiction. In R. L. Spitzer, M. B. First, J. B. W. Williams, & M. Gibbon (Eds.), *Treatment companion to the DSM–IV–TR casebook* (2nd ed., pp. 53–65). Washington, DC: American Psychiatric Association.

Ball, S. A., Rounsaville, B. J., Tennen, H., & Kranzler, H. R. (2001). Reliability of personality disorder symptoms and personality traits in substance dependent inpatients. *Journal of Abnormal Psychology, 110,* 341–352.

Ball, S. A., & Young, J. E. (2000). Dual focus schema therapy for personality disorders and substance dependence: Case study results. *Cognitive and Behavioral Practice, 7,* 270–281.

Beck, A. T., Freeman, A., & Davis, D. D. (2004). *Cognitive therapy of personality disorders* (2nd ed.). New York: Guilford Press.

Beck, A. T., Rush, A. J., Shaw, B. F., & Emery, G. D. (1979). *Cognitive therapy of depression.* New York: Guilford Press.

Beck, A. T., Wright, F. D., Newman, C. F., & Liese, B. S. (1993). *Cognitive therapy of substance abuse.* New York: Guilford Press.

Brotchie, J., Meyer, C., Copello, A., Kidney, R., & Waller, G. (2004). Cognitive representations in alcohol and opiate abuse: The role of core beliefs. *British Journal of Clinical Psychology, 43,* 337–342.

Brownell, K. D., Marlatt, G. A., Lichtenstein, E., & Wilson, G. T. (1986). Understanding and preventing relapse. *American Psychologist, 41,* 765–782.

Calache, J., Martinez, R., Verhulst, S. J., Bourgeois, M., & Peyre, R. (1994). Dysfunctional attitudes in depressed and non-depressed substance abusers: An exploratory study. *European Psychiatry, 9,* 77–82.

Carroll, K. M. (1997a). Manual guided psychosocial treatment: A new virtual requirement for pharmacotherapy trials. *Archives of General Psychiatry, 54,* 923–928.

Carroll, K. M. (1997b). Relapse prevention as a psychosocial treatment: A review of controlled clinical trials. In G. A. Marlatt & G. R. VandenBos (Eds.), *Addictive behaviors: Readings on etiology, prevention, and treatment* (pp. 697–717). Washington, DC: American Psychological Association.

Cecero, J. J., Nelson, J. D., & Gillie, J. M. (2004). Tool and tenets of schema therapy: Toward the construct validity of the Early Maladaptive Schema Questionnaire—Research Version (EMSQ–R). *Clinical Psychology & Psychotherapy, 11,* 344–357.

Chabrol, H., Massot, E., Chouicha, K., Montovany, A., & Roge, B. (2001). Study of dysfunctional beliefs in adolescent cannabis use using the Questionnaire of Anticipatory, Relief-Oriented, and Permissive Beliefs for Drug Addiction. *Journal de Therapie Comportementale et Cognitive, 11,* 105–108.

Decouvelaere, F., Graziani, P., Gackiere-Eraldi, D., Rusinek, S., & Hautekeete, M. (2002). Hypothesis of existence and development of early maladaptive schemas in alcohol-dependent patients. *Journal de Therapie Comportementale et Cognitive, 12,* 43–48.

Denoff, M. S. (1988). An integrated analysis of the contribution made by irrational beliefs and parental interactions to adolescent drug abuse. *International Journal of the Addictions, 23,* 655–669.

Ellis, A., McInerney, J. F., DiGiuseppe, R., & Yeager, R. J. (1988). *Rational-emotive therapy with alcoholics and substance abusers.* New York: Psychology Practitioner Guidebooks.

Hill, C. V., Oei, T. P., & Hill, M. A. (1989). An empirical investigation of the specificity and sensitivity of the Automatic Thoughts Questionnaire and Dysfunctional Attitudes Scale. *Journal of Psychopathology and Behavioral Assessment, 11,* 291–311.

Iliardi, S. S., & Craighead, W. E. (1999). The relationship between personality pathology and dysfunctional cognitions in previously depressed adults. *Journal of Abnormal Psychology, 108,* 51–57.

Iliardi, S. S., Craighead, W. E., & Evans, D. D. (1997). Modeling relapse in unipolar depression: The effects of dysfunctional cognitions and personality disorders. *Journal of Consulting and Clinical Psychology, 65,* 381–391.

Kadden, R., Carroll, K. M., Donovan, D., Cooney, N., Monti, P., Abrams, D., et al. (1992). Cognitive–behavioral coping skills therapy manual: A clinical research guide for therapists treating individuals with alcohol abuse and dependence. In M. E. Mattson (Ed.), *Project MATCH Monograph Series* (Vol. 3; DHHS Publication No. 94-3724). Rockville, MD: NIAAA.

Kovacs, M., & Beck, A. T. (1978). Maladaptive cognitive structures in depression. *American Journal of Psychiatry, 135,* 525–533.

Lee, C. W., Taylor, R. G., & Dunn, J. (1999). Factor structure of the schema questionnaire in a large clinical sample. *Cognitive Therapy and Research, 23,* 441–451.

Loper, A. B. (2003). The relationship of maladaptive beliefs to personality and behavioral adjustment among incarcerated women. *Journal of Cognitive Psychotherapy, 17,* 253–266.

Marlatt, G. A., & Gordon, J. R. (1985). *Relapse prevention.* New York: Guilford Press.

Mihaescu, G., Secahud, M., Cottraux, J., Velardi, A., Heinze, X., Finot, S. C., & Baettig, D. (1997). Le questionnaire de schemas cognitifs de Young: Traduction et validation preliminaire [Young's cognitive schemas questionnaire: Translation and preliminary validation]. *L'Enchephale, 23,* 200–208.

Monti, P. M., Abram, D. B., Kadden, R., & Cooney, N. (1989). *Treating alcohol dependence: A coping skills training guide.* New York: Guilford Press.

Petrocelli, J. V., Glaser, B. A., Calhoun, G. B., & Campbell, L. F. (2001). Early maladaptive schemas of personality disorder subtypes. *Journal of Personality Disorders, 15,* 546–559.

Ramsey, S. E., Brown, R. A., Stuart, G. L., Burgess, E. S., & Miller, I. W. (2002). Cognitive variables in alcohol dependent patients with elevated depressive symptoms: Changes and predictive utility as a function of treatment modality. *Substance Abuse, 23,* 171–182.

Schmidt, N. B., Joiner, T. E., Young, J. E., & Telch, M. J. (1995). The Schema Questionnaire: Investigation of psychometric properties and hierarchical structure of a measure of maladaptive schemas. *Cognitive Therapy and Research, 19,* 295–321.

Segal, Z. V. (1988). Appraisal of the self-schema construct in cognitive models of depression. *Psychological Bulletin, 103,* 147–162.

Stopa, L., Thorne, P., Waters, A., & Preston, J. (2001). Are the short and long forms of the Young Schema Questionnaire comparable and how well does each version predict psychopathology scores? *Journal of Cognitive Psychotherapy, 15,* 253–272.

Terjesen, M. D., DiGiuseppe, R., & Gruner, P. (2000). A review of REBT research in alcohol abuse treatment. *Journal of Rational–Emotive and Cognitive Behavior Therapy, 18,* 165–179.

Waller, G., Meyer, C., & Ohanian, V. (2001). Psychometric properties of the long and short versions of the Young Schema Questionnaire: Core beliefs among bulimic and comparison women. *Cognitive Therapy and Research, 25,* 137–147.

Weissman, A., & Beck, A. T. (1978, March). *Development and validation of the dysfunctional attitude scale: A preliminary investigation.* Paper presented at the annual meeting of the American Educational Research Association, Toronto, Ontario, Canada.

Welburn, K., Coristine, M., Dagg, P., Pontefract, A., & Jordan, S. (2002). The Schema Questionnaire—Short Form: Factor analysis and relationship between schemas and symptoms. *Cognitive Therapy and Research, 26,* 519–530.

Whisman, M. A. (1993). Mediators and moderators of change in cognitive therapy of depression. *Psychological Bulletin, 47,* 837–845.

Young, J. E. (1994). *Cognitive therapy for personality disorders: A schema-focused approach.* Sarasota, FL: Professional Resource Exchange.

Young, J., & Brown, G. (1994). *Schema Questionnaire* (2nd ed.). Unpublished instrument.

Young, J. E., Klosko, J. S., & Weishaar, M. E. (2003). *Schema therapy: A practitioner's guide.* New York: Guilford Press.

7

SCHEMA-FOCUSED COGNITIVE–BEHAVIORAL THERAPY FOR EATING DISORDERS

GLENN WALLER, HELEN KENNERLEY, AND VARTOUHI OHANIAN

Up until the mid-1990s, conventional cognitive–behavioral therapy (CBT) for the eating disorders (e.g., Fairburn, 1997) was based largely on models of psychopathology that were developed 2 decades ago (e.g., Fairburn, 1981; Garner & Bemis, 1982). These were largely maintenance models, which address the factors that sustain the eating disorder once it has developed but do not attempt to explain its etiology. Trials of CBT based on such models have demonstrated an impressive effectiveness rate among relatively specific groups, particularly bulimia nervosa and binge-eating disorder (Agras, Walsh, Fairburn, Wilson, & Kraemer, 2000; Fairburn et al., 1995; Fairburn & Harrison, 2003; Vitousek, 1996; Waller & Kennerley, 2003; Wilson, 1999). However, it has become clear that those early models, and the therapies developed from them, are not sufficient to deal with a range of eating disorders (e.g., Hollon & Beck, 1994). For example, they

---

Names have been changed to preserve anonymity. Our use of female examples here and throughout (and the use of female pronouns) simply reflects the fact that this population is predominantly female. We use the same principles and practice in working with male cases.

139

are no more effective than some other therapies in anorexia nervosa. Finally, there is virtually no evidence that CBT (or any other therapy) is effective in the treatment of the other atypical eating disorders, such as anorexia nervosa or bulimia nervosa that do not meet full diagnostic criteria (Fairburn & Harrison, 2003; Waller & Kennerley, 2003; Wilson, 1996, 1999). This pattern of findings has resulted in the development of a second set of CBT maintenance models of the eating disorders. For example, Fairburn, Shafran, and Cooper (1999) suggested a model of anorexia nervosa that addresses the fundamental relevance of belief systems concerning control (as put forward by Slade, 1982). They subsequently developed a transdiagnostic model of the eating disorders (Fairburn, Cooper, & Shafran, 2003) that eschews diagnostic differentiation. These models remain to be tested therapeutically to determine whether they have greater value than the previously mentioned existing models.

At the same time as the development of this second wave of maintenance models of the eating disorders, it was suggested that such models might not be sufficient to account for the phenomenology of the eating disorders because they do not take sufficient account of past experiences as causal factors and of the role of such experiences in the ongoing psychopathology. As far back as 1994, Hollon and Beck suggested that meaningful models need to incorporate other levels of cognition.

Cooper (1997) and Waller and Kennerley (2003) have concluded that the schema level of representations (cognitive, emotional, behavioral, and somatic) is the most likely to aid in the development of broader CBT models of the eating disorders. Unlike the more here-and-now maintenance models, these broader models require a deeper understanding of the role of past experiences in the development of eating disorders and related behaviors, detailing the roles played by unconditional core belief systems, affective states, and somatic states in generating those behaviors. A complex model of functioning is necessary to explain many features of the eating disorders that are relatively resistant to existing CBT for the eating disorders, such as very poor self-esteem, body-image disturbance, perfectionism, dissociation, multiple impulsive behaviors, compulsive pathology, and personality pathology (e.g., Fichter, Quadfleig, & Reif, 1994; Sansone & Fine, 1992; Waller, 1997). The resilience of these psychological phenomena suggests a need to develop models of the eating disorders that take account of the schema-level representations that might underpin them, and to develop interventions accordingly.

In discussing the management of eating disorders, we have deliberately chosen to use the term *schema-focused cognitive–behavioral therapy* (SFCBT). Although this term possibly goes against current trends in the field of schema therapy (e.g., Young, Klosko, & Weishaar, 2003), we have adopted the term because of the crucial importance of behavioral change (both as a mechanism of change and as a target for that change) when working with the eating disorders. An exclusive focus on the cognitive element of these disorders is not likely to be effective.

Although it is important to develop an SFCBT that can improve treatment outcomes with the eating disorders, it is also crucial to not ignore the advances that have been made in the field in the past 2 decades. Therefore, the developments that are discussed and advocated here should be seen as having the potential to augment rather than replace existing therapy outcomes. Such innovations can comfortably coexist with the first-wave and the developing second-wave CBT maintenance models, as well as with other developments in CBT that might be applicable to the eating disorders (e.g., dialectical behavior therapy: Linehan, 1993; Wiser & Telch, 1999; interpersonal cognitive therapy: Safran & Segal, 1990). The long-term goal must be to determine criteria for matching treatments to individual patients' needs.

For current purposes, we have focused on the eating disorders as they are defined in the standard diagnostic schemes (anorexia nervosa, bulimia nervosa, eating disorder not otherwise specified or atypical cases), rather than considering simple obesity or compulsive eating. This distinction reflects the literature to date, which identifies a core cognitive pathology that is specific to the eating disorders (overevaluation of the importance of eating, weight, and shape; e.g., Fairburn et al., 2003; Waller, 1993) rather than to other eating-related difficulties.

SCHEMAS IN THE EATING DISORDERS

Recent years have yielded a number of studies of schemas in the eating disorders. Conclusions from this literature are limited by the use of the term *schema* in different ways. Although there appears to be agreement that the schema is a mental structure of meaning that is derived from experience, some authors have used the term to describe a purely cognitive construct (e.g., Cooper, 1997), discounting the noncognitive processes (e.g., behavior, emotion) that are inherent in the concept. Furthermore, Cooper, Cohen-Tovée, Todd, Wells, and Tovée (1997) focus only on self-schemas in their conceptualization of the eating disorders. In contrast to this limited framework, outside the world of eating disorders, cognitive therapists have developed models of meaning that integrate cognitive with noncognitive elements (e.g., Beck, 1996). To add further confusion, some authors use the term *schema* to describe what appear to be conditional beliefs as well as unconditional beliefs. For example, in describing "central schemas that interfere with treatment progress," Padesky and Greenberger (1995) described a patient who "believed he would be worthless *if* [emphasis added] he followed

TABLE 7.1
The Relationship Between Unconditional Beliefs
and Schema Development

Cognitions regarding the self	Cognitions regarding other people and the world	Cognitions regarding the future	Possible schemas (using Young's nomenclature)
Worthless; unlovable	Judgmental, but can be adjusted	My performance or ability will redeem me	Unrelenting standards
Worthless; unlovable	Judgmental, but can be adjusted	Precarious; I have to make the best of it	Vulnerability to harm
Worthless; unlovable	Judgmental and harsh	Hopeless and lonely	Abandonment

the advice of someone else" (p. 29). An example of an unconditional belief is the belief of an individual that she is worthless regardless of setting, other people's actions, or circumstances.

When studying depression, Beck developed his concept of the cognitive triad (Beck, Rush, Shaw, & Emery, 1979)—a triangle of interacting beliefs about self, others or the world, and the future. Beck recognized that the interplay of these beliefs helps to shape people's schemas, which in turn influence their interpretations, emotional responses, and behaviors. People generally function well when the cognitive triad is relevant to reality: when their interpretations are realistic and their responses are appropriate. However, that is not always the case. Table 7.1 illustrates how this triangle of interacting beliefs might manifest as particular schemas. Those schemas might then predispose a person to an eating disorder, which may or may not manifest itself. For example, unrelenting standards could drive restrictive anorexia; a need to dissociate from a vulnerability to harm schema might drive bulimic behaviour; a painful abandonment schema might trigger comfort eating in someone with a binge-eating disorder.

A pioneer of SFCBT, Young (1994) described early maladaptive schemas as consisting of both unconditional cognitive content (core beliefs about the self, others and the world, and the future) and cognitive processes (e.g., schema maintenance and coping mechanisms). When a schema is activated, those processes maintain the cognitive content, often via the behavioral, affective, and somatic manifestations of those schemas. Other cognitive therapists have also postulated models to capture the rich multi-modal quality of the schema (e.g., Power, 1997; Teasdale & Barnard, 1993); these models allow complex information processing to occur effortlessly and rapidly. For example, the following case demonstrates modes reflecting the self, emotion, and motivation:

Amelia believed herself to be unlovable and unattractive, and believed that others were judgmental of her appearance. She had a precarious sense of the future, but strove to maintain high standards in her performance and appearance. This constellation of core beliefs made sense of her low self-esteem, her difficulty maintaining her relationships, her anxiety, and her comfort-eating. When, one day, a colleague said, "You look well," her interpretation (colored by her belief system) was extreme: "He thinks that I look fat." This interpretation activated her schema, triggering a powerful felt sense of ugliness, fatness, and self-revulsion, resulting in a physiological reaction of nausea, a flood of adrenaline, and the feeling of fear. She also had an uneasy sense of déjà vu and a fleeting image of being rejected. This promoted a drive to protect herself through escape: through eating to dissociate or through exiting the situation. In an instant, she experienced something powerfully awful that she could not easily put into words, but that served to confirm that she was unattractive, that others were judgmental, and that her future was painful.

Research Findings

Studies to date have addressed schema content (core beliefs and associated behaviors) and process, establishing the psychometrics of measures designed for general populations (e.g., Young, 1994) and specifically for the eating disorders (e.g., Cooper et al., 1997). They have also considered the etiology of schemas in the eating disorders, and their relevance to treatment. Table 7.2 summarizes this literature.

The research evidence generally demonstrates that pathological schemas are present in the eating disorders, and that they are associated with the pathogenic factors that are predicted by the broad schema model (e.g., negative parenting; physical and emotional trauma). There is case material indicating treatment efficacy (e.g., Kennerley, 1997; Ohanian, 2002), although this evidence base is, so far, highly limited. The relevant study populations are all women, unless otherwise specified, which matches the patterns of prevalence of the eating disorders. Most are self-report measures, and there is a need to develop convergent evidence through the use of other methodologies (e.g., experimental, observational) that emphasize behavioral mechanisms.

Gaps in the Literature

Although the literature to date is extensive, it has a number of deficiencies. First, it is largely focused on women and fails to address schemas in children and adolescents of both sexes or in men. Second, it has been based on the most common diagnostic categories, which means that it fails

TABLE 7.2

Summary of Empirical Studies Regarding Schema Content and Process in Eating Disorders

Domain	Conclusions	References
Psychometrics	▪ Full and short versions of the Young Schema Questionnaire (205 and 75 items) have good internal reliability and fit Young's proposed structure. ▪ Eating Disorders Belief Questionnaire has good psychometric properties. ▪ Young-Rygh Avoidance Inventory, Young Compensatory Inventory and Young Parenting Inventory all have good psychometric properties, but not as per proposed structure.	▪ Waller, Meyer, & Ohanian (2001); Waller et al. (2000) ▪ Cooper et al. (1997) ▪ Luck et al. (2005); Spranger et al. (2001) ▪ Hartt & Waller (2001); Lawson et al. (2003)
Background experiences	▪ Reported history of sexual abuse associated with unhealthy core beliefs and schema processes. ▪ Unhealthy family function associated with schema content and schema process. ▪ Core beliefs mediate trauma-eating relationships.	▪ Emanuelli et al. (2004); Leung, Thomas, & Waller (2000); Sheffield, Waller, Emanuelli, Murray, & Meyer (2005) ▪ Leung, Thomas, & Waller (2000); Waller, Meyer, Ohanian, Elliott, et al. (2001)
Schema content	▪ Eating-disordered patients have more pathological core beliefs than do normal subjects. ▪ Eating-disordered patients have more pathological core beliefs than do dieters. ▪ Specific beliefs associated with bingeing and vomiting behaviors, but variable patterns of linkage. ▪ Specific associations of core beliefs with unhealthy eating attitudes. ▪ Minimal differences between core beliefs of patients with different eating disorders. ▪ Some specific differences between eating-disordered and depressed patients.	▪ Cooper et al. (1997); Cooper & Hunt (1998); Cooper & Turner (2000); Waller et al. (2000) ▪ Cooper & Hunt (1998); Cooper & Turner (2000) ▪ Leung et al. (1999); Waller (2003); Waller et al. (2000) ▪ Waller et al. (2002) ▪ Cooper & Hunt (1998); Cooper & Turner (2000); Leung et al. (1999); Waller (2003) ▪ Cooper & Hunt (1998); Shah & Waller (2000); Waller, Shah, et al. (2001)

Schema processes	Attentional bias toward and rapid processing of personal threat cues, especially abandonment (automatic processing).	McManus et al. (1996); Meyer & Waller (1999); Patton (1992); Rieger et al. (1998); Waller & Mijatovich (1998)
Maintenance/surrender	Cognitive avoidance of personal threat cues (strategic processing).	Meyer et al. (2005); Waller et al. (1996)
▪ avoidance	Anorexia nervosa has high levels of (a) primary avoidance of emotion through personal and social control (schema compensation) and (b) secondary control of emotion through behavioral and somatic control (schema avoidance).	Luck et al. (2005)
▪ compensation	Experimental evidence of schema compensation in anorexia.	Mountford et al. (2004)
	Bulimia nervosa has high levels of secondary control of emotion through behavioral and somatic means (schema avoidance).	Luck et al. (2005); Spranger et al. (2001)
Treatment	Negative core beliefs predict poor outcome from conventional CBT for bulimia.	Leung, Waller, & Thomas (2000)
	Case studies showing positive outcome of SFCBT for eating disorders.	Kennerley (1997); Waller & Ohanian (1999)
	Case studies showing positive outcome from imagery rescripting in bulimia nervosa (resistant to conventional CBT).	Cooper (2003); Ohanian (2002)

Note. CBT = cognitive–behavioral therapy; SFCBT = schema-focused cognitive–behavioral therapy.

to contribute systematically to an understanding of those individuals with eating disorders who do not meet full criteria for anorexia nervosa, bulimia nervosa, or binge-eating disorder (approximately 50% of the clinical population; Fairburn & Harrison, 2003). Third, although the studies have used a range of methodologies, most have been cross-sectional or correlational. Thus, only a small number have established direct links to eating behavior. Finally, although this literature has established the nature and origins of schema-level pathology in the eating disorders, it remains deficient at the level of treatment studies. Systematic studies are required to match and complement the CBT studies that have taken place in the field of the eating disorders over the past 2 decades. These studies will need to develop from case series all the way to randomized control trials.

PROPOSED SCHEMA-FOCUSED MODELS OF THE EATING DISORDERS

Building on the literature outlined earlier, Waller (2004) has developed preliminary SFCBT models of the eating disorders. These models are intended to account for a range of phenomena in the eating disorders, including the similarity of cognitive content and the discrepancies in cognitive processing across different types of eating disorder. Rather than being related to specific eating disorders, they address the role of schema content and process in restrictive–compulsive pathology and in bulimic–impulsive pathology. Thus, they are able to account for common features across the eating disorders, as well as disparate elements. These models can accommodate the comorbidity of restrictive and bulimic cognitions and behaviors in the majority of cases, and are not confined to the subset of patients with eating disorders who meet full criteria for diagnoses of anorexia nervosa or bulimia nervosa (e.g., Fairburn & Harrison, 2003).

These models are predicated on the homogeneity of schema content across the eating disorders, with high mean levels of negative core beliefs (Young Schema Questionnaire—Short Form [YSQ–S] scores on scales such as abandonment, emotional deprivation, and defectiveness or shame) in all eating disorders (see Table 7.2). It is hypothesised that restrictive and bulimic pathologies differ in their patterns of schema processes. Although both appear to serve the function of affect regulation, the key difference between the two pathologies is the point in the cognition–emotion–behavior chain at which the individual makes any effort to reduce her experience of intolerable emotional states. Primary avoidance of affect involves the individual in attempting to avoid the affect being triggered in the first instance, whereas secondary avoidance involves reduction of the affect after it has been triggered. There is some preliminary evidence in support of these models (e.g.,

Luck, Waller, Meyer, & Lacey, 2005; Mountford, Waller, Watson, & Scragg, 2004; Spranger, Waller, & Bryant-Waugh, 2001), but further testing is required.

Schema Compensation in Restrictive Eating Pathology

Restrictive behavior achieves primary avoidance of negative affect (avoiding the possibility of negative affect being triggered in the first place) through a process of schema compensation. In this process, a countervailing compensatory schema and related behavior are activated to avoid the emotion being experienced. For example, when a person with anorexia undertakes a task, a fear of failure schema might be activated and there is a risk of feeling depressed. So that the intolerable negative affect is not triggered, an unrelenting standards schema is activated (manifesting in perfectionist behaviors) that reduces the danger of that affect being experienced. Other such compensatory schemas include subjugation, emotional inhibition, self-sacrifice, and social isolation, each of which has behavioral manifestations. The same process seems to be central to a range of compulsive problems, which are (unsurprisingly, given the proposed common cognitive process) often comorbid with the restrictive eating disorders. These problems include obsessive–compulsive disorder, compulsive exercise, and compulsive self-harm (Waller, 2004). Thus, it is probably parsimonious to see restrictive–anorexic behavior as a part of a cluster of compulsive behaviors, with a common root in the cognitive process of schema compensation.

Schema Avoidance in Bulimic Eating Pathology

Bulimic behavior achieves secondary avoidance of negative affect (reducing the experience of affect once it has been experienced) through a process of schema avoidance (i.e., behavioral methods are used to block awareness of the affect in the short term). For example, someone with bulimia who is stood up on a date might experience the activation of existing abandonment and mistrust–abuse schemas, which results in feelings of loneliness and anger. In light of the high levels of emotional inhibition that are present in such individuals, the behavior of bingeing is reinforced (in the short term) by its capacity to reduce this negative emotional arousal (e.g., McManus & Waller, 1995; Root & Fallon, 1989). Again, a similar pattern of emotional blocking can be seen in other behaviors that are often comorbid with bulimic behaviors, such as self-harm, alcohol abuse, and risky sexual behaviors. The specific behavior(s) are hypothesized to be driven by

- experience across the life span (e.g., the child whose parents modeled the use of alcohol to deal with distress versus parents who used food to calm the child when upset);

- immediate availability of the behavior (e.g., self-harm may be easier to carry out than binge-eating during a working day); and
- the speed and duration of action of the behavior (e.g., to reduce loneliness feelings, self-harm is rapidly effective but often short-lived, binge-eating takes longer but gives a more lasting effect, and alcohol use takes still longer to achieve a result but the effects can last all day).

Again, it is probably parsimonious to see bulimic behavior as a part of a cluster of impulsive behaviors, with a common root in the cognitive process of schema avoidance.

Within these models, it is important to consider the function of the behavior, rather than categorize by the behavior per se. For example, some individuals plan apparently impulsive behaviors (e.g., "When I get home this evening, I will binge/drink/cut myself, so I can cope with the day"). In such a case, the strategy appears more consistent with primary avoidance of affect, a compulsive strategy, allowing the individual to avoid becoming distressed. We have found that a useful way of explaining the difference between the schema processes of compensation and avoidance in the eating disorders is to evoke the analogy of two gardeners, both of whom have a morbid fear that their perfect lawn (control over life) will be ruined by the activity of moles (painful schemas), which create molehills (perceived loss of emotional control). The gardener with bulimia deals with the problem by going out every time that a molehill develops and banging it back down with a spade; the gardener with anorexia simply lays concrete over the garden to stop the molehills from ever developing. The common theme is that both strategies result in a loss of the desired perfect lawn, and the moles (and fear of molehills) remain.

Multiple Processes in Mixed Cases

Of course, clinical experience and the literature show that most cases of the eating disorders are not purely restrictive or bulimic: Restrictive efforts are common in the bulimic disorders (e.g., Fairburn, 1997), and bulimic behaviors are found in a large proportion of those with anorexia nervosa. These schema models can be amalgamated to explain this overlap, with individuals using both primary and secondary avoidance of negative affect (schema compensation and avoidance, respectively) to allow the maximum avoidance of negative affect. The specific schema process used depends on the nature of the trigger, the strength of the core belief laid down by early experience, and the nature and rapidity of onset of the "hot" cognitions that are activated by the interaction of the trigger and the core belief.

For example, an adult with a history of abuse might experience very negative and powerful hot cognitions when reminded of a sexual trauma, resulting in an inability to avoid the experience of distress and a need to rely on blocking behaviors. In contrast, if the same person is reminded of a less distressing trauma, the negative hot cognitions might be milder and might be reduced through activation of a perfectionist behavior used to avoid experiencing the affect at all. Thus, the same individual can use different schema strategies in response to different matches between specific triggers and core beliefs.

Relationship to Maintenance Models of the Eating Disorders

The reliance in the current models on understanding the role of early experience and schemas is sharply at variance with early models of the eating disorders (e.g., Fairburn, 1981, 1997). However, those models have not been static. Fairburn, Cooper, and Shafran (2003) have more recently proposed a transdiagnostic model of the eating disorders, which can be mapped onto this SFCBT model to some extent. Although their model is proposed as a maintenance one, which eschews understanding of factors that contribute to the origins of those cognitions and behaviors, many features in that model can be reframed within the context of the schema model. For example, their description of core low self-esteem has much in common with defectiveness core beliefs, affect regulation is similar to the secondary avoidance of affect (schema avoidance), and clinical perfectionism (similar to unrelenting standards, in SFCBT terms) serves the function of primary avoidance of emotion (schema compensation). Thus, the apparent distinction between this maintenance CBT model and SFCBT models of the eating disorders is misleading; the two are potentially complementary.

TREATMENT

We would argue that any treatment for the eating disorders depends on the use of the assessment to generate a working set of hypotheses about the disorder—the individual formulation, which reflects that person's experience rather than a diagnosis. However, the formulation remains hypothetical, and will require frequent updating in light of the evidence that emerges from therapy. As we find that many patients can focus on only one part of the formulation at any time, it may be more the task of the therapist to keep the broader picture in mind during the early stages of treatment, simply sharing relevant aspects of the conceptualization in a user-friendly manner and at the appropriate time.

Although it is not the immediate topic here, it should be remembered that eating disorders require substantial medical monitoring throughout treatment. In cases in which there is medical risk because of restrictive or bulimic behaviors, these medical problems must be treated as a priority. Examples of dangerous symptoms include cardiac complications (e.g., brady-cardia, arrhythmias); low blood pressure and fainting; muscular weakness; physical damage (e.g., tears to the esophagus); electrolyte imbalance resulting from purging behaviors; and skeletal damage resulting from osteoporosis or excessive exercise. Kaplan and Garfinkel (1993) and Birmingham and Beumont (2004) provided further details of identification and management of medical risks.

Preliminary Considerations

As stated earlier, there are some well-validated treatments for the eating disorders. Inherent in those approaches are elements that we consider vital to the treatment of all patients with eating disorders. Those elements include forming a therapeutic alliance based on an agreed agenda for change, psychoeducation, introduction to the CBT model and techniques, motivational enhancement, and behavioral experimentation with the aims of reducing dietary restriction and chaos and reducing the anxiety associated with such changes in intake.

We advocate the use of conventional CBT in the early part of treatment for the eating disorders (e.g., Fairburn, Marcus, & Wilson, 1993; Fairburn et al., 2003) rather than beginning therapy with a schema-focused approach. As CBT has a more established empirical basis, and in the interests of economy of effort on the part of the therapist and client, it should be the default option for treatment unless there are early indices that the individual is not engaging in or benefiting from treatment. The decision to move to more complex (and costlier) therapeutic endeavors should be made only when there is evidence that this early approach to treatment is inadequate, when the formulation justifies a schema-focused approach, and if the therapist is sufficiently skilled and resourced to offer SFCBT.

Despite the overall benefits of conventional CBT in the eating disorders, some individual patients will not benefit from this evidence-based therapy. Therefore, it is necessary to consider who is likely to fail to benefit. In CBT in general, early signs such as failure to complete homework tasks or self-monitoring indicate that treatment is likely to be less effective. In the eating disorders, Agras, Crow, Halmi, Mitchell, Wilson, and Kraemer (2000) have demonstrated that a failure to reduce purging behavior in the early part of treatment (six sessions) is a specific predictor of poor outcome of conventional CBT for bulimia nervosa. There are also suggestions that very poor self-esteem and impulsive behaviors are predictive of failure with this approach (e.g., Fairburn et al., 2003). We recommend that such cases should be considered for other therapies that have a clear and overt structure such as cognitive analytic therapy (e.g., Treasure & Ward, 1997), interpersonal psychotherapy (e.g., Agras, Walsh, et al., 2000; Fairburn et al., 1995) or structured focal dynamic psychotherapy with a behavioral element (e.g., Murphy, Russell, & Waller, 2005). Although the evidence base for such therapies is less extensive than that for cognitive–behavioral approaches, they each have the strength of emphasizing the interpersonal issues that are commonly found to be relevant to eating pathology (e.g., Steiger, Gauvin, Jabalpurwala, Seguin, & Stotland, 1999).

Therefore, we suggest that the initial part of treatment for the eating disorders should be derived from existing CBT models and clinical recommendations. However, rather than completing such a course of therapy without reflection, it is more appropriate to treat this initial period as experimental, bearing in mind the possibility of using SFCBT to augment therapy if the conventional CBT is not proving helpful. If appropriate, we recommend that this change of emphasis should be considered after four to eight sessions. Such a time frame allows the individual a chance to respond to conventional CBT (Agras, Crow, et al., 2000) and allows time to reformulate in light of the failure to engage with and respond to conventional CBT for the eating disorders. Thus, assessment continues throughout this period.

Assessment and Evaluation

We use a range of tools to assist in the assessment of eating disorders. In each case, these are useful both in identifying relevant schemas and in evaluating meaningful change. In keeping with our earlier point, it is important to keep the eating behaviors and associated distress as clear and critical targets for change. These make more meaningful targets than does diagnostic change. Therefore, the full assessment needs to include reliable and robust measures of eating attitudes and behaviors and related experiences, such as the Eating Disorders Inventory (Garner, 1991), structured interviews, and behavioral recording (e.g., frequency of bingeing and purging). Necessary biological assessments are equally important (e.g., weight as a proportion of height; potassium levels wherein there is a high frequency of purging).

Self-Report Measures of Schema Content and Process

In terms of schemas per se, we have found Young's measures (Schema Questionnaire; Compensation Inventory; Avoidance Inventory; Parenting Inventory) to be clinically useful. They provide valuable material for discussion, often in association with self-help guides (Young, 1999; Young &

Klosko, 1993), enabling the patient to see patterns in her own thinking and behavior. However, although the subscales that Young has proposed for the Schema Questionnaire appear to be robust (e.g., Schmidt, Joiner, Young, & Telch, 1995), the subscales that emerge from factor analysis of the other measures are not as Young proposed (e.g., Luck et al., 2005). Cooper et al. (1997) have developed a measure of cognitions in the eating disorders that includes a measure of core beliefs, but that scale (negative self-beliefs) is a unitary one that lacks the clinical richness of Young's measures. One might argue that it is a more parsimonious measure, but it has two drawbacks relative to Young's measures. First, it does not address schema processes. Second, the unitary measure is very focused on the individual's perceived failings and fails to take account of the importance of core beliefs about other people, the world, and the future. Core beliefs such as abandonment are very socially oriented and are central to eating pathology (e.g., Meyer & Waller, 1999), and there is clear evidence that social triggers are important in the eating behaviors (e.g., Steiger et al., 1999). Such findings mean that Cooper and coworkers' parsimony results in the potential loss of important clinical information.

Information From Interview and Interaction With the Patient

No self-report measure will ever be sufficient, so the psychometrics outlined earlier should be treated as indicative, requiring elaboration and clarification in the assessment. For example, patients can idealize or exaggerate their experience when completing self-report measures, and our clinical experience indicates that it is common to see a temporary increase in Schema Questionnaire scores once patients begin to examine their beliefs in light of their experience to date.

In some cases, what we label as a maladaptive schema may be adaptive (e.g., a subjugation schema in an adolescent who is still living in a hostile family environment). Such information should be clear from a fuller assessment, and will have marked implications for the treatment options. For example, the priority for the adolescent might be to create a safe environment before tackling core beliefs.

Additional relevant idiosyncratic information can be gathered in many ways. Padesky (1994) suggested first asking the individual to complete phrases such as "I am . . ." and "Others are . . . ." This task is unlikely to target key beliefs in all patients, but some do respond to this simple cueing. Another approach, which is inevitably associated with Beckian cognitive therapy, is Socratic inquiry—the technique of systematic but gentle questioning, facilitating the patient's understanding or expression of fundamental beliefs. Sensitive and difficult information can also be shared through a range of different media—drawings, telephone calls, poems, analogies, and so on. In this way, a patient can often express something painful or frightening indirectly. Of course, the material is less likely to reflect hot cognitions, but it is possible to communicate an understanding that will assist the therapist and client. Other information might be available only in more subtle ways, and can best be identified by close attention to the process and content of therapy. For example, consider this common experience:

> Gemma had begun to engage fully in treatment, after an initial period of failing to engage with the therapist and cancelling appointments for a variety of reasons. However, during one session, the therapist explained that he would not be able to make a session in 3 weeks' because he was taking leave. Gemma became very distant and appeared uninterested in the session. As she was leaving at the end of the session, she announced that she really did not feel that she needed treatment, and she did not see any point in returning.

What had happened in this case was that the abandonment schema she had struggled with when entering the therapeutic relationship had been triggered by the therapist's piece of news, and her immediate conclusion was that the treatment was about to be withdrawn. As is often the case with such responses, the clinician is best advised to use them in the session to explore the possibility that this catastrophic reaction is triggered in other interpersonal situations. In a manner similar to the psychodynamic work of Malan (1979), the clinician might aim to determine how those responses relate to past experiences.

It is also important to consider a lack of what appear to be normal responses. For example,

> Fiona was first seen 4 weeks after she had given birth for the first time, and the infant was with her throughout the assessment. Fiona engaged well and appeared to be very clear and forthcoming about her bulimia and about the origins and maintenance of those behaviors. She described her family as close and supportive all through her life, and attributed her problems to being raped at the age of 14. At the end of the first session, she apologized that she would not be able to make the same day the next week, as she was going to her parents' home (across the United Kingdom) so that her parents could see the baby for the first time.

What became clear (with some thought between sessions about what was wrong with this picture) was that there was a contradiction. Fiona's parents were described as close and supportive, yet had not seen their new granddaughter over the first month of her life. When this point was raised at the next session, Fiona soon acknowledged that she tended to present her home life as perfect because she had grown up in an invalidating environment. Her distress at her family's lack of support led her to believe that she simply did not understand the world. Therefore, she felt that she had no right to see other people negatively. This information enabled the identification of an emotional inhibition schema (an unconditional belief that it is unacceptable or dangerous to experience or express affect, with associated avoidant behaviors), which had led to her other relationships being highly insecure. That core belief had not been identified on the Schema Questionnaire. This example demonstrates how one can draw information from interaction with the patient.

Finally, behavior outside the formal session can be indicative, and can often be flagged by the way in which others describe the patient (e.g., the referral letter from another clinician) or by the way that the patient interacts with the therapist. For example, subjugation and self-sacrifice schemas are often apparent when the patient habitually asks the therapist how she is during the walk from the waiting area to the therapy room. Abandonment schemas (with the implicit invitation for the therapist to confirm those belief systems by discharging the patient) often manifest first in poor attendance, or by the patient describing feeling like a fraud because there are people in the waiting room who are more needy. It is also important to note the activation of schema processes and content that can result from the clinician being out sick or taking leave.

Addressing the patient's interactions inside and outside the session can be indicative of the problems that the person experiences in everyday life. Such indications can provide an important adjunct to assessment, giving clear targets for treatment and evaluation. Safran and Segal (1990) have developed an invaluable approach that uses such interpersonal processes as a medium for exploration and change, within the traditional framework of Beckian cognitive therapy.

Once established, fundamental belief systems can be usefully represented as a set of visual analog scales that reflect the conviction with which a schema or a core belief is held. Patients in treatment can then use these scales to review the strength of their beliefs as therapy progresses. These scales serve as simple, easily repeated gauges of progress that do not require the regular completion of long schema questionnaires.

Schema-Focused Cognitive–Behavioral Therapy Formulation of the Eating Disorders

As always, the purpose of a psychological assessment is the development of a personalized conceptualization of a patient's problems, which addresses the "Why me?" "Why now?" and "Why isn't it going away?" questions, and which generates hypotheses concerning treatment. So often, the first therapeutic step is helping the patient to see the processes that drive and maintain her difficulties, giving her a perspective that allows her to stand back and make sense of the problem. The following case example gives an example of an SFCBT formulation in a case of an eating disorder.

Carla was a bright and talented 22-year-old who was on sick leave because her bulimia and depressed mood interfered with her ability to work. On assessment, it became apparent that she veered from over-restricting her diet and excessive exercise to binge-eating and spitting and purging. She also lacerated her arms and legs, and appeared to put herself at risk of assaults from her father and uncle (see the following section titled "Schema Content").

Relevant background: From 3 to 16 years old, she was subjected to physical, emotional, and sexual abuse from father and uncle. She was told that this was a punishment. Her mother was unprotective, and her sister was not subjected to sexual abuse. The family was also active in a church that "taught children to obey adults and fear God's wrath."

Schema content: A somatic experience of intense discomfort, which did not readily map onto language. The associated assumption was "I can't cope with this—I must stop it." Core beliefs and derived assumptions included "I am bad and should be punished/deserve to be hurt/am unlovable;" "I am abnormal and will never fit in, so I must try to appear as normal as possible;" "I am a failure, and so I must achieve to compensate;" "Others are harmful (unless they prove otherwise), but should be pleased and pacified;" "Others do not understand;" "The world is a hostile place, and I must stay on top to survive;" and "My future is bleak—I will be abandoned and miserable." These cognitions were linked with feelings of high anxiety and hopelessness, and memories of traumatic incidents often emerged as flashbacks.

Assumptions that specifically promote problem behaviors: "I can't cope with the distress unless I binge/exercise/cut;" "It will all be all right when I have perfect control;" "If I don't function at 100%, I have failed; therefore, if I can't be 100% good, I'll be 100% bad;" "They will listen if I do something dramatic/allow something dramatic to happen to me;" and "It is right that I should be in pain."

- Triggers for schema activation: chronic, critical inner voice; weight changes; perceived failure; and interpersonal stress.
- Basic responses to her inner world: avoidance, deflection, and compliance
- Behaviors to stave off schema activation (schema compensation): starvation and compulsive exercise, attempts to achieve high standards in appearance and performance, and interpersonal avoidance (except of children).
- Behaviors to switch off activated schemas: excessive exercise; binge-eating, followed by spitting and purging; and self-injury.
- Behaviors consistent with schemas: self-inflicted and other-inflicted injury, and being careless regarding personal health and safety. Such

behaviors included binge-eating and cutting. Carla appeared to struggle with a drive to behave in a way that was consistent with her fundamental belief system (because of a comforting familiarity), and this struggle perhaps contributed to her constant urge to binge-eat and self-harm (schema-avoidant behaviors).

- Maintenance: Carla's eating disorder was maintained because of the impact of her behaviors, and because her responses to those behaviors ultimately served to fuel them.

Her perceptions were colored by her schemas. For example, a benign disagreement was construed as a rejection, which confirmed negative self- and other-beliefs; and an unexpected glimpse of herself in a mirror revealed to her "a monster" that must be got rid of. Her excessive coping strategies were unsustainable and maintained her view of herself as a failure, unlovable, bad, and so on. Her attempts to avoid schema activation reinforced her beliefs that she was a failure, impoverished her social confidence, and reduced her hope of coping. In addition, her social isolation deprived her of support, and the behaviors of her family confirmed that she was abusable and not worthy of protection.

However, Carla's eating disorder remained compelling because, in the short term, it served so many functions: the comfort of "doing the right thing," the physiological kick of starving or bingeing, the veiled communication of need, the possibility of destroying the despised body and perhaps killing herself, the facilitating of social avoidance or withdrawal, and the satisfaction of being excessively in control or out of control.

SCHEMA-FOCUSED COGNITIVE–BEHAVIORAL THERAPY TECHNIQUES

Several important points about treatment have already been raised. First, SFCBT should be an active and justifiable choice with patients with more complex eating disorders who are not responsive to proven methods. Second, the identification of schema content and processes is necessarily multifactorial. Third, the targets of the treatment also need to be modified to take account of whether the core beliefs and coping strategies (although maladaptive) remain relevant in the current environment (e.g., in a demanding and abusive relationship, it might well be adaptive to retain unrelenting high standards). Fourth, as in all cases, the treatment should be related to the patient's individual formulation (and should be amended as that formulation is developed across treatment). As the formulation needs to incorporate both schema-level cognitions and processes and the specific eating pathology (cognitions and behaviors), the treatment will need to consider both levels of pathology in parallel.

Once the decision to undertake SFCBT is made, a number of approaches are helpful in producing change in the core beliefs and schema processes that drive eating-disordered behaviors and conditional beliefs. These approaches include preparation work, specific cognitive and behavioral techniques used to target core beliefs and schema maintenance processes, certain therapeutic tools, the management of dissociation, and the use of imagery rescripting to modify schemas that are not coded verbally. Particular attention is paid to this last skill, given the nature of the negative early experiences of many patients with eating disorders (e.g., Fallon & Wonderlich, 1997).

Preparation

First, it is essential to assess the client's personal and systemic resources. Can change be tolerated and supported? Is there a risk that the patient could suffer as a consequence of making changes, or that her children might suffer in the process? It is essential to carry out as full a systemic evaluation as possible, as the patient is unlikely to live in isolation and many with complex presentations have dysfunctional backgrounds.

Explaining Schema-Driven Problems and Schema Maintenance

The therapist has the task of sharing a complicated and still somewhat controversial psychological concept with the patient. Padesky (1990) has developed the prejudice metaphor to aid the therapist in explaining the role of schemas. This metaphor is used to explain that schemas act like prejudices, biasing one's processing of information and leading one to reach conclusions that are unfair—in this case, to the individual who holds the schema. Also, Young (1994; Young & Klosko, 1993) has written very accessible client guides to schema-focused therapy.

Basic Mood and Stress Management Skills

Complex clients can be at risk of relapse from the outset. Their progress is often fragile, and the complexities of their interpersonal and intrapersonal life are such that change can provoke major stresses, which can undermine progress. For this reason they need a rapid-access "first aid kit" of basic mood and stress management skills that will help them through difficult patches, and that will also provide the starting point of relapse management. Such skills would include relaxation and controlled breathing, distraction, problem solving, activity scheduling, and graded behavioral experiments. These techniques can be readily taught. Although their use may offer only temporary respite in some instances, respite could make a situation bearable or could ward off strong urges to self-harm. As long as these strategies are not perceived by the patient as safety behaviors, but rather as skills that add to a repertoire of adaptive coping techniques, they can contribute to the patient's sense of agency from the early stages of therapy.

Addressing Fears Regarding Change

The use of comprehensive validation (Geller, Williams, & Srikameswaran, 2001; Linehan, 1993) and examination of the pros and cons of change (e.g., Serpell & Treasure, 2002; Serpell, Treasure, Teasdale, & Sullivan, 1999) are critical in allowing the individual to contemplate change without the fear of being criticized or doomed to fail. Such work should help the patient to anticipate the stress of change, both personal and systemic.

Cognitive and Behavioral Change

The emphasis of the next stage is on helping the individual to build new and adaptive belief systems, thus overcoming the problematic unconditional beliefs that are common in the eating disorders. The following tools and techniques are valuable with this clinical group.

Continuum Work

The continuum technique or scaling (Beck, Freeman, & Davis, 2004) is used to address the dichotomous quality of problem schemas. Problem core beliefs and associated assumptions are often extreme: for example, Carla's view that "Unless I am exceedingly good/bad, I will not be distinctive, and I will have to face my reality of being utterly worthless." The aim of continuum work is to help the client to risk moving away from inflexible, polarized categories. Once Carla and her therapist have reflected on the pros and cons of dichotomous processing and its unhelpfulness is apparent, scaling can be used to introduce the possibility of degree and flexibility (in Carla's case, the aim was to help her to understand that her performance did not have to be perfect, but could be "good enough"). One way of developing this skill is to ask the patient to map continua for qualities in others that make up worth (e.g., size, goodness, success). Having established a series of continua, Carla has become familiar with the concept of scaling, and can be encouraged to review her assessment of her self in comparison to others and, finally, to review her sense of worth.

Continuum work often offers the possibility of further behavioral testing. Like many of the schema-change strategies we outline in this chapter, it is best used in creative combination with other techniques.

Positive Data Logs

The positive data log (Greenberger & Padesky, 1995; Padesky, 1994) is used to help clients build a tangible body of evidence that counterbalances an extreme view. This log consists of a diary or list of all the positive self-attributes and achievements of the patients.

Titling such a list "Why I am good enough" can be very helpful, as it directs the patient away from perfection and emphasizes a more realistic view of the self. A separate list is kept on past and present achievements (under headings, e.g., academic, work related, personal, or social), which the patient adds to regularly as she attempts behavioral experiments and succeeds in therapy. This reminder of reality can challenge schemas and negative automatic thoughts as they get triggered. Reading both lists daily is encouraged.

> Carla believed herself worthless, but recognized qualities in others that she considered made them acceptable. She listed these attributes and labeled her list the "Basically OK" checklist, which she then applied to herself. She gradually realized that she had most of the attributes that she felt made a person "basically OK," and in doing so developed a new belief about herself, which began to occlude "I am worthless."

Prediction Log

Padesky (1994) suggested that the logging technique can be further used in the form of a prediction log, a record of predictions and actual occurrences, which again gives the patient tangible data to use in reevaluating beliefs. For example,

> Clara predicted that she could cope with extreme distress (triggered by schema activation) only by dissociating through binge-eating or self-injury. As part of her therapy, she had developed distraction and visualization skills that served as a reasonable substitute for her impulsive behaviors. Thus, she was able to use these to undermine the prediction that served to maintain her difficulties.

Historical Review

Patients are helped to develop a historical perspective on the genesis of their beliefs and behavioral patterns, in the context of environmental factors across the life span. The review helps individuals to understand that their behaviors and cognitions make sense in the context of their development, rather than simply being irrational and proof of madness or defectiveness. This understanding assists individuals in carrying out the necessary shifts in attribution that allow them to reduce their perception of negative events as being caused by agents that are internal, stable, and global (Young, 1990; see next section).

Shifts in Attribution

A key issue is assisting the patient to shift her attributions regarding the origins and the maintenance of the schemas. Schema dialogue is an important tool in this process (see next section). The individual can be encouraged (through Socratic questioning) to consider alternative explanations for why an event or set of events occurred. The aim is to achieve a shift from attributing negative events internally, globally, and stably (e.g., "I was to blame for the physical abuse I experienced, and therefore I am a defective person who deserved or needed that treatment. The bingeing stops me thinking how terrible I am"), and to attribute them externally, more specifically and flexibly (e.g., "Well, I guess that I did not actually do anything to encourage my father to abuse me. As he was also doing it to my little sister, maybe he was to blame. Maybe I can view the abuse as being something that happened to me, rather than being about who I was and remain"). It is also important to encourage a shift from attributing positive events to others or to chance ("I passed that exam only by luck. The only thing that I can do reliably well is to restrict my intake") and toward attributing those events to the self ("I tried as hard as I always do, and I did well as I always do; maybe I am good at this if I put in the effort"), to generate a more normal pattern of positive attributional bias.

Schema Dialogue

In this powerful intervention technique, patients are asked to role-play the schema, elaborating on the thoughts and feelings consistent with the schema., Patients are subsequently encouraged to use their "healthy" side to counter the arguments of the schema. Patients find this part more difficult to carry out and often need the therapist to guide them in pointing out the evidence that refutes the schema. This refutation results in weakening the impact of the negative schema, by developing a viable alternative. It may be easier for patients to change chairs when role-playing the schema and the healthy self. Doing so helps distance the patient from the schema.

In point–counterpoint (Young, 1990), the therapist plays the "healthy" or rational part and the patient plays the schema side or emotional part and then they switch roles. In this exercise, both therapist and patient speak as the patient—that is, they both use the *I* pronoun. Again, this exercise helps the patient to establish some distance from the schema and use rational arguments modeled by the therapist. The therapist should attempt to use the same words as the patient when role-playing, to make it more relevant to the patient's experience. It may be necessary during this role-play for both patient and therapist to come out of role and discuss areas that the patient finds particularly difficult to work on. The therapist needs to evaluate the effectiveness of the technique by asking the patient how helpful she finds it in changing her belief.

The decision to use this technique should be collaborative, as many patients may feel reluctant to do this role-play. The therapist should also ensure that he or she is not being confrontational when role-playing the rational part of the mind or making the patient feel criticized.

Using Others as a Reference Point

Patients are often objective when considering other people's beliefs, and can realize the discrepancy between what they believe to be true for themselves and what they believe is true about other people. A helpful strategy is to have patients consider how other people (e.g., friends, their own children) would see the same experience if it happened to them. This strategy helps to identify the distortion in the belief. The therapist can then encourage patients to apply this insight to themselves, distancing themselves from their schema and challenging it more effectively.

Body Image Restructuring

When the meaning that drives a problem is held in a somatic form, it is often best tackled as felt-sense. In Carla's case, she could not tolerate normal body weight as easily as she could over- or underweight. Body imagery, or somatic, work focused on helping her articulate how her body felt at different weights. Imagining herself at a normal weight left her feeling "terrified, I'm asking for it, dirty, weak and inviting [of sexual abuse]." Therapy focused on helping her develop an alternative felt-sense by directing her to describe how she needed to feel in her body if she were to overcome this problem. She aimed for bodily sensations that communicated "confidence, strength, protection" and was eventually able to generate this somatic experience. She was then able to tolerate the feelings of being at normal weight.

Behavioral Tests

As patients develop new perspectives and possibilities, they need to reality-test them to confirm their veracity. To help patients transform new ideas into tangible experiences, therapists can ask questions such as "And how might you check that out?"; "If that were the case, what could you do differently next time?"; and "That sounds like a good principle; how might you put it into practice?"

Therapeutic Tools

A range of conventional tools are useful in the practice of SFCBT in the eating disorders. These tools include those oriented toward disorders with a specific behavioral profile and treatment targets such as eating disorders. In particular, we find diaries and flashcards invaluable in helping the patient to take control of behaviors. However, some tools merit particular attention because of their relevance to disorders in which dissociation is relevant.

Diaries and Dysfunctional Thought Records

The aim of keeping such records is to help patients identify and distance themselves from the problem schema. From this more detached stance, they are often better able to restructure their distorted view regarding the self, others, and the future. Diaries and thought records can prompt patients to more effectively identify, question, and challenge their automatic thoughts, which thereby reduces negative affect. Eventually, with time and practice, patients will experience new, more accurate automatic thoughts. Diaries are often best introduced in stages so as not to overwhelm patients, and tailored to meet the patients' needs, as described by Greenberger and Padesky (1995). They can include whatever information is relevant to therapy at a particular time (e.g., records of mood changes, identification of schemas, and evidence for and against the particular schema that is being examined). Reviewing the patient's current life experiences, uncovering all the evidence that seems to support or disconfirm the schema, and then critically examining it will enable the patient to critically reevaluate the problem schema. The schema diaries can be used to challenge the negative beliefs relating to the past as well as the present and the future.

Self-monitoring of eating habits should include information on food eaten and weight control measures used as well as thoughts and feelings. These records will enable both patient and therapist to identify the circumstances that gave rise to the problems.

Pie Charts

A technique that patients find very helpful is to construct a pie chart comprising all their positive attributes, with one segment representing their body or appearance. This visual representation helps to remind them of who they are as a whole person, showing how insignificant their physical appearance is in relation to their whole self and thereby challenging the emphasis they place on their body, weight, and shape.

Therapy Notebook

A therapy notebook is particularly helpful for those who struggle to recall key points emerging from the session or the details of assignments and so on. They can also be used to record formulations, copy helpful diagrams, or chart weights. They are also useful for recording significant between-session events such as experiences that support a new perspective or relapse management. In this way, the client has a tangible log of progress with personal guidelines and achievements, which can be used for reference.

Therapy Tape

This is an excellent aide-mémoire for the client and (with the client's permission) an invaluable adjunct to the therapist's supervision. It is particularly advisable to tape imagery sessions for the client to listen to later on, as well as for the therapist to use to evaluate the session.

Self-Harm Prevention Plans

This form of relapse prevention (or management) should be introduced if therapists consider their client at risk of self-harm. These plans typically consist of commitments to create a safe environment, lists of alternative behaviors, statements and behavioral intentions to avert self-harm, and practical information (e.g., key telephone numbers). It is also essential to work within the context of a multidisciplinary approach that ensures contact between professionals, to reduce the risk of self-harm. For example,

> Carla agreed not to keep razor blades or laxatives in her apartment, and not to visit her father alone. She listed running and painting among her alternative behaviors; running enabled her to inflict pain on her body, whereas painting allowed her to express her hatred of it in a nondamaging way. When she felt the urge, she referred to a coping statement: "Although I feel desperate to hurt, I know that it makes matters worse and that I can take the edge off the urge by using my visualization exercise, by running until I'm numb. If it gets too tempting I will phone Janie (telephone number) or Meena (telephone number) or the helpline (telephone number) or my doctor (telephone number) or the psychiatric registrar as a last resort (telephone number)." This statement was written on a small card, which Carla carried with her.

Flashcards

The role of flashcards is to invalidate the criticisms that the patient grew up with and is now directing at herself as an adult. These are written on a piece of paper or an index card and incorporate the most powerful evidence for and counterevidence against the schemas. They are usually developed by the therapist, in collaboration with the patient. Patients are encouraged to carry these flashcards with them so that they can read them repeatedly and have them at hand whenever a schema is activated. In light of the stubborn nature of schemas, the aim of flashcards is to help the patient repeatedly go over the evidence that challenges the schema, thus weakening it and developing a viable, alternative perspective and, as a result, more functional coping strategies. For patients with eating disorders with borderline characteristics, it may be more effective to have the therapist write out the flashcards; some patients prefer to have the therapist's voice on tape because this keeps them more anchored in a healthier and more objectively accurate reality.

Mini-Flashcards

These are very brief cue cards, derived from Young's (1990) flashcards. These carry four cues to help the patient: identify the problem emotion (and motivation); label the process (rather than assuming personal weakness); generate an alternative possibility; and direct herself to an adaptive response. One of Carla's mini-flashcards helped her to resist binge-eating triggered by weight gain, and she attached it to her weighing scales:

I feel   disappointed in myself and want to binge into oblivion.

Because   my "Bad" and "Misfit" and "Failure" beliefs are kicking in and they hurt!

However   if I distract myself, the urge weakens and I'll show them I'm not a failure.

Therefore   I'm going to get out of the apartment and I'm going to get active.

Recovery and Relapse-Prevention Workbook

In the late stages of treatment, we find it helpful to encourage patients to develop their own workbooks, detailing the methods that have worked for them. In this way, they can attribute positive change to their own efforts and understand and continue to implement the skills that they have developed.

Managing Dissociation

Dissociation is commonly associated with the eating disorders, and often serves to help the person to escape from or avoid a painful experience (e.g., an activated schema or a traumatic flashback). This detachment from current distress is often the function of the impulsive or compulsive behaviors witnessed in the eating disorders. Managing dissociation involves first discovering its function and the means by which it is achieved. Then, more benign alternatives can be developed, serving the same function. Finally, if the purpose of distraction is an avoidance that is ultimately unhelpful, graded exposure can be introduced.

Among other things, Carla used excessive physical exercise to achieve a state of dissociation. She exercised "until I feel as though my insides are dead and my mind is numb." In this way, she dealt with feelings of somatic and emotional distress that she predicted that she could not otherwise tolerate. She learned to deal with both the somatic and emotional distress by substituting her new, positive felt-sense for punishing exercise. Later, she embarked on a graded exposure program to help her learn to tolerate emotional distress in a systematic fashion, using her positive felt-sense as the safe base to which she could return if she felt overwhelmed by emotion.

Kennerley (1996) detailed specific approaches for reducing dissociation that are useful in treating the eating disorders. Those approaches include helping the patient to feel safe in therapy (to avoid dissociation during sessions), identifying and avoiding triggers to dissociation, distraction (e.g., focusing on the present environment rather than the past event), grounding (through the use of grounding words or phrases, safe images, or pleasant objects), and cognitive restructuring (e.g., reducing dichotomous thinking about the traumatic memory).

Imagery Rescripting

Imagery is one of the most powerful experiential techniques within schema-focused therapy, and has support in the clinical literature (e.g., Arntz & Weertman, 1999; Hackmann, 1998; Smucker, Dancu, Foa, & Niederee, 1995). Edwards (1990) and Layden, Newman, Freeman, and Morse (1993) suggested that imagery gives more direct access to primitive schemas, in which meanings have been coded in pictorial form or other sensory modalities (making them inaccessible through analysis of current automatic thoughts alone). Identification of the schemas can be achieved through using imagery in the assessment phase, particularly in cases in which the individual has a tendency to intellectualize and avoid emotion. Thus, one can ask a patient to recall a painful childhood experience and question her about the conclusion she is arriving at about herself, other people, and the future. Once the "rules for living" (Layden et al., 1993) are identified and the hidden evidence maintaining the schemas is revealed, modification of these schemas can then take place.

Goals

Imagery rescripting is not about denying the past or changing the details of the critical event, but about helping the patient to reexamine and reevaluate the meanings associated with the early experience to arrive at more realistic alternative conclusions. It is not a form of catharsis, because simply recalling a memory is not sufficient for change. The key schemas need to be identified and modified for change to occur. The fact that patients often say something to the effect of "I understand it in my head. I know that I am not bad or to blame, but I still *feel* bad; I do not feel any different particularly in certain situations" indicates that the patient has gained intellectual insight, but is experiencing difficulty in achieving a commensurate emotional insight. Although sometimes this insight can be achieved (with time) through verbal techniques, at other times the use of language (in the form of activation of verbal automatic thoughts or assumptions) will not effect emotional shift, and relapse or incomplete remission is the result.

Contextual Issues

Imagery rescripting is a very powerful tool because of the high affect that is evoked when the schema is triggered in the image. Therefore, enough time should be allowed to focus on induction and debriefing, and it should not be used at the end of the session. It should not be used with a patient who has not yet developed trust with the therapist or with one who is in crisis. If a patient has a history of dissociation, particularly flashbacks (see earlier discussion titled "Managing Dissociation"), then the therapist should ensure that the patient has learned to use grounding techniques (e.g., Kennerley, 1996) and proceed at a slower pace. If severe abuse is going to be the subject matter for imagery rescripting, then the therapist should teach patients self-soothing behaviors, relaxation techniques, and safe images before commencing, particularly if the client presents with a history of self-harm.

Methods

It is important to choose the appropriate subject matter for doing imagery work. One possibility is to work on past events that have been already identified by the patients as being critical in their lives, and which they still recall vividly because of their being associated with high levels of affect. It is helpful to start with the earliest events, as these would be more significant in the laying down of early maladaptive schemas. Another alternative is to focus on a current event in the patient's life or on an issue that has emerged in a therapy session (regarding which the patient's emotional reaction was exaggerated). Once the link is made with a similar event in the past then a pattern or theme can be identified, giving a clue to the underlying schemas. Then, appropriate imagery rescripting can take place on the early negative memory.

During imagery rescripting, the patient should be encouraged to close her eyes and to describe the event in great detail, including memories that are coded in sensory modalities (i.e., smells, colors, touch, tone of voice). Attention should be focused on thoughts, feelings, and the content of memory—more specifically, thoughts about the self, and expectations of the future and of other people as a result of the event. The whole session should be conducted in the present tense, with the patient using the *I* pronoun. Several imagery sessions can focus on one significant early memory or on different critical childhood events before schema modification takes place. Throughout the imagery exercise, the therapist should assess the modification of the belief by asking the "child" patient about her thoughts and feelings and how much she believes what she is being told. It is essential for the therapist to observe a client's nonverbal behavior during the imagery as this may provide important clues as to what is going on in the image over and above what the client is reporting.

In imagery, the schema (with its associated affect) is evoked, thus providing the basis for a reexamination of the validity of the schema and for restructuring its cognitive components. This evocation of the schema can be achieved by bringing the adult patient (or a safe person chosen by the child patient) into the childhood image to empower the child with the knowledge, empathy, and rationality of the adult patient or safe person. The safe person can be a real person or a representation of what the child needs to feel good and safe (e.g., a god, fairies, dead person, or a famous figure). Another way of doing this imagery exercise is to have a dialogue between the child patient and the significant adults from whom they learned a particular schema. The child is encouraged to talk back to the adults in the image and express her needs and feelings. So, by responding as the child or as an adult, the patient can defend and nurture her image of herself in earlier life. In this way, the patient can restructure the meanings attached to the early negative experiences, changing the rules for living that were adopted as a result. This new, corrective information is recorded in memory, helping to empower the individual to change the schema in her current life as well as the schema processes (i.e., including dysfunctional coping mechanisms, e.g., bingeing, starving, and purging), learning and adopting healthier ways of coping.

Therapists should always explain the rationale for imagery rescripting in ways that are understood and accepted by the patient, so that the imagery work is collaborative rather than being forced onto the patient. It is essential for patients to have a cognitive foundation so that the experiential exercises can make sense to them and thus produce maximum change. The therapist needs a sound working knowledge of cognitive therapy and schema-focused CBT to interweave imagery with more verbally based techniques.

The Course of Schema-Focused Cognitive–Behavioral Therapy

Schema-focused cognitive–behavioral therapy usually takes longer than more conventional CBT approaches to the eating disorders (e.g.,

Fairburn et al., 2003) because of the more complex nature of the majority of cases for which SFCBT is appropriate, with their more deep-rooted cognitive structures and behavioral patterns. We often find that the early stages are characterized by a need to focus on engagement and therapeutic relationship issues, as well as the more overt cognitive and behavioral tasks. However, as the core beliefs become less unconditional and the compensatory behaviors reduce, it becomes easier to work at the level of direct cognitive challenges and behavioral experiments. With this shift to a more conventional pattern of CBT, more disorder-specific cognitions (e.g., the critical importance of weight; body image) can be addressed directly.

With many of our clients, relapse is not prevented but managed. Their progress is characterized by a series of setbacks, each providing insights into the nature of the particular person's eating disorder. Thus, the idea of relapse management should be presented from the outset, and a long-term personal coping strategy will evolve.

The distinction between setbacks and relapse should be explained to the patients, and they should be helped to have realistic expectations of themselves. Thus, aiming never to overeat, starve, or purge should be discussed, explored, and challenged. The risks of extreme dieting and relapse should be explained whether or not the patient is overweight. Identifying early warning signals and triggers to binge eating, vomiting, use of laxatives, excessive exercise, and so on and planning alternative coping strategies for these behaviors will be helpful. The patient should be encouraged to

- identify schemas and cognitive distortions, and develop challenges; patients should be particularly alert to the use of double standards and dichotomous thinking;
- use their positive data log and achievement list, diaries, and flashcards to undermine vulnerabilities and get back on track;
- be aware of situations that may trigger the eating problem and schemas, and take steps to change these situations;
- have a regular, but reasonably flexible, eating plan regardless of what goes on in life, and plan the day accordingly;
- acknowledge progress and reward herself for dealing with problems without resorting to unhelpful eating patterns;
- review why a setback has occurred and learn from this experience, tackling a setback sooner rather than later;
- develop a support network and healthy relationships; and
- ask friends for help, call the therapist for advice, have booster sessions, and revisit the recommended bibliography.

Toward the end of treatment, the therapist should consider tapering off sessions while strongly encouraging the rehearsal of these relapse-prevention strategies.

Training, Supervision, and Support

Training in the appropriate techniques is vital for any clinician using SFCBT (James, 2001). Thus, it should go without saying that it is crucial for practitioners to seek competent supervision of their clinical work. This supervision needs to be delivered by a practitioner who is both skilled in conventional CBT for the eating disorders and knowledgeable about the roles of core beliefs and schema processes in disorders with restrictive–compulsive and bulimic–impulsive features. Such supervision should incorporate consideration and discussion of relevant interpersonal issues—namely, the way in which the client's schemas interact with those of the therapist. Because of the complexity of such cases and the potential for interpersonal issues arising during SFCBT with the eating disorders, weekly supervision meetings are likely to be necessary. The nature of the treatment (as outlined earlier) means that the supervision needs to address both the eating cognitions and behaviors and the schema-level cognitions in parallel. When working with the more complex client with an eating disorder, it is also beneficial to operate in a broadly supportive environment, rather than being a lone practitioner.

IMPLICATIONS FOR FUTURE RESEARCH INTO THE OUTCOME OF SFCBT IN THE EATING DISORDERS

Schema-focused cognitive–behavioral therapy should be used with due caution (James, 2001) when working with the eating disorders. As has been indicated earlier (and as is true of most disorders), one of the key gaps in the literature is the lack of systematic research into the effectiveness of SFCBT in treating eating pathology, or indeed any other psychopathology. Our clinical experience suggests that it is most likely to be effective in those cases in which factors reduce the efficacy of conventional, maintenance-model CBT (e.g., comorbid dissociation, personality disorder and very poor self-esteem, history of trauma). However, SFCBT can be a longer and more costly treatment than conventional CBT, and needs to be used only when other forms of CBT or therapy can be shown to be inadequate or are unlikely to be effective. There is clearly a need for research that will enable treatment matching on the basis of psychological and social functioning at presentation, but so far there is little evidence of what those criteria are.

The evidence to date suggests that the appropriate unit of analysis when treating the eating disorders is likely to be the impact of SFCBT on restrictive and bulimic pathology, rather than on diagnosis per se. This approach allows the full range of cases to be addressed (Fairburn et al., 2003; Waller, 1993). It is likely to be necessary to determine which components and techniques of SFCBT will be most relevant to the different elements of the eating disorders (e.g., body image disturbance, purging). Such treatment is likely to depend on the identification and modification of both schema content (core beliefs, sensations) and process (schema compensation and avoidance), and future research should examine the links between changes in these features and behavioral change. Such an analysis should establish the necessity and sufficiency of this form of treatment.

REFERENCES

Agras, W. S., Crow, S. J., Halmi, K. A., Mitchell, J. E., Wilson, G. T., & Kraemer, H. C. (2000). Outcome predictors for the cognitive behavior treatment of bulimia nervosa: Data from a multisite study. *American Journal of Psychiatry, 157,* 1302–1308.

Agras, W. S., Walsh, B. T., Fairburn, C. G., Wilson, G. T., & Kraemer, H. C. (2000). A multicenter comparison of cognitive–behavioral therapy and interpersonal psychotherapy for bulimia nervosa. *Archives of General Psychiatry, 57,* 459–466.

Arntz, A., & Weertman, A. (1999). Treatment of childhood memories: Theory and practice. *Behaviour Research and Therapy, 37,* 715–740.

Beck, A. T. (1996). Beyond belief: A theory of modes, personality and psychopathology. In P. M. Salkovskis (Ed.), *Frontiers of cognitive therapy* (pp. 1–25). New York: Guilford Press.

Beck, A. T., Freeman, A., & Davis, D. D. (2004). Cognitive therapy of personality disorders (2nd ed.). New York: Guilford Press.

Beck, A. T., Rush, A. J., Shaw, B. F., & Emery, G. (1979). *Cognitive therapy of depression.* New York: Guilford Press.

Birmingham, C. L., & Beumont, P. J. V. (2004). *Medical management of eating disorders: A practical handbook for healthcare professionals.* Cambridge, England: Cambridge University Press.

Cooper, M. (1997). Cognitive theory in anorexia nervosa and bulimia nervosa: A review. *Behavioural and Cognitive Psychotherapy, 25,* 113–145.

Cooper, M. (2003, July). *The effects of using imagery to modify core beliefs in bulimia nervosa.* Paper presented at the British Association of Behavioral and Cognitive Psychotherapy conference, Warwick, England.

Cooper, M., Cohen-Tovée, E., Todd, G., Wells, A., & Tovée, M. (1997). The Eating Disorder Belief Questionnaire: Preliminary development. *Behaviour Research and Therapy, 35,* 381–388.

Cooper, M., & Hunt, J. (1998). Core beliefs and underlying assumptions in bulimia nervosa and depression. *Behaviour Research and Therapy, 36,* 895–898.

Cooper, M., & Turner, H. (2000). Underlying assumptions and core beliefs in anorexia nervosa and dieting. *British Journal of Clinical Psychology, 39,* 215–218.

Edwards, D. J. A. (1990). Cognitive therapy and the restructuring of early memories through guided imagery. *Journal of Cognitive Psychotherapy: An International Quarterly, 4*, 33–50.

Emanuelli, F., Meyer, C., Dennis, L., Snell, R., Waller, G., & Lacey, J. H. (2004). *Perceived parental behaviors in the eating disorders: The utility of the Young Parenting Inventory*. Manuscript submitted for publication.

Fairburn, C. G. (1981). A cognitive behavioral approach to the treatment of bulimia. *Psychological Medicine, 11*, 707–711.

Fairburn, C. G. (1997). Eating disorders. In D. M. Clark & C. G. Fairburn (Eds.), *Science and practice of cognitive behavior therapy*. Oxford, England: Oxford University Press.

Fairburn, C. G., Cooper, Z., & Shafran, R. (2003). Cognitive behavior therapy for eating disorders: A "transdiagnostic" theory and treatment. *Behaviour Research and Therapy, 41*, 509–528.

Fairburn, C. G., & Harrison, P. J. (2003). Eating disorders. *The Lancet, 361*, 407–416.

Fairburn, C. G., Marcus, M. D., & Wilson, G. T. (1993). Cognitive behavior therapy for binge eating and bulimia nervosa: A comprehensive treatment manual. In C. G. Fairburn & G. T. Wilson (Eds.), *Binge eating: Nature, assessment and treatment* (pp. 361–404). New York: Guilford Press.

Fairburn, C. G., Norman, P. A.,Welch, S. L., O'Connor, M. E., Doll, H. A., & Peveler, R. C. (1995). A prospective study of outcome in bulimia nervosa and the long-term effects of three psychological treatments. *Archives of General Psychiatry, 52*, 304–312.

Fairburn, C. G., Shafran, R., & Cooper, Z. (1999). A cognitive–behavioral theory of anorexia nervosa. *Behaviour Research and Therapy, 37*, 1–13.

Fallon, P., & Wonderlich, S. A. (1997). Sexual abuse and other forms of trauma. In D. M. Garner & P. E. Garfinkel (Eds.), *Handbook of treatment for eating disorders* (pp. 394–414). New York: Guilford Press.

Fichter, M., Quadfleig, N., & Reif, W. (1994). Course of multi-impulsive bulimia. *Psychological Medicine, 24*, 591–604.

Garner, D. M. (1991). *Eating Disorder Inventory–2*. Odessa, FL: Psychological Assessment Resources.

Garner, D., & Bemis, K. M. (1982). A cognitive–behavioral approach to anorexia nervosa. *Cognitive Therapy and Research, 6*, 123–150.

Geller, J., Williams, K. D., & Srikameswaran, S. (2001). Clinician stance in the treatment of chronic eating disorders. *European Eating Disorders Review, 9*, 374–380.

Greenberger, D., & Padesky, C. A. (1995). *Mind over mood: Change the way you feel by changing the way you think*. New York: Guilford Press.

Hackmann, A. (1998). Working with images in clinical psychology. In A. S. Bellack & M. Hersen (Eds.), *Comprehensive clinical psychology* (Vol. 6, pp. 301–318). Oxford, England: Pergamon Press.

Hartt, J., & Waller, G. (2001). Child abuse, dissociation, and core beliefs in bulimic disorders. *Child Abuse and Neglect, 26,* 923–938.

Hollon, S. D., & Beck, A. T. (1994). Cognitive and cognitive–behavioral therapies. In A. E. Bergin & S. L. Garfield (Eds.), *Handbook of psychotherapy and behavioral change* (pp. 428–466). Chichester, England: Wiley.

James, I. (2001). Schema therapy: The next generation, but should it carry a health warning? *Behavioural and Cognitive Psychotherapy, 29,* 401–408.

Kaplan, A. S., & Garfinkel, P. E. (1993). *Medical issues and the eating disorders: The interface.* New York: Brunner/Mazel.

Kennerley, H. (1996). Cognitive therapy of dissociative symptoms associated with trauma. *British Journal of Clinical Psychology, 35,* 325–340.

Kennerley, H. (1997, July). *Managing complex eating disorders using schema-based cognitive therapy.* Paper presented at the British Association of Cognitive and Behavioral Psychotherapy conference, Canterbury, England.

Lawson, R., Waller, G., Corstorphine, E., Ganis, C., & Luck, A. (2003). *Cognitive content and process in multi-impulsive eating disorders.* Manuscript submitted for publication.

Layden, M. A., Newman, C. F., Freeman, A., & Morse, S. B. (1993). *Cognitive therapy of borderline personality disorder.* Boston: Allyn & Bacon.

Leung, N., Thomas, G. V., & Waller, G. (2000). The relationship between parental bonding and core beliefs in anorexic and bulimic women. *British Journal of Clinical Psychology, 39,* 203–213.

Leung, N., Waller, G., & Thomas, G. V. (1999). Core beliefs in anorexic and bulimic women. *Journal of Nervous and Mental Disease, 187,* 736–741.

Linehan, M. M. (1993). *Cognitive–behavioral treatment for borderline personality disorder: The dialectics of effective treatment.* New York: Guilford Press.

Luck, A., Waller, G., Meyer, C., Ussher, M., & Lacey, J. H. (2005). The role of schema processes in the eating disorders. *Cognitive Therapy and Research, 29,* 717–732.

Malan, D. H. (1979). *Individual psychotherapy and the science of psychodynamics.* London: Butterworth-Heineman.

McManus, F., & Waller, G. (1995). A functional analysis of binge-eating. *Clinical Psychology Review, 15,* 345–363.

McManus, F., Waller, G., & Chadwick, P. (1996). Biases in the processing of different forms of threat in bulimic and comparison women. *Journal of Nervous and Mental Disease, 184,* 547–554.

Meyer, C., & Waller, G. (1999). The impact of emotion upon eating behavior: The role of subliminal visual processing of threat cues. *International Journal of Eating Disorders, 25,* 319–326.

Meyer, C., Serpell, L., Waller, G., Murphy, F., Treasure, J., & Leung, N. (2005). Cognitive avoidance in the strategic processing of ego threats among eating-disordered patients. *International Journal of Eating Disorders, 38,* 30–36.

Mountford, V., Waller, G., Watson, D., & Scragg, P. (2004). An experimental analysis of the role of schema compensation in anorexia nervosa. *Eating Behaviors, 5*, 223–230.

Murphy, S., Russell, L., & Waller, G. (2005). Integrated psychodynamic therapy for bulimia nervosa and binge eating disorder: Theory, practice and preliminary findings. *European Eating Disorders Review, 13*, 383–391.

Ohanian, V. (2002). Imagery rescripting within cognitive behavior therapy for bulimia nervosa: An illustrative case report. *International Journal of Eating Disorders, 30*, 352–357.

Padesky, C. (1990). Schema as self-prejudice. *International Cognitive Therapy Newsletter, 6*, 5–6.

Padesky, C. (1994) Schema change processes in cognitive therapy. *Clinical Psychology and Psychotherapy, 1*, 267–278.

Padesky, C., & Greenberger, D. (1995). *Clinician's guide to Mind Over Mood.* New York: Guilford Press.

Patton, C. J. (1992). Fear of abandonment and binge eating: A subliminal psychodynamic activation investigation. *Journal of Nervous and Mental Disease, 180*, 484–490.

Power, M. (1997). Conscious and unconscious representations of meaning. In M. Power & C. Brewin (Eds.), *The transformation of meaning in psychological therapies* (pp. 57–73). Chichester, England: Wiley.

Rieger, E., Schotte, D. E., Touyz, S. W., Beumont, P. J. V., Griffiths, R., & Russell, J. (1998). Attentional biases in eating disorders: A visual probe detection procedure. *International Journal of Eating Disorders, 23*, 199–205.

Root, M. P. P., & Fallon, P. (1989). Treating the victimized bulimic. *Journal of Interpersonal Violence, 4*, 90–100.

Safran, J. D., & Segal, Z. V. (1990). *Interpersonal process in cognitive therapy.* New York: Basic Books.

Sansone, R. A., & Fine, M. A. (1992). Borderline personality disorder as a predictor of outcome in women with eating disorders. *Journal of Personality Disorders, 6*, 176–186.

Schmidt, N. B., Joiner, T. E., Young, J. E., & Telch, M. J. (1995). The Schema Questionnaire: Investigation of psychometric properties and the hierarchical structure of a measure of maladaptive schemas. *Cognitive Therapy and Research, 19*, 295–321.

Serpell, L., & Treasure, J. (2002). Bulimia nervosa: Friend or foe? The pros and cons of bulimia nervosa. *International Journal of Eating Disorders, 32*, 164–170.

Serpell, L., Treasure, J., Teasdale, J., & Sullivan, V. (1999). Anorexia nervosa: Friend or foe? *International Journal of Eating Disorders, 25*, 177–186.

Shah, R., & Waller, G. (2000). Parental style and vulnerability to depression: The role of core beliefs. *Journal of Nervous and Mental Disease, 188*, 19–25.

Sheffield, A., Waller, G., Emanuelli, F., Murray, J., & Meyer, C. (2005). Links between parenting and core beliefs: Preliminary psychometric validation of the Young Parenting Inventory. *Cognitive Therapy and Research, 29,* 787–802.

Slade, P. (1982). Towards a functional analysis of anorexia nervosa and bulimia nervosa. *British Journal of Clinical Psychology, 21,* 167–179.

Smucker, M. R., Dancu, C., Foa, E. B., & Niederee, J. L. (1995). Imagery rescripting: A new treatment for survivors of childhood sexual abuse suffering from posttraumatic stress. *Journal of Cognitive Psychotherapy: An International Quarterly, 9,* 3–17.

Spranger, S. C., Waller, G., & Bryant-Waugh, R. (2001) Schema avoidance in bulimic and non-eating disordered women. *International Journal of Eating Disorders, 29,* 302–306.

Steiger, H., Gauvin, L., Jabalpurwala, S., Seguin, J. R., & Stotland, S. (1999). Hypersensitivity to social interactions in bulimic syndromes: Relationship to binge eating. *Journal of Consulting and Clinical Psychology, 67,* 765–775.

Teasdale, J. D., & Barnard, P. J. (1993). *Affect, cognition and change: Remodelling depressive thought.* Hove, England: Erlbaum.

Treasure, J., & Ward, A. (1997). Cognitive analytic therapy in the treatment of anorexia nervosa. *Clinical Psychology and Psychotherapy, 4,* 62–71.

Vitousek, K. B. (1996). The current status of cognitive behavioral models of anorexia nervosa and bulimia nervosa. In P. M. Salkovskis (Ed.), *Frontiers of cognitive therapy* (pp. 383–418). New York: Guilford Press.

Waller, G. (1993). Why do we diagnose different types of eating disorder? Arguments for a change in research and clinical practice. *Eating Disorders Review, 1,* 74–89.

Waller, G. (1997). Drop-out and failure to engage in individual outpatient cognitive–behavior therapy for bulimic disorders. *International Journal of Eating Disorders, 22,* 35–41.

Waller, G. (2003). Schema-level cognitions in patients with binge eating disorder: A case control study. *International Journal of Eating Disorders, 33,* 458–464.

Waller, G. (2004). *A schema-based cognitive behavioral model of the aetiology and maintenance of restrictive and bulimic pathology in the eating disorders.* Manuscript submitted for publication.

Waller, G., Dickson, C., & Ohanian, V. (2002). Cognitive content in bulimic disorders: Core beliefs and eating attitudes. *Eating Behaviors, 3,* 171–178.

Waller, G., & Kennerley, H. (2003). Cognitive–behavioral treatments. In J. Treasure, U. Schmidt, & E. Furth (Eds.). *Handbook of eating disorders* (pp. 233–252). Chichester, England: Wiley.

Waller, G., Meyer, C., & Ohanian, V. (2001). Psychometric properties of the long and short versions of the Young Schema Questionnaire: Core beliefs among bulimic and comparison women. *Cognitive Therapy and Research, 25,* 137–147.

Waller, G., Meyer, C., Ohanian, V., Elliott, P., Dickson, C., & Sellings, J. (2001). The psychopathology of bulimic women who report childhood sexual abuse:

The mediating role of core beliefs. *Journal of Nervous and Mental Disease*, *189*, 700–708.

Waller, G., & Mijatovich, S. (1998). Preconscious processing of threat cues: Impact on eating among women with unhealthy eating attitudes. *International Journal of Eating Disorders*, *24*, 83–89.

Waller, G., & Ohanian, V. (1999, April). *Cognitive behavioural treatment of complex cases of bulimia: Use of schema-focused therapy and imagery rescripting*. Paper presented at the International Conference on Eating Disorders, London, England.

Waller, G., Ohanian, V., Meyer, C., & Osman, S. (2000). Cognitive content among bulimic women: The role of core beliefs. *International Journal of Eating Disorders*, *28*, 235–241.

Waller, G., Shah, R., Ohanian, V., & Elliott, P. A. (2001). Core beliefs in bulimia nervosa and depression: The discriminant validity of Young's Schema Questionnaire. *Behavior Therapy*, *32*, 139–153.

Waller, G., & Thomas, G. V. (2000). Outcome of group cognitive–behavior therapy for bulimia nervosa: The role of core beliefs. *Behaviour Research and Therapy*, *38*, 145–156.

Waller, G., Watkins, H., Shuck, V., & McManus, F. (1996). Bulimic psychopathology and attentional biases to ego threats among non-eating-disordered women. *International Journal of Eating Disorders*, *20*, 169–176.

Wilson, G. T. (1996). Treatment of bulimia nervosa: When CBT fails. *Behaviour Research and Therapy*, *34*, 197–212.

Wilson, G. T. (1999). Cognitive behavior therapy for eating disorders: Progress and problems. *Behaviour Research and Therapy*, *37*, S79–S95.

Wiser, S., & Telch, C. F. (1999). Dialectical behavior therapy for binge-eating disorder. *Journal of Clinical Psychology*, *55*, 755–768.

Young, J. E. (1990). *Cognitive therapy for personality disorders: A schema focused approach* (1st ed.). Sarasota, FL: Professional Resource Exchange.

Young, J. E. (1994). *Cognitive therapy for personality disorders: A schema focused approach* (2nd ed.). Sarasota, FL: Professional Resource Exchange.

Young, J. E. (1999). *Cognitive therapy for personality disorders: A schema focused approach* (3rd ed.). Sarasota, FL: Professional Resource Exchange.

Young, J. E., & Klosko, J. S. (1993). *Reinventing your life*. New York: Plume.

Young, J. E., Klosko, J. S., & Weishaar, M. E. (2003). *Schema therapy: A practitioner's guide*. New York: Guilford.

8

CASE FORMULATION AND COGNITIVE SCHEMAS IN COGNITIVE THERAPY FOR PSYCHOSIS

ANTHONY P. MORRISON

Cognitive–behavioral therapy (CBT), including schema-focused approaches to the understanding and treatment of psychosis, has developed considerably over the past decade. There is now a recognition that cognitive models of psychosis can account for significant aspects of the development and maintenance of psychosis, especially in relation to the distress and disability that can be associated with psychotic experiences (Chadwick & Birchwood, 1994; Garety, Kuipers, Fowler, Freeman, & Bebbington, 2001; Morrison, 1998a, 2001).

Numerous randomized controlled trials have demonstrated the efficacy of CBT for people with psychosis, typically as an adjunct to medication (Kuipers et al., 1997; Sensky et al., 2000; Tarrier et al., 1998; Turkington, Kingdon, & Turner, 2002). In fact, several meta-analyses concluded that CBT for psychosis is efficacious and should be provided routinely (Gould, Mueser, Bolton, Mays, & Goff, 2001; Rector & Beck, 2001). Effectiveness studies also suggest that it can be implemented in routine clinical settings (Morrison, Renton, Dunn, Williams, & Bentall, 2004). In light of the strong evidence in support of CBT for psychosis, CBT is now included in National

Institute for Clinical Excellence (2003) guidelines for the treatment of schizophrenia.

On the basis of such evidence, it would seem reasonable to suggest that all patients experiencing distress associated with psychotic experiences should be offered access to CBT. The remainder of this chapter outlines an approach to the delivery of cognitive therapy (CT) that incorporates schemas in case conceptualizations and includes the utilization of schema-focused intervention strategies.

The structure, process, and principles of CT for people with psychosis is very similar to those developed for people with emotional disorders (Beck, 1976). Thus, it begins with developing a therapeutic relationship and socializing the patient to a cognitive model. The process of therapy begins with assessment and engagement, after which a list of problems and goals are developed collaboratively and a case formulation is developed. Intervention strategies are selected on the basis of the formulation, and are evaluated in an ongoing manner. Therapy finishes with relapse prevention and the development of a therapeutic blueprint. Each aspect is considered in more detail later.

The characteristics of CT include being collaborative, time limited, problem oriented, and educational, involving guided discovery and the inductive method. The structure of CT for psychosis also parallels the structure of standard CT. Thus, sessions start with a review of current mental state and feedback from the previous session, followed by the setting of an agenda. Agenda setting is performed collaboratively, with both client and therapist contributing to the process. The agenda typically involves a review of the previous week's homework task(s) and one or two discrete session targets that are based on the model or formulation, followed by the assignment of new homework, feedback, and a summary of the current session. Time should be allocated to each agenda item and a timekeeper agreed on; the agenda should not be rigidly adhered to, but rather seen as a guide to ensure productive use of the limited time available.

The aims of CT for psychosis are worth considering. The primary aim is to reduce the distress experienced by people with psychosis and to improve their quality of life. The aims of CT do not necessarily include reducing the frequency of psychotic symptoms, but rather focus on helping patients to achieve the goals that they have set in relation to the problems that they have identified.

MALADAPTIVE SCHEMAS AND PSYCHOSIS

In many ways, maladaptive schemas are important in working with people with psychosis. They can be related to the development and maintenance of psychotic experiences and can cause distress in their own right in people with psychosis, and certain psychotic beliefs can be conceptualized as schema. These issues need to be addressed in each phase of therapy: assessment and engagement, development of a case formulation, intervention, and relapse prevention.

In working with people with psychotic experiences, it is important to consider relevant early experiences that may have contributed to the development of current difficulties, both psychotic and nonpsychotic. Life events in childhood contribute to the development of schemas and dysfunctional assumptions or rules that guide behavior and the selection of information-processing strategies (Beck, 1976; Wells & Matthews, 1994).

Particular events that are important to assess specifically include childhood sexual and physical abuse, given the high prevalence of such experiences in people with psychosis (Read, Agar, Argyle, & Aderhold, 2003). Read and Argyle (1999) found that the content of just over half (54%) of the "schizophrenic" symptoms of abused adult inpatients was obviously related to the abuse; for example, a woman who had been sexually abused by her father from age 5 heard "male voices outside her head and screaming children's voices inside her head." Bebbington et al. (2004) used interview-based data on 8,580 adults from the British National Survey of Psychiatric Morbidity to test the hypothesis that a range of early victimization experiences contributes to vulnerability to psychosis. They found that those people with psychosis were 15.5 times more likely to have experienced sexual abuse than those without any mental disorder, and had a higher odds ratio than that of any other diagnostic group. Another large study of the general population from the Netherlands ($N = 4,045$) concluded that their "results suggest that early childhood trauma increases the risk for positive psychotic symptoms. This finding fits well with certain models that suggest that early adversities may lead to psychological and biological changes that increase psychosis vulnerability" (Janssen et al., 2004, p. 38). Similar experiences in adulthood should also be examined. A general assessment of family life, cultural and spiritual upbringing, school experiences, and friendships should also be included.

The influence of life experiences on the development of knowledge and beliefs about self, world, and others should be considered. Assessment should include an analysis of a client's schemas, which are unconditional statements about themselves, the world, and other people (e.g., "I am unlovable," "Other people will exploit you," and "The world is hostile"). The conditional beliefs or rules that people adopt to compensate for these core beliefs, often occurring in the form of "if . . . then" statements (e.g., "If I am perfect, then I will be lovable"), should also be assessed. The compensatory strategies that are behavioral expressions of such rules (e.g., striving for perfection) should also be identified.

Procedural beliefs, which guide the selection of information-processing strategies, should also be assessed (Wells & Matthews, 1994). Procedural beliefs are largely implicit representations of metacognitive knowledge that influence processing and often operate outside of conscious awareness (Wells & Matthews, 1994). However, such beliefs can be explicit; such beliefs that are particularly relevant to people with psychosis include beliefs about the meaning and usefulness of paranoia and suspiciousness (e.g., "Being paranoid means you won't get caught unawares") or beliefs about unusual perceptual experiences (e.g., "Seeing things that others don't means that you are going mad" or "Hearing voices provides me with company"). It is important to inquire about any advantages that such psychotic experiences or beliefs may have for the person, and how these modes of operating developed over time and are related to past and current environment. This information can be highly valuable for the development of a cognitive case conceptualization.

The role of schemas is especially important in the collaborative development of a historical or developmental case formulation. Common schemas that are encountered in people with distressing psychotic experiences include the following: "I am bad," "I am unlovable," "I am vulnerable," "I am different," "Others are not to be trusted," and "The world is dangerous." These beliefs can help to explain the seemingly bizarre appraisals of ambiguous events and can also be used to help predict difficulties in therapy, such as lack of trust in the therapeutic relationship, belief that one is unworthy of therapist input, or difficulties in homework completion.

Schemas often appear to be related to the development of psychotic experiences. The early experiences and beliefs about self, world, and others that are at the core of schemas are frequently apparent in the expression of unusual experiences and beliefs. For example, many people with persecutory ideas have had aversive or genuine persecutory experiences in childhood or early adulthood, and it is clear that these are related to the development of overgeneralized threat beliefs or specific idiosyncratic ideas about conspiracies and ongoing persecution. It has been suggested that such ideas reflect underlying low self-esteem and are a defense against self-discrepancies (Bentall, Corcoran, Howard, Blackwood, & Kinderman, 2001). The content of hallucinatory experiences similarly can reflect the content of core beliefs; for example, voices often comment on early experience or are highly critical of the patient, reflecting both negative beliefs about themselves and negative expectations about the behavior of others. It is also common for grandiose ideas to be compensatory in nature, reflecting an implicit low self-esteem. Although delusional beliefs are often viewed as being highly resistant to change and inflexible, evidence suggests that this is not the case. There are similarities between the rigidity and impairment associated with schemas or core beliefs and many delusional ideas, and it is clear that delusional ideation can fluctuate in terms of conviction and impairment naturalistically (Garety & Hemsley, 1994) as well as in response to verbal challenging and behavioral testing (Chadwick & Lowe, 1990).

Schema change methods are of considerable importance in CT for people with psychosis. See the Intervention section for more details about these approaches.

ASSESSMENT AND ENGAGEMENT

Assessment of a person with psychosis is extremely similar to a cognitive–behavioral assessment of a nonpsychotic patient. After setting the scene and explaining confidentiality and the practicalities of therapy, the therapist usually finds it helpful to begin with an analysis of a recent problematic incident. The aim of this analysis is to generate information that will be useful in understanding the development and maintenance of problems and in suggesting change strategies, as well as to begin to socialize the person to a cognitive model and way of viewing his or her difficulties. It can also promote hope and suggest ways for achieving change.

Engagement is an important aspect of therapy throughout the process but is vital in the early phases. Strategies that can help to promote engagement include emphasizing the collaborative nature of CT and focusing on distress and the early development of a list of shared goals for therapy (this process is described in greater detail shortly). A sound therapeutic relationship based on warmth, acceptance, and empathy is required to promote engagement. Flexibility regarding timing and duration of appointments, choice of venue, and therapeutic style are all important too. It is important to explicitly address expectations regarding therapy and people's previous experiences of mental health services, and the role of interpersonal schemas should be considered with regard to engagement; for example, if someone believes that he or she is vulnerable and other people not to be trusted, then it is obviously going to be difficult for that person to engage in a therapeutic relationship and take risks within that context. Use of the patient's own language and some patience on the part of therapist appear to be particularly important when working with people with psychosis (e.g., avoiding the use of words such as *schizophrenia* unless the patient introduces them), and regular supervision from a suitably qualified and experienced practitioner also seems crucial to successful engagement of patients. A more detailed discussion of assessment and engagement strategies can be found in Morrison, Renton, et al. (2003).

It is common for assessment to begin with an analysis of problem maintenance. This can be done by examining recent situations in terms of events, thoughts, feelings, and behaviors and collaboratively searching for

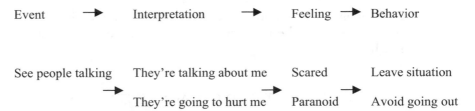

Figure 8.1. Analysis of problem maintenance.

meaningful links between these factors. For example, such a framework could be applied to ideas of reference as shown in Figure 8.1.

As stated earlier, an important aim of the assessment phase of CT is the development of a shared list of problems and goals. Problems should be described quite generally at first, and be phrased in a more specific manner after additional information is gained. The goals that are set in relation to the problems should then be made as SMART as possible (i.e., make the goals specific, measurable, achievable, realistic, and time-limited). An example of a problems and goals list is provided in Exhibit 8.1.

The establishment of such a shared list of problems and goals that can then be collaboratively prioritized is a central part of CT, and is invaluable in engaging patients. It is worth noting that the problem lists of people with psychosis frequently do not include or prioritize psychotic experiences,

EXHIBIT 8.1
An Example Problem and Goal List

Problem: Hearing distressing voices that stop me from going out.
Goal: Within 10 weeks, to reduce the distress associated with the voices from 80% to 40%, or to increase the belief that "I can go out despite the voices" from 10% to 50% conviction.

Problem: Feeling paranoid in social situations.
Goal: Within 10 weeks, to reduce the belief that "Other people are talking about me" from 100% to 60%, or to reduce anxiety when in such social situations from an average of 75% to an average of 40%.

Problem: Feeling hopeless about the future.
Goal: Within 4 weeks, to have increased the belief that "Things can change for the better" from 10% to 50%.

Problem: Not having a job.
Goal: Within 4 weeks, to meet with an appropriate person who can advise me regarding employment opportunities and training schemes.

whereas interpersonal issues, such as family or sexual relationships, meaningful daytime activities, and emotional problems such as anxiety, depression, and anger all feature commonly (Birchwood, 2003; Morrison, Renton, et al., 2003). In fact, the issues that are highlighted as most important by people with psychosis, such as understanding of self, empowerment, meaningful activities, and relationships, are similar to those identified by others (Deegan, 1988). The strategies that are described later for formulating and intervening with distressing psychotic experiences assume that they are identified as problems and prioritized by the patient; if they are not, then the usual methods devised for dealing with nonpsychotic problems are equally applicable to people with psychosis.

FORMULATION

Once the assessment process has been completed, an idiosyncratic case formulation can be developed. These can range from very basic event–thought–feeling–behavior chains, as outlined earlier, to fairly complex historical formulations that incorporate relevant early experiences, schemas and assumptions, critical incidents, and current environmental factors. The level of formulation that is required depends on a number of factors including the type of problem that is being analyzed and the question that is being asked (e.g., "How can I reduce the distress associated with hearing voices?" may require a fairly basic maintenance level of analysis, whereas "Why am I experiencing my current problems?" would require a much more detailed, developmental perspective). It is useful to adopt a parsimonious approach, using the simplest approaches when possible, but always having knowledge regarding early experiences and the schemas and assumptions that have been formed as a result of these. These experiences and beliefs can be incorporated in the explicit, shared case conceptualization if the presenting problems appear complex or have interpersonal aspects to them, if the person is asking for an understanding of how his or her problems developed, or if progress is proving difficult when therapy is at a maintenance level. In addition, it can be useful to provide a historical or developmental perspective to facilitate normalizing people's psychotic experiences (e.g., if a person's abusive history makes sense of current paranoid ideation).

All formulations should ideally be based on an empirically supported cognitive model of the difficulties in question. If people are prioritizing psychotic experiences, then a useful approach to the developmental or historical case conceptualization can be derived from a model of psychosis. This cognitive account of psychotic symptoms (Morrison, 2001) suggests that the cultural acceptability of interpretations determines whether someone is viewed as psychotic or not, and that these interpretations are influenced

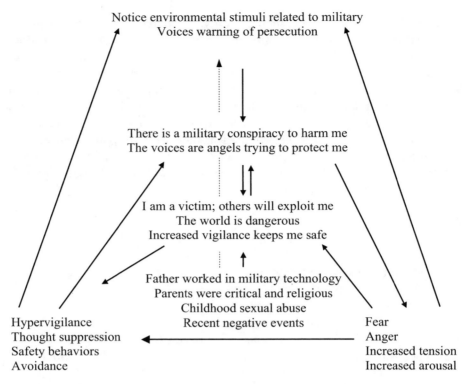

Notice environmental stimuli related to military
Voices warning of persecution

There is a military conspiracy to harm me
The voices are angels trying to protect me

I am a victim; others will exploit me
The world is dangerous
Increased vigilance keeps me safe

Father worked in military technology
Parents were critical and religious
Childhood sexual abuse
Recent negative events

Hypervigilance
Thought suppression
Safety behaviors
Avoidance

Fear
Anger
Increased tension
Increased arousal

Figure 8.2. An idiosyncratic formulation of the cognitive model of psychosis.

by life experiences and beliefs (schemas and assumptions). It also suggests that it is the initial interpretation of psychotic experiences, and the way in which people respond to such experiences, that determines whether or not the experience will cause distress and recur. This model of psychosis is also easily translated into an idiosyncratic case conceptualization that can explain the development and maintenance of psychosis.

For example, Harry, a 25-year-old man, had a history of adversity in his childhood. He was sexually abused by a family friend, and his parents did not believe him when he disclosed this. His father was in the military and was involved in classified work regarding new technologies for espionage purposes. Both his parents were strict disciplinarians and were devout Catholics. These early experiences led Harry to develop beliefs about himself being vulnerable to harm, other people being untrustworthy, and the world being a dangerous and unpredictable place. He also developed a belief that it was important to be vigilant for threat, and as a result he was permanently on red alert for interpersonal danger. At the age of 21, Harry had a stressful time in which a relationship ended, he was physically assaulted in the street by two strangers, and he lost his part-time job. These events were followed by a period of sleep disturbance and anxiety. Over time, Harry started to become suspicious of others, suspecting that they might be involved in some kind of conspiracy against him; he became increasingly preoccupied with this idea, deciding that it was probably organized by the military and may have something to do with his father. He began to hear voices that confirmed these beliefs and warned him about potential sources of persecution (e.g., his parents, people in the street, and electronic audiovisual equipment). His religious background led him to interpret these voices as guardian angels who were trying to protect him (he later made links in therapy between his desire for protection in adulthood and his lack of protection in child-hood). Once convinced of the conspiracy, he tried to avoid leaving the house, if possible, and ceased contact with his parents. In addition, he tried to suppress thoughts of the conspiracy and adopted several safety behaviors such as going out only in the dark, varying his routes, trying to disguise himself, and carrying a knife. These behaviors served to maintain his beliefs regarding the conspiracy. This formulation is illustrated in Figure 8.2.

INTERVENTION

Once a case conceptualization has been collaboratively developed, intervention strategies can be collaboratively discussed and chosen on the basis of what is likely to achieve quick success or what will have the most significant effect on quality of life. Most change strategies can be described as being verbal reattribution methods or behavioral reattribution methods; each is considered in more detail later, and particular emphasis is placed on schema change strategies.

Verbal Strategies

There are a variety of verbal strategies for the facilitation of change that can be useful when used on the basis of a case conceptualization.

Advantages and Disadvantages

It is particularly important to consider the advantages and disadvantages of a particular belief or experience at the outset, prior to attempting to change a belief, even if the belief in question is associated with distress. Positive beliefs about psychotic experiences include the advantages of being paranoid, such as safety and excitement, or beliefs about the benefits of hearing voices, such as that the voices are benevolent (Chadwick & Birchwood, 1994), and that the voices provide companionship or relaxation (Miller, O'Connor, & DiPasquale, 1993). The origins of psychotic experiences can be explored within this context, as they may have developed as coping or survival strategies (e.g., paranoia is helpful if one is in a very dangerous or abusive environment; Romme & Escher, 1989, suggested that voices frequently evolve as a coping response to trauma). Negative symptoms can also be conceptualized in a similar way (Morrison, Renton, et al., 2003); for example, flat affect can be functional if previous experience has taught someone that strong emotions are punished (e.g., by physical violence in the family home or playground) and poverty of speech can be adaptive if one has been emotionally or physically abused for saying the wrong thing.

If significant advantages are identified, then these should be evaluated with regard to current usefulness (e.g., although paranoia may have been appropriate for a previous situation, things may have changed in the current environment). Alternative sources of the benefits that are identified should be considered. For example, if someone's self-esteem is maintained by a belief that he or she is special and is, therefore, being targeted by a government's espionage organization, then it is important to provide alternative sources of self-esteem prior to reducing conviction in this problematic belief. At times, it may be necessary to recognize that the benefits of a psychotic experience outweigh the disadvantages, and that other ways of providing the advantages are not achievable or realistic; in such cases, the patient should be supported to make his or her own decision.

Evidential Analysis

A standard procedure in CT is to examine the evidence for and against a particular thought or interpretation of events (Wells, 1997). Once a specific thought or belief is identified and agreed on as being problematic, then two columns can be used to collate evidence for and against the particular belief. The evidence should be elicited Socratically, with questions such as "What makes you think that this is true?" and "Is there anything that is incompatible with your belief?" Consideration of modulating factors can also be helpful in generating evidence, as can questions specifically related to the content of the belief. This process can identify other psychotic experiences or beliefs that can also be evaluated with verbal reattribution techniques (e.g., examining alternative explanations).

Generation of Alternative Explanations

The generation of alternative explanations is another strategy that can reduce the distress associated with psychotic experiences. Delusional ideas and beliefs about voices are open to examination and it is important to help patients consider a wide variety of possible explanations for their experiences. Brainstorming exercises and the consideration of what other

EXHIBIT 8.2
Alternative Explanations and Degrees of Belief

The people are laughing because . . .	
Initial belief: They are laughing at me	95%
They are nervous and it is a nervous laugh	25%
They are telling a joke	50%
They are laughing at someone else in the center	40%
I am imagining them laughing	1%
They have taken nitrous oxide (laughing gas)	0%

people have suggested or would suggest can facilitate this process. The alternative explanations that are generated should be rated for degree of belief or conviction on an ongoing basis, and recent problematic situations and moderators can be evaluated in relation to consistency with each explanation. For example, John believed that people at his local day center were laughing at him. He was encouraged to generate as many possible explanations for the most recent incident that he had reported. This process yielded the list in Exhibit 8.2.

It can be useful to place each explanation into a pie chart to ensure that the total adds up to 100%, and in such circumstances it is useful to leave the most distressing explanation until last and then rerate the initial belief.

Normalization

The use of normalizing information can help to combat the negative effects of stigma, reduce distress, and help to provide information to facilitate the generation of alternatives. Normalization is particularly important as many people with psychotic diagnoses identify stigma and discrimination as being the most distressing or difficult aspect of their mental health problem. Normalizing information can include facts and figures about the prevalence of psychotic experiences and beliefs in the general population; for example, 5% of the population hear voices at any given time (Tien, 1991), and up to 70% of the general population endorse beliefs that could be labeled as delusional (Verdoux et al., 1998). This information can be extremely liberating for people who believed they were the only person with such experiences, or that such experiences automatically meant that they were mad (emphasizing the fact that many of these experiences are not pathological). Information about the links between certain life events and specific psychotic experiences can also be helpful in reducing distress (e.g., there is evidence suggesting that auditory hallucinations are linked to experiences such as childhood trauma [Read et al., 2003] and that discrimination is related to delusional ideation [Janssen et al., 2003]). A summary of the normalizing approach to the understanding of psychosis is provided elsewhere (Kingdon & Turkington, 1994).

Behavioral Strategies

The use of behavioral strategies within a cognitive case conceptualization can be an extremely effective way of achieving belief change and, therefore, reducing distress (Chadwick & Lowe, 1990). Behavioral experiments are a vital component of CT, and safety behaviors that are used to prevent the feared outcomes associated with psychosis can be particularly important to address.

Behavioral Experiments

Behavioral experiments are an important component of effective CT for psychosis. Beliefs about voices and delusional ideas are frequently translatable into testable hypotheses, which can be collaboratively investigated by patient and therapist. Behavioral experiments should be designed very carefully to ensure a no-lose outcome, and predictions should be stated in a concrete way. The possible results should be reviewed in advance to ensure that the outcome is meaningful and that they will not be dismissed or accommodated within the problematic belief system. Examples of behavioral experiments include using activity scheduling to evaluate beliefs about the consequences of activity or the lack of pleasure (which can be extremely helpful for negative symptoms such as anhedonia, avolition, and apathy) or exposure to feared situations to evaluate beliefs about voices or paranoid ideas.

Safety Behaviors

Safety behaviors were first identified in relation to anxiety disorders, and are behaviors that are adopted to prevent a feared outcome (Salkovskis, 1991). They are problematic for people if they prevent disconfirmation of the catastrophic beliefs about the feared outcome. It has been noted that people with psychotic experiences frequently use safety behaviors (Morrison, 1998b), and empirical studies have demonstrated the presence of such behaviors in people with persecutory delusions (Freeman, Garety, & Kuipers, 2001) and in people experiencing distressing auditory hallucinations. Examples of such safety behaviors include avoidance of particular places, hypervigilance and selective attention, and idiosyncratic strategies to prevent psychosis-related fears. People who are experiencing voices that produce anxiety are typically associated with safety behaviors. For example, if people believe that their voices will make them go mad, then they will adopt behaviors designed to maintain mental well-being (e.g., thought suppression, monitoring for signs of impending madness, staying in the company of others or trying to relax), which prevent disconfirmation of this belief and may actually increase the frequency or intensity of the voices. If people believe that they are being persecuted, then they may develop extensive avoidance behavior, or more subtle strategies such as taking different routes to the shops, being hypervigilant for men in suits, suppressing signs of arousal, or avoiding eye contact, which can be similarly problematic. Such safety behaviors can be manipulated to demonstrate their counterproductive effects, and are amenable to being dropped in behavioral experiments to evaluate the relevant beliefs (i.e. people can stop using their safety behaviours in order to test out what happens).

Schema Change Methods

There are several useful strategies for dealing with schemas and related issues (e.g., the themes of people's voices that often reflect core beliefs held about self, world, and others) in people with psychotic experiences. After we discuss the rationale for schema-focused work that can be presented to patients, we will discuss these strategies.

A Rationale for Schema Work: The Prejudice Model

A useful strategy to help clients see how their core beliefs can operate much like a prejudicial belief, with incoming information being processed differently according to whether it is consistent with, or contradicts, the existing belief, has been described by Christine Padesky (1993). This technique can be applied most easily to unconditional schematic beliefs, such as "I am unlovable" or "I am bad," and entails the examination of this processing style in the maintenance of a specific prejudicial belief held by someone known to the client, but a belief with which the client disagrees. The use of this analogy allows the illustration of how a process of ignoring, distorting, or making an exception of incoming contradictory information, versus the ready acceptance of confirmatory information, maintains a belief, even when it is not true. Once clients understand the concepts, they can be encouraged to think about how they would go about changing this other person's prejudicial belief.

For example, John believed himself to be unlovable. His socialist politics meant that he was extremely opposed to racism. When asked to consider how a racist was able to develop such a belief, he recognized it was a result of learning and experience. He was also able to identify how a racist might ignore information that was inconsistent with his belief (e.g., people from ethnic minorities performing valuable roles in society or acts of generosity) and how such a person is motivated to search for information that confirms his or her belief (e.g., news items relating to crimes committed by people from such backgrounds). John was able to make links between this process and the development and maintenance of his own beliefs about himself being unlovable, and to consider what implications this would have for evaluating, and possibly changing, those beliefs.

This process has the additional benefit of allowing the client to consider how difficult changing a long-held and extreme belief might be, and how long it might take. This knowledge can be helpful when the model is applied to the client's own belief in preparation for the process of change. All of the other verbal and behavioral strategies described within this chapter are applicable as schema change methods; however, some specific strategies can be useful for targeting such long-standing beliefs.

Historical Testing

Historical testing provides the client with an opportunity to reevaluate a lifetime of "evidence" supporting a schematic belief and to search for counterevidence (Padesky, 1994). It can be done by breaking the client's life down into blocks (e.g., blocks of 3 years) and, within each period, experiences that seem to support the problematic belief can be recorded and then questioned and reevaluated with Socratic dialogue. A search is made for experiences that do not support the schema in question, and these are similarly recorded. Summaries are made at the end of each block, and these summaries are likely to contain the seeds of an alternative belief. This process can be lengthy and difficult, and such a review may take place over several sessions.

For example, Marsha heard voices that were critical and hostile, frequently telling her that she was a bad and evil person and instructing her to harm herself. These voices caused her a great deal of distress, and she believed that the voices were those of her dead parents. In addition to considering the evidence for and against this interpretation of the voices as well as other possible explanations for these phenomena, the therapist felt that some evaluation of the accuracy of the statements that the voices made about her self-worth would be useful. Marsha was able to identify many pieces of "evidence" from her life history that were supportive of her self-view as being bad, evil, and worthless. However, the use of a historical test allowed her to take notice of information that was initially overlooked or dismissed (e.g., positive relationships with neighbors, a teacher, and a grandparent), as well as providing a structure for reevaluating the "evidence for" column (e.g., deciding that her mother's criticism of her as a child may have been related to her mother's own depression and therefore negative view of other people, rather than Marsha's being an evil 3-year-old).

Criteria Continua

The criteria continua technique begins with the identification of alternative, adaptive schematic beliefs that patients would like to endorse, if they did not hold their existing, problematic belief (Padesky, 1994). An adaptive continuum is constructed, with the absence of the positive characteristic related to the belief at one end, and its greatest possible presence at the other (e.g., "not good at all" and "as good as it is possible to be"). Current ratings on this scale are obtained (they usually are very low initially), and the client can, at this stage, be asked to rate other people, including extreme examples, on the same scale. This activity alone can change the client's self-rating, as it introduces the notion of relativity, and it is very difficult for the client to maintain an extremely low initial rating if extreme examples are used.

Objective criteria for obtaining a high rating on the scale are then discussed, using the people the patient placed higher than him- or herself on the scale. A list of these criteria can then be agreed on by client and therapist, and a new subcontinuum can be constructed for each. The client then rates him- or herself on each criteria continua, and is likely to rate him- or herself as higher on these than he or she did on the original, overall scale. The client is then encouraged to rerate the overall scale, taking account of the new information. Diaries and positive data logs may be needed to record examples of the relevant characteristics.

For example, Marsha (mentioned earlier) held a very negative view of herself, believing that she was bad and evil, and viewed her badness as justification for her persecution (what is termed *punishment paranoia*; Chadwick & Trower, 1997). She was asked to put people from her current social network, her family, and famous or historical figures on a continuum of goodness. She started herself out very low; however, in comparison with people such as Adolf Hitler and other more recent war criminals, infamous murderers, and rapists, she recognized that she had overestimated her own badness. In addition, it became clear that many of the people she rated as being good had qualities such as generosity and trustworthiness. With some questioning, it became evident to her that she herself possessed high levels of these characteristics, and she was asked to keep a diary to confirm this fact.

Orthogonal Continua

Similar to the criteria continua strategy, the orthogonal continua method allows clients to plot data on orthogonal axes to evaluate and challenge the accuracy of an underlying assumption (an "if . . . then" statement or rule). For example, one of the reasons that Marsha believed that she was being persecuted was that she believed that others knew how bad she was and, therefore, were motivated to punish and conspire against her. As her belief about being bad was at times impervious to other change methods, an orthogonal continuum was constructed with "not at all good" to "as good as other people" as the x-axis, and "completely persecuted" to "completely safe" as the y-axis. She was then asked to place people she knew of, both people from her own life and social networks and people from history, the media, and current affairs, at appropriate places against each axis. It became evident to Marsha that being bad was not necessarily incompatible with being safe and unpunished, and that many good people were persecuted. This knowledge was useful for her at times when she was unable to challenge her belief that she was a bad person, at least allowing her to question the previously automatic inference that this badness would lead to persecution and harm.

Surveys

Surveys can be very useful when dealing with patients' misinterpretations of the world or to gather evidence about their current concerns. This technique involves encouraging the patient to gather answers to a set question by asking other people (the advantage of this method is that patients can select the group whose answers will be most relevant and credible to them). It can also be useful for a therapist to conduct such a survey on the patient's behalf. In Marsha's case, her perception of herself as different was normalized successfully with a survey method. She asked people that she knew and respected if they had felt different in the eyes of other people at some stage of their life; she was surprised to find that all seven of the people that she asked responded positively to this question.

Positive Data Logs

When clients have been introduced to the prejudice metaphor, positive data logs or diaries can be introduced to the client as a way of obtaining and storing information that is consistent with an alternative, more adaptive belief. Once a negative schema, such as "I am unlovable," has been identified, then the client can be asked about an alternative belief he or she would like to hold (e.g., "If you were not unlovable, what would you like to be true?"). Once an alternative self-belief has been generated that is acceptable to the client, then work can begin to elicit information that supports this new belief. It is important to keep written records of this information over a considerable period, as this positive data log represents the alternative core belief. The client is initially likely to be unable to store such information internally, and without a positive data log, evidence is likely to be discarded or misinterpreted to support the old negative schema. For example, Marsha successfully developed a new, more positive belief about herself as a person by keeping records of her acts of generosity and being a trustworthy person, and was able to produce this as evidence to challenge the voices when they were critical and abusive toward her.

Imagery

Some research has demonstrated that people with psychotic experiences have recurrent images associated with them (Morrison et al., 2002) and that these images are often associated with high affect. For example, people who hear voices frequently have an image of the perceived source of their voice (e.g., a celebrity, a relative, or a spiritual being) or an image that is associated with the content of the voices. Patients with paranoid thoughts often have images of their persecutors or images that are associated with their feared outcomes (e.g., being assaulted or killed). Such images can be a useful way of accessing personal meaning and schemas, and can be modified to become less distressing or powerful using techniques such as those described by Hackmann (1998).

Trauma-Related Strategies

In light of the high prevalence of trauma in patients with psychosis (Morrison, Frame, & Larkin, 2003; Read, 1997), it is likely that treatment strategies that have been developed for patients with posttraumatic stress disorder (PTSD) or dissociative disorders may be helpful. Such strategies include examining the idiosyncratic meaning of the trauma and developing an explanatory narrative for the trauma to aid contextualization in memory (Ehlers & Clark, 2000). In addition, strategies for dissociation, such as the use of grounding and distraction techniques, refocusing, and cognitive restructuring, can be helpful (Kennerley, 1996).

Adjustment, Emotional Dysfunction, and Recovery

Once people with psychosis have recovered from the distress associated with their psychotic experiences, many other factors that are potential targets for psychological intervention with CT should be examined. Such difficulties should also be considered at the beginning of CT, as many patients prioritize problems that are traditionally viewed as comorbid as being more distressing than their experience of psychosis. It has been suggested that a greater emphasis should be placed on the emotional problems that are frequently associated with psychosis, rather than psychotic experiences themselves, and that CBT should focus on these issues rather than attempting to become a "quasi-neuroleptic" (Birchwood, 2003). For example, a significant literature suggests that PTSD is a common problem for people with psychosis (Mueser et al., 1998), which is unsurprising given the prevalence of traumatic life events in people with psychosis (Mueser et al., 1998; Read, 1997). It is also worth considering that people with psychosis frequently develop PTSD in response to their treatment experiences or the psychotic symptoms themselves (Frame & Morrison, 2001; McGorry et al., 1991). For example, the belief that you are being persecuted by a government intelligence agency is likely to be as traumatic as actually being persecuted, and the belief you are hearing the voice of the devil who is attempting to possess you and make you harm others is also likely to be highly traumatic.

Depression and hopelessness are also common responses to an episode of psychosis (Birchwood, Iqbal, Chadwick, & Trower, 2000), as is social anxiety (Turnbull & Bebbington, 2001), and such problems are appropriate targets for CT. Emphasis on promoting personal recovery should also be incorporated within CT for people with psychosis, and the development of personal goals and valued social roles should be encouraged. It is also important to facilitate access to appropriate education or employment (Warner, 1985). Research by service users with personal experience of psychosis (Pitt, Kilbride, Nothard, & Morrison, 2004) has suggested that recovery is a process that involves rebuilding the self (in terms of understanding self and empowering the self), rebuilding life (in terms of rebuilding social life and engaging in meaningful activities), and hope for a better future (considering the possibilities of positive change). Although CT is well suited to targeting such themes and delivering such outcomes, it must explicitly address these factors.

CONCLUSIONS

Cognitive therapy for people with psychosis is effective, and people with psychosis can benefit in terms of reduced distress and frequency of psychotic experiences in addition to reduced emotional difficulties. The utilization of cognitive and behavioral strategies, including schema-focused techniques, which are derived from an idiosyncratic case formulation, can be extremely helpful in improving quality of life.

REFERENCES

Bebbington, P. E., Bhugra, D., Brugha, T., Singleton, N., Farrell, M., Jenkins, R., et al. (2004). Psychosis, victimisation and childhood disadvantage: Evidence from the second British National Survey of Psychiatric Morbidity. *British Journal of Psychiatry*, 185, 220–226.

Beck, A. T. (1976). *Cognitive therapy and the emotional disorders*. New York: International Universities Press.

Bentall, R. P., Corcoran, R., Howard, R., Blackwood, R., & Kinderman, P. (2001). Persecutory delusions: A review and theoretical integration. *Clinical Psychology Review, 22,* 1–50.

Birchwood, M. (2003). Pathways to emotional dysfunction in first-episode psychosis. *British Journal of Psychiatry, 182,* 373–375.

Birchwood, M., Iqbal, Z., Chadwick, P., & Trower, P. (2000). Cognitive approach to depression and suicidal thinking in psychosis. 1. Ontogeny of post-psychotic depression. *British Journal of Psychiatry, 177,* 516–521.

Chadwick, P., & Birchwood, M. (1994). The omnipotence of voices: A cognitive approach to auditory hallucinations. *British Journal of Psychiatry, 164,* 190–201.

Chadwick, P., & Lowe, C. F. (1990). The measurement and modification of delusional beliefs. *Journal of Consulting and Clinical Psychology, 58,* 225–232.

Chadwick, P., & Trower, P. (1997). To defend or not to defend: A comparison of paranoia and depression. *Journal of Cognitive Psychotherapy, 11,* 63–71.

Deegan, P. E. (1988). Recovery : The lived experience of rehabilitation. *Psychosocial Rehabilitation Journal, 11,* 11–19.

Ehlers, A., & Clark, D. M. (2000). A cognitive model of posttraumatic stress disorder. *Behaviour Research and Therapy, 38,* 319–345.

Frame, L., & Morrison, A. P. (2001). Causes of posttraumatic stress disorder in psychotic patients. *Archives of General Psychiatry, 58,* 305–306.

Freeman, D., Garety, P. A., & Kuipers, E. (2001). Persecutory delusions: Developing the understanding of belief maintenance and emotional distress. *Psychological Medicine, 31,* 1293–1306.

Garety, P. A., & Hemsley, D. R. (1994). *Delusions.* London: Psychology Press.

Garety, P. A., Kuipers, E., Fowler, D., Freeman, D., & Bebbington, P. E. (2001). A cognitive model of the positive symptoms of psychosis. *Psychological Medicine, 31,* 189–195.

Gould, R. A., Mueser, K. T., Bolton, E., Mays, V., & Goff, D. (2001). Cognitive therapy for psychosis in schizophrenia: An effect size analysis. *Schizophrenia Research, 48,* 335–342.

Hackmann, A. (1998). Working with images in clinical psychology. In A. S. Bellack & M. Hersen (Eds.), *Comprehensive clinical psychology: Volume 6. Adults: Clinical Formulation and Treatment* (pp. 301–318). Amsterdam: Pergamon Press.

Janssen, I., Hanssen, M., Bak, M., Bijl, R. V., de Graaf, R., Vollebergh, W., et al. (2003). Discrimination and delusional ideation. *British Journal of Psychiatry, 182,* 71–76.

Janssen, I., Krabbendam, L., Bak, M., Hanssen, M., Vollebergh, W., Graaf, R., & van Os, J. (2004). Childhood abuse as a risk factor for psychotic experiences. *Acta Psychiatrica Scandinavica, 109,* 38–45.

Kennerley, H. (1996). Cognitive therapy for dissociative symptoms associated with trauma. *British Journal of Clinical Psychology, 35,* 325–340.

Kingdon, D. G., & Turkington, D. (1994). *Cognitive-behavioral therapy of schizophrenia.* Hove, England: Erlbaum.

Kuipers, E., Garety, P., Fowler, D., Dunn, G., Bebbington, P., Freeman, D., & Hadley, C. (1997). The London-East Anglia randomised controlled trial of cognitive-behavior therapy for psychosis I: Effects of the treatment phase. *British Journal of Psychiatry, 171,* 319–327.

McGorry, P. D., Chanen, A., McCarthy, E., van Riel, R., McKenzie, D., & Singh, B. S. (1991). Post traumatic stress disorder following recent onset psychosis. *Journal of Nervous and Mental Disease, 179,* 253–258.

Miller, L. J., O'Connor, E., & DiPasquale, T. (1993). Patients' attitudes to hallucinations. *American Journal of Psychiatry, 150,* 584–588.

Morrison, A. P. (1998a). A cognitive analysis of the maintenance of auditory hallucinations: Are voices to schizophrenia what bodily sensations are to panic? *Behavioural and Cognitive Psychotherapy, 26,* 289–302.

Morrison, A. P. (1998b). Cognitive behavior therapy for psychotic symptoms in schizophrenia. In N. Tarrier, A. Wells, & G. Haddock (Eds.), *Treating complex cases: The cognitive-behavioral therapy approach* (pp195–216). Chichester, England: Wiley.

Morrison, A. P. (2001). The interpretation of intrusions in psychosis: An integrative cognitive approach to hallucinations and delusions. *Behavioural and Cognitive Psychotherapy, 29,* 257–276.

Morrison, A. P., Beck, A. T., Glentworth, D., Dunn, H., Reid, G., Larkin, W., & Williams, S. (2002). Imagery and psychotic symptoms: A preliminary investigation. *Behaviour Research and Therapy, 40,* 1063–1072.

Morrison, A. P., Frame, L., & Larkin, W. (2003). Relationships between trauma and psychosis: A review and integration. *British Journal of Clinical Psychology, 42,* 331–353.

Morrison, A. P., Renton, J. C., Dunn, H., Williams, S., & Bentall, R. P. (2004). *Cognitive therapy for psychosis: A formulation-based approach.* London: Psychology Press.

Morrison, A. P., Renton, J. C., Williams, S., Dunn, H., Knight, A., Kreutz, M., et al. (2004). Delivering cognitive therapy to people with psychosis in a community mental health setting: An effectiveness study. *Acta Psychiatrica Scandinavica, 110,* 36–44.

Mueser, K. T., Goodman, L. B., Trumbetta, S. L., Rosenberg, S. D., Osher, F. C., Vidaver, R., et al. (1998). Trauma and posttraumatic stress disorder in severe mental illness. *Journal of Consulting and Clinical Psychology, 66,* 493–499.

National Institute for Clinical Excellence. (2003). *Schizophrenia: Core interventions in the treatment and management of schizophrenia in primary and secondary care.* London: Author.

Padesky, C. A. (1993). Schema as self-prejudice. *International cognitive therapy newsletter, 5/6,* 16–17.

Padesky, C. A. (1994). Schema change processes in cognitive therapy. *Clinical Psychology and Psychotherapy, 1,* 267–278.

Pitt, L., Kilbride, M., Nothard, S., & Morrison, A. P. (2004). *Service users' subjective experiences of recovery from psychosis: A user-led research study.* Manuscript in preparation.

Read, J. (1997). Child abuse and psychosis: A literature review and implications for professional practice. *Professional Psychology: Research and Practice, 28,* 448–456.

Read, J., Agar, K., Argyle, N., & Aderhold, V. (2003). Sexual and physical abuse during childhood and adulthood as predictors of hallucinations, delusions and thought disorder. *Psychology and Psychotherapy, 76,* 1–22.

Read, J., & Argyle, N. (1999). Hallucinations, delusions, and thought disorder among adult psychiatric inpatients with a history of child abuse. *Psychiatric Services, 50,* 1467–1472.

Rector, N., & Beck, A. T. (2001). Cognitive behavioral therapy for schizophrenia: An empirical review. *Journal of Nervous and Mental Disease, 189,* 278–287.

Romme, M., & Escher, A. (1989). Hearing voices. *Schizophrenia Bulletin, 15,* 209–216.

Salkovskis, P. M. (1991). The importance of behavior in the maintenance of anxiety and panic: A cognitive account. *Behavioral Psychotherapy, 19,* 6–19.

Sensky, T., Turkington, D., Kingdon, D., Scott, J. L., Scott, J., Siddle, R., et al. (2000). A randomized controlled trial of cognitive-behavioral therapy for persistent symptoms in schizophrenia resistant to medication. *Archives of General Psychiatry, 57,* 165–172.

Tarrier, N., Yusupoff, L., Kinner, C., McCarthy, E., Gladhill, A., Haddock, G., & Morris, J. (1998). A randomized controlled trial of intense cognitive behavior therapy for chronic schizophrenia. *British Medical Journal, 317,* 303–307.

Tien, A. Y. (1991). Distribution of hallucinations in the population. *Social Psychiatry and Psychiatric Epidemiology, 26,* 287–292.

Turkington, D., Kingdon, D., & Turner, T. (2002). Effectiveness of a brief cognitive-behavioral therapy intervention in the treatment of schizophrenia. *British Journal of Psychiatry, 180,* 523–527.

Turnbull, G., & Bebbington, P. E. (2001). Anxiety and the schizophrenic process: Clinical and epidemiological evidence. *Social Psychiatry and Psychiatric Epidemiology, 36,* 235–243.

Verdoux, H., Maurice-Tison, S., Gay, B., Van Os, J., Salamon, R., & Bourgeois, M. L. (1998). A survey of delusional ideation in primary-care patients. *Psychological Medicine, 28,* 127–134.

Warner, R. (1985). *Recovery from schizophrenia: Psychiatry and political economy.* New York: Routledge & Kegan Paul.

Wells, A. (1997). *Cognitive therapy for anxiety disorders.* London: Wiley.

Wells, A., & Matthews, G. (1994). *Attention and emotion.* London: LEA.

9

MALADAPTIVE SCHEMAS AND CORE BELIEFS IN TREATMENT AND RESEARCH WITH COUPLES

MARK A. WHISMAN AND LISA A. UEBELACKER

It has long been recognized that cognitions are important for relationship functioning. For example, the first published scientific book on psychological factors in marital happiness included a discussion of specific attitudes that were associated with happiness (Terman, Buttenwieser, Ferguson, Johnson, & Wilson, 1938), and cognitive interventions have long been included in treatment manuals for couples therapy (e.g., Jacobson & Margolin, 1979). Over the years, theoretical and empirical advances have resulted in greater understanding of the types of relationship cognitions that seem to be important to relationship functioning (Epstein & Baucom, 2002).

One type of cognition that seems to be important for relationship functioning is schemas. Although the term *schema* has been used in many fields of study, and although there are a variety of definitions for the term, the construct has been used by A. T. Beck (1967) and others in two general ways (cf. Hollon & Kriss, 1984). First, the term schema has been defined in terms of cognitive prepositional constructs, which represent generalities, themes, or patterns of cognitive content. This definition, for example, best fits Young's (1990; Young, Klosko, & Weishaar, 2003) theory of early maladaptive schemas. Self-report questionnaires, which focus on the content of cognitions, are generally used to operationalize schemas according to this definition. Second, the term schema has been defined in terms of cognitive structural constructs, which focus on how information is stored and organized, and how such structures guide the processing of information. This definition, for example, best fits Marcus's (1977) perspective of self-schema. Information-processing and performance-based measures are generally used to operationalize schemas according to this definition, insofar as such measures focus on the functioning of schemas.

In this chapter, we review the literature on schemas associated with relationship functioning and couples therapy. First, we review the literature on interview and questionnaire studies of relationship schemas, as viewed from cognitive–behavioral and attachment perspectives. We then review the literature on information-processing and performance-based measure of relationship schemas, focusing on research evaluating relationship scripts and partner schemas. Next we present a treatment model for working with relationship schemas in couples therapy, on the basis of the tenets of cognitive therapy. Finally, we offer some suggestions for future research on relationship schemas.

SELF-REPORT STUDIES OF COGNITIVE SCHEMAS

Two sets of literature describe cognitive content that may constitute key schemas about relationships that are relevant for working with couples. The first is the literature on cognitive–behavioral theory. Baucom and Epstein (Baucom, Epstein, Sayers, & Sher, 1989; Epstein & Baucom, 2002) reviewed two types of broad relationship beliefs: assumptions and standards. Assumptions are beliefs about the nature of close relationships in general as well as specific people (i.e., one's partner and one's self). Standards are beliefs about the way relationships should be or the way partners should behave. Long-standing and strongly held assumptions and standards have an impact on emotions and behaviors, and may serve to organize one's perception of the world. Assumptions and standards are most likely to be associated with relationship problems and distress to the extent that they are unrealistic or too extreme or rigid or, in the case of standards, not being met in the relationship. The second broad area of the relevant literature is the literature on adult attachment. An attachment style reflects a set of interconnected cognitions, emotions, behaviors, and drives. There is evidence that underlying schemas about one's partner and one's self play a large role in defining different types of attachment styles. We discuss each set of literature in turn.

Cognitive–Behavioral Theory

As described earlier, relationship standards are beliefs about the way relationships should be, or how people in relationships should think, feel, or behave in different situations. Although there are obviously an unlimited number of types of relationship standards an individual might hold, Baucom and colleagues (Baucom, Epstein, Daiuto, et al., 1996; Baucom, Epstein, Rankin, & Burnett, 1996) have argued that three areas are particularly important. The first is standards for boundaries within a couple—that is, the degree of independence versus interdependence that each member of the couple should have. This area includes standards for the amount of time couples should spend together, and the degree to which they should share thoughts and feelings with each other. The second important set of standards relates to power and control within the couple unit. These standards define acceptable practices within the process of decision making, as well as the degree to which outcomes should reflect a compromise between partners versus one partner's desires or decisions prevailing. The third important area in which individuals often have standards is that of investment in the couple relationship, as evidenced through completion of instrumental tasks (e.g., chores) and behaviors that show caring or affection.

Baucom, Epstein, Daiuto, et al. (1996) found that individuals who reported high levels of marital satisfaction tended to believe that couples should spend time together and share thoughts and feelings with each other, that decision making should be egalitarian, and that partners should show high levels of investment. In addition to finding that the content of the standard was important, they found that whether or not one's standards were being met in one's relationship was also associated with marital satisfaction as well as with other types of cognitions and with behavior. Individuals who reported that their standards were not being met tended to attribute the cause of relationship problems to their partner and to see the cause as global and stable; they also reported that they responded to relationship problems with negative behavior of their own.

One other standard that has received some attention in research is the belief that partners should be able to read each other's minds. This particular standard may be associated with a lack of communication about important issues and subsequent hurt feelings when one is misunderstood or one's needs are not cared for. Indeed, research has shown that this belief is associated with overall relationship dissatisfaction, critical and defensive behavior on the part of the partner, and dysfunctional attributions made for a partner's behavior (i.e., that his or her behavior was because of lack of love or malicious intent; Eidelson & Epstein, 1982; Epstein, Pretzer, & Fleming, 1987). This standard may be a particular problem when it leads to lack of communication about important issues, misunderstandings, and hurt feelings.

Cognitive–behavioral researchers have also discussed the importance of relationship assumptions. That is, one may make assumptions about one's self, or one's partner—for example, that he or she is trustworthy and faithful, or, alternatively, that he or she cannot be trusted. One may also make assumptions about relationships—either one's current relationship or relationships in general. For example, after a series of relationship breakups, one might assume that all one's relationships are destined to failure.

As with standards, one may make an unlimited number of assumptions about relationships, and these assumptions may promote a positive or negative view of relationships. However, certain relationship assumptions that have implications for communication and problem solving have received particular attention in the research literature. For example, the assumption that disagreement is destructive to relationships has consistently been shown to be associated with couples' distress (Bradbury & Fincham, 1993; Eidelson & Epstein, 1982; Emmelkamp, Krol, Sanderman, & Ruphan, 1987; Epstein et al., 1987; Moller & Van Zyl, 1991). Other assumptions that are associated with relationship dissatisfaction include the belief that partners cannot change or improve their relationship, and the belief that men and women are very different in terms of their personalities and what they need from a relationship (Bradbury & Fincham, 1993; Eidelson & Epstein, 1982; Epstein et al., 1987). That the latter belief is associated with couples dissatisfaction is particularly concerning, given that it is the central tenet of several popular self-help books. Greater endorsement of unrealistic assumptions and standards has also been correlated with other relationship outcomes, such as negative problem-solving behavior (Bradbury & Fincham, 1993).

A final issue that bears mentioning is the impact that affairs or other relationship betrayals may have on positive relationship assumptions (e.g., my partner is trustworthy). For instance, upon discovery of an affair, an individual may find that many of his or her vital assumptions—about one's self and partner, and about relationships in general—have been violated (Gordon & Baucom, 2003). This violation of positive assumptions can have a large impact on emotions and behaviors. After a betrayal, positive assumptions are replaced with negative assumptions; it is only as the hurt partner begins to forgive that his or her assumptions may become more positive. In support of this model, Gordon and Baucom (2003) found that individuals who were in later stages of forgiveness after a relationship betrayal had more positive assumptions about themselves and their partner.

Adult Attachment

In his seminal writing on attachment, Bowlby (1969) suggested that, on the basis of their experiences with their caregivers, children develop internal working models of close relationships. In a similar fashion, Hazan and Shaver (1987) hypothesized that adults form attachments to their adult romantic partners, and have an internal working model of adult romantic relationships. Bartholomew and Horowitz (1991) subsequently suggested that adult attachment styles could be characterized by two cognitive dimensions, both of which may be characterized as schemas. The first concerns one's view of oneself, as either worthy or not worthy of love; the second concerns one's view of others, as either trustworthy or unreliable. By crossing positive versus negative models of self with positive versus negative models of others, Bartholomew and Horowitz derived four different attachment styles. *Securely* attached individuals view themselves as worthy and others as trustworthy. They are comfortable both with intimacy and with autonomy. *Preoccupied* individuals have a negative view of self but a positive view of others. As the label suggests, these individuals become overinvolved in close relationships and tend to depend on others for a sense of self-worth. *Fearful–avoidant* individuals have a negative view of both themselves and others, and therefore they are fearful of intimacy and avoid relationships with other people. Finally, *dismissing* individuals have a positive view of themselves but a negative view of others; these individuals may also avoid relationships with others. They report that they prefer being independent, and that close relationships are not important to them.

Other researchers have suggested another variation on two cognitive dimensions (or schemas) that may underlie attachment styles. Individuals may vary on (a) avoidance, or the degree to which they are comfortable with being close to others, and (b) anxiety, or the degree to which they are anxious about relationships, including being afraid of being abandoned and wanting excessive closeness (Feeney, 1999). Specific attachment styles can, in turn, be mapped on this two-dimensional structure insofar as a negative model of others is closely associated with avoidance, whereas a negative model of self is closely associated with anxiety about abandonment (Brennan, Clark, & Shaver, 1998).

Research has shown that adult attachment is associated with satisfaction with marital and other romantic relationships (for a review, see Mikulincer, Florian, Cowan, & Cowan, 2002). In other words, securely attached individuals are more satisfied with their partner relationships. In particular, couples in which both partners are securely attached seem to be the most satisfied with their relationships (Senchak & Leonard, 1992). Secure attachment is associated with increased trust and respect for one's partner

(Kirkpatrick & Davis, 1994) as well as more supportive and less rejecting communication patterns during problem solving (Kobak & Hazan, 1991). Also, people who are securely attached are more likely to be in a stable romantic relationship than those who do not have a secure attachment style (Mikulincer et al., 2002).

Worth noting, particular attachment styles are similar to some of what Young et al. (2003) have called early maladaptive schemas—that is, beliefs about oneself and others that develop early in life and have an enduring negative impact. For example, they describe an abandonment schema, in which a person does not believe that significant others will be available as a stable source of support when they are needed, and a self-sacrifice schema, in which a person focuses on meeting others' needs to the exclusion of their own. As with attachment styles, these schemas likely have serious implications for relationship functioning.

INFORMATION-PROCESSING AND PERFORMANCE-BASED STUDIES OF COGNITIVE SCHEMAS

In this section, we review studies that have used information-processing or performance-based procedures for studying cognitive schemas related to relationship functioning. Baldwin (1992) proposed that research on processing of social information could benefit from considering "relational schemas," which he defined as "cognitive structures representing regularities in patterns of interpersonal relatedness" (p. 461). According to this model, a relational schema consists of three elements: "an interpersonal script for the interactional pattern, a self-schema for how self is experienced in that interpersonal situation, and a schema for the other person in the interaction" (p. 461). Although we are unaware of any information-processing research on the association between self-schemas and relationship outcomes such as couple satisfaction, there has been some research on information-processing aspects of relationship scripts and partner-schemas. Therefore, we use Baldwin's model of the three elements of relational schemas as a heuristic for organizing the research on information-processing and performance-based measures of relationship schemas.

Relationship scripts refer to key events that take place in romantic relationships as well as the order in which those events occur. Scripts are typically evaluated by having people generate an ordered list of steps that usually occur in a particular relationship event or stage, or sorting lists generated by other people. These methods have been used, for example, to study scripts for dating and sexual encounters. The association between scripts and relationship outcomes (e.g., relationship satisfaction), however, has rarely been evaluated. In an exception, Holmberg and MacKenzie (2002) had dating couples complete personal relationship scripts (based on the past and future development of their own relationship) and normative relationship scripts (based on how relationships typically develop). They found that "correspondence between personal and normative scripts, and agreement between partners on personal scripts, predicted several measures of relationship well-being" (p. 777). This line of research could be expanded by evaluating correspondence between partners and between personal and normative versions of other types of relationship scripts, such as scripts for discussing problems in a relationship or seeking support from a partner.

Baldwin, Fehr, Keedian, Seidel, and Thomson (1993) used a lexical decision task to study the perspective that interpersonal scripts could be formulated as a series of if . . . then contingencies ("If I do X, then my partner will do Y"). In a lexical decision task, participants read a string of letters and try to identify as quickly as possible whether it is a word or not. On the basis of previous findings that reaction times for words are quicker if a context that is related to the target words has been provided (i.e., people are quicker to recognize the stimulus word *nurse* if they have just read the word *doctor*), these authors hypothesized that contextual effects would also be found for interpersonal outcomes an individual automatically associates with various behaviors, including those behaviors associated with the interpersonal domains of dependency, trust, and closeness. Consistent with this perspective, it was found, for example, that when the context stem was "If I trust my partner, then my partner will _____," securely attached individuals were quicker to identify *care* whereas avoidant individuals were quicker to identify *hurt*. Future research could look at the association between individual differences in this type of information processing and relationship outcomes such as satisfaction and stability.

In addition to scripts (and self-schemas), the other element in Baldwin's (1992) relational schemas is schemas about the other, or partner schemas. In one study on partner schemas, Reifman and Crohan (1993) had individuals in dating relationships describe their partners in a card-sorting task used to assess cognitive complexity. Individuals were asked to form groups of attributes or traits that went together in describing an aspect of their partner; they could make as many groups as they desired. Results indicated that greater redundancy in the card-sorting task (i.e., greater use of the same versus unique attributes to describe different facets of the partner) was associated with greater commitment and positive affect and less negative affect being felt toward the partner. The authors concluded that "when a perceiver repeatedly uses similar attributes to describe the partner over the different facets of the partner's life, it may be easier for the perceiver to maintain a consistently positive view of the partner" (p. 479).

Whisman and Delinsky (2002) developed an information-processing measure of partner schemas based on an incidental recall paradigm. In this paradigm, participants are instructed to indicate whether personal adjectives, which differ in valence or likableness, describe their partner. Immediately after all the adjectives have been presented, they are asked to recall as many of the words as possible. It was found that marital satisfaction was (a) negatively associated with the number of negative adjectives endorsed, (b) positively associated with the number of positive adjectives endorsed, and (c) negatively associated with the number of negative adjectives endorsed and subsequently recalled. Moreover, these associations remained significant when depression was controlled for, which indicated that they were not due to the shared association with negative affective states. These findings suggest that relationship distress may be associated with negative recall bias, such that "negative information is more schematic for dissatisfied spouses, making it easier for them to retrieve negative information about their partners" (p. 624).

Although relatively limited in number, the studies that have found information-processing measures of relational schemas to be associated with relationship outcomes argue for continued development and use of information processing in the study of relationship functioning. There is also some evidence that information-processing measures of relationship schemas may also moderate the impact of other variables on relationship functioning. For example, Fincham, Garnier, Gano-Phillips, and Osborne (1995) found that a measure of accessibility (i.e., reaction time) for evaluative judgments about the partner and the marriage moderated the association between marital satisfaction and (a) expectations of partner behavior for an upcoming interaction for husbands and (b) attributed responsibility for negative marital events for husbands and wives. It was found that expectations and attributions were more strongly associated with marital satisfaction for partners with more accessible evaluative judgments.

TREATMENT IMPLICATIONS

In the sections that follow, we provide an overview of assessment and intervention for relationship schemas in the context of couples therapy. More detailed information about the application of cognitive theory and treatment as applied to relationship difficulties can be found in Dattilo and Padesky (1990), A. T. Beck (1998), and Whisman and Weinstock (2002). In addition, the inclusion of cognitive interventions within a behavioral framework for working with couples can be found in Epstein and Baucom (2002).

Assessment

In clinical practice, standards, assumptions, and cognitions associated with attachment can be assessed with self-report questionnaires and clinical interviewing. Instruments that assess schemas may be used in several ways in therapy. First, they may be used diagnostically, insofar as inspection of endorsed items and total scores may provide information about important relationship cognitions to target in therapy. Second, completing these instruments may provide partners with new insights into their own patterns of thinking, and may allow them to view some of their beliefs as a particular way of viewing the world rather than as absolute truth. Third, these instruments may serve as a springboard to discussion, in which the therapist helps partners to explore the origins of these beliefs and the implications that they have for the relationship. Finally, these instruments may be used to measure change in therapy.

Self-Report Assessment of Standards and Assumptions

Two self-report assessment instruments that may be useful in clinical practice are the Relationship Belief Inventory (RBI; Eidelson & Epstein, 1982) and the Inventory of Specific Relationship Standards (ISRS; Baucom, Epstein, Rankin, et al., 1996). The RBI is a 40-item scale that assesses five relationship beliefs, including two standards ("Partners should be able to read each other's minds" and "One should be a perfect sexual partner") and three assumptions ("Disagreement is destructive to relationships," "Partners cannot change themselves or their relationship," and "Men and women have very different personalities and needs"). The ISRS is a 60-item scale that assesses relationship standards on three dimensions: boundaries, control and power, and relationship investment. Within those dimensions, a variety of content areas related to marriage are considered (e.g., finances, affection, household chores). Individuals are asked about the extent to which they endorse a particular standard, whether or not the standard is met in their relationship, and how upsetting it is when the standard is not being met.

Self-Report Assessment of Adult Attachment

The Relationship Questionnaire (Bartholomew & Horowitz, 1991) is an adaptation of an earlier measure (Hazan & Shaver, 1987) of assessing attachment types. It consists of four paragraphs, each describing one of four attachment styles (secure, preoccupied, dismissing, and fearful). Individuals are asked to read each paragraph and then select the one that best describes them, or rate how well each paragraph describes them on a continuous scale. This questionnaire may be used as a very quick measure of attachment style. However, this measure has been criticized because it requires an individual to make a judgment about whether a group of statements are true, and does not allow the individual to consider each statement separately. For these reasons, as well as for the fact that that there is no evidence for a true attachment typology (Fraley & Waller, 1998), it may be preferable to assess attachment with a dimensional measure. One commonly used dimensional measure is the Experiences in Close Relationships—Revised (ECR–R; Fraley, Waller, & Brennan, 2000). The ECR–R is a 36-item self-report attachment measure derived from an item response theory analysis of most of the existing self-report measures of adult romantic attachment. It yields scores on two subscales, avoidance (or discomfort with closeness and discomfort with depending on others) and anxiety (or fear of rejection and abandonment).

Interview Assessment of Relationship Schemas

Clinical interviewing is also an important assessment tool for understanding relationship cognitions. First, clinicians can begin to formulate hypotheses about key relationship cognitions simply by asking about the nature of the problem for which a couple is seeking therapy. For example, in an initial interview, a woman might state, "I just don't think he cares about me. He always complains about his life, his job, his problems, but he never asks me about my day or how I'm feeling." This statement reflects an important assumption, namely, that her husband does not care about her. Another example of a problem might be conflict over a wife going out "with the girls" every Friday night. Although the exact nature of the conflict will need to be explored further, one possibility is that spouses have differing standards for how much time they should spend together. Or the husband may have a pattern of anxious attachment, and may be constantly fearful that his wife will abandon him. Therefore, he interprets her nights out as a chance to get away from him. Although the clinician may not choose to pursue a line of questioning that will elicit cognitions at this particular time, he or she can start to build a list of hypotheses about underlying relationship schemas that may be causing or maintaining relationship conflict.

When the clinician has a hypothesis about a particular schema that he or she thinks is operating and is important, he or she will want to test that hypothesis. For example, a clinician may hypothesize that one member of a couple believes that the partner ought to be able to know what that member wants without the person explicitly stating his or her desires. Some cognitions may be elicited through direct questioning. For example, standards may be assessed by asking partners what an "ideal" relationship would look like, and focusing on areas that Baucom and colleagues (Baucom, Epstein, Daiuto, et al., 1996; Baucom, Epstein, Rankin, et al., 1996) proposed are important—that is, how much time partners would spend together, how much they would share their feelings and thoughts, how they would handle disagreements, and how they would show affection. In general, use of the words *should, must, have to,* and the like signal that a standard is being voiced. Clinicians will want to pay particular attention to standards that seem unattainable or unrealistic, and standards that differ between partners, as these are likely to be associated with relationship dissatisfaction.

In-Session Assessment of Relationship Schemas

In addition to questionnaire and interview assessments of relationship schemas occurring at the beginning of therapy, assessments also take place throughout the course of therapy. Thus, there is a close link between assessment of and intervention with relationship cognitions. At all points in therapy, an important question facing a couples therapist is when to assess for and intervene with relationship cognitions. For example, if a couple is talking about a problem in their relationship during the session, the therapist must decide among various options, including whether to let the couple continue uninterrupted to collect information on the content and process of their problem solving, intervene to teach them communication and problem-solving skills, or interrupt the discussion and assess, educate, and intervene in terms of cognition. A particularly important indicator for working with cognitions is change in affect, as indicated by change in nonverbal (e.g., facial expression, posture) or verbal (e.g., voice tone or inflection) behavior. For example, a clinician noted that one member of a couple became very teary-eyed as the partner described a recent argument. The clinician asked what was going through the person's mind, to which the person replied, "I have this dreadful fear that he doesn't love me or want to be with me" (which is an example of a core schema relating to fear of abandonment). As discussed elsewhere (J. S. Beck, 1995; Safran, Vallis, Segal, & Shaw, 1986), it has been proposed that certain cognitions are going to be accessible only when the person is experiencing the same affective state that is characteristic of when the person is experiencing his or her problems. Thus, a change in affect (e.g., a marked change in sadness, anxiety, anger), which can occur spontaneously or can be elicited through imagery, role-play, or other methods, may indicate the presence of "hot" cognitions, and therefore, a change in affect is the single most important marker for pursuing a cognitive intervention.

Once a therapist has decided to pursue a cognitive intervention, the first step is to identify the cognition that has been activated. The basic question for identifying cognitive activity is "What was going through your mind just then?" (J. S. Beck, 1995). This question is a therapist's point of access for identifying relationship cognitions. According to the cognitive perspective, environmental events (in this case, relationship events or part-ner behaviors) elicit stream-of-consciousness or automatic thoughts. These automatic thoughts that people have in response to ongoing events in their lives are the cognitions that are first addressed in therapy. The therapist helps partners recognize the automatic thoughts that are triggered by relationship events and that are associated with changes in their mood.

Whereas asking individuals what was going through their minds when they noticed changes in the person's mood is a good method for assessing automatic thoughts, the primary method for identifying core beliefs or sche-mas is the use of the downward arrow (Burns, 1980). After a partner has articulated an automatic thought that the therapist believes may be directly related to an underlying belief or schema, the therapist asks for the meaning of the automatic thought, assuming it were true. As discussed by J. S. Beck (1995), there are two ways of asking about meaning, which are likely to get at different levels of cognitions. First, asking "What does this thought mean to you?" is likely to elicit intermediate beliefs, such as the if . . . then contingencies evaluated by Baldwin et al. (1993), whereas asking, "What does this thought mean about you?" (or "your partner" or "your relationship") is likely to elicit core beliefs (i.e., schemas). The therapist continues to ask about the meaning of the person's cognition until one or more important beliefs are uncovered. For example, consider a couple that is having a disagreement in which one partner is angry and so the therapist stops the conversation. The therapist then asks the angry partner what his automatic thoughts are; he reports thinking, "She is so inconsiderate." Questioning about what he meant by his partner being inconsiderate reveals the core relationship beliefs that "she doesn't care about me" and "she would leave me if she had a chance."

Intervention

Once a partner has learned to identify relationship cognitions, the therapist can proceed to work with the person in changing them. A therapist would first work with helping partners change their beliefs in a session, and then encourage them to practice these methods on their own between sessions. There are several different ways of modifying cognitions. The following descriptions are offered as examples of ways of modifying both automatic thoughts and relationship schemas; a more comprehensive list of methods for modifying cognitions can be found elsewhere (e.g., J. S. Beck, 1995; Dattilo & Padesky, 1990).

In one method, the therapist and partner can work together to evaluate the evidence regarding the cognitions. To do so, they first ask, "What is the evidence that supports this thought?" Cognitions do not develop in a vacuum, and it is often helpful for a person, as well as his or her partner, to consider and review the basis for the cognition. Such a discussion can often engender positive feelings from the partner, as the partner hears the person discussing experiences that contributed to his or her cognition, which in turn helps the partner see the person in a different light (e.g., a person's perception of his or her partner's withdrawal from conflict is seen not as a manipulative effort to control the conversation but as a pattern that was learned in early childhood through interactions with parents). The therapist then works with the person to answer the question "What is the evidence against this thought?" Some people are able to generate responses to this question fairly easily, although others will need help from the therapist or the partner, or both, to generate counterevidence, at least during the early stages of modifying a particular cognition. The technique of evaluating evidence for a belief is particularly well suited to working with assumptions. For example, a wife who did not believe her husband still loved her was encouraged to think of specific things he did that showed him he did love her (e.g., asking her about her work, preparing dinner, arranging a night out).

A second method for evaluating cognitions is constructing an alternative explanation for the event. Therapists can work with partners in coming up with other ways of explaining an upsetting event, such as a negative partner behavior. We have found that generating alternative explanations is particularly helpful for working with negative attributions. For example, a wife who attributed her husband's diminished interest in sex to a loss of love could be encouraged to consider alternative explanations for his behavior, such as increased stress at work and anxiety about the failing health of his parents. Because both partners are in therapy together, this wife may then have the immediate opportunity to discuss and evaluate the alternative explanations for her husband's behavior with him directly.

A third method for evaluating beliefs is to ask partners to consider what they would tell a friend in a similar situation. This strategy may be most appropriate for working with unrealistic relationship standards or expectations. People often hold belief systems for themselves that are very different from those they hold for other people, and encouraging partners to consider what they would tell someone else in a similar situation helps them more clearly see their double standard. This awareness is often useful in helping people change the unrealistic or unobtainable standards they hold for their partner and their relationship.

A fourth method for evaluating cognitions is to conduct a behavioral experiment. Although experiments are appropriate for modifying most types of relationship cognitions, they are particularly important for cognitions that are associated with avoidance of situations that would provide disconfirming evidence. For example, a person who endorses the belief that disagreement is destructive to a relationship may be hesitant to bring up things about the relationship that are bothering him or her because of fears that the partner would become angry or upset. As an experiment, this person could be encouraged to bring up a subject that is bothering him or her and see if the partner reacts in the anticipated negative ways. The partner, in turn, might be coached to behave in a positive manner that does not confirm the dysfunctional belief. Young et al. (2003) called this method *pattern breaking*, and it consists of having people behave in ways that are counter to underlying schemas. They provide several suggestions for building motivation for pattern breaking, including reviewing advantages and disadvantages of maintaining versus changing behavior, having the person reward him- or herself for behaving in a new way, and developing an understanding of the early-childhood origins of a current maladaptive behavior. These strategies may easily be adapted for work with couples: For example, both partners could participate in rewarding one or both partners for behaving in new ways. In addition, one way to build understanding and empathy between partners is for them each to have a better understanding of childhood origins of current maladaptive, schema-driven behavior. This knowledge may decrease blame.

In addition to standard cognitive therapy interventions for working with relationship cognitions, the relationship schemas may also be modified with techniques outlined by Young and Gluhoski (1997). In essence, schema-focused strategies for couples therapy are similar to those used in individual therapy, as discussed by Young et al. (2003) and other chapters in this volume. For example, couples can be encouraged to write out alternative responses to core schemas through the use of a diary or flashcards, to be read when the schemas are activated.

Thus far, the discussion of treatment implications of schemas in couples therapy has focused on modifying the content of such schemas. However, as reviewed earlier, researchers have also identified information-processing effects associated with relationship outcomes. How then can couples therapists work at modifying information-processing biases? Although little has been written about clinical implications of information-processing biases from a couples therapy perspective, suggestions have been made for managing such biases from an individual therapy perspective, which can be tailored to couples therapy.

To the extent that distressed couples have more negative expectations and more negative perceptions of their partners, then therapeutic interventions designed to improve memory for positive outcomes and events may be expected to improve satisfaction. Gotlib and Krasnoperova (1998) have proposed that completing a detailed log or diary of positive events, as well as keeping reminders of positive events, might help to improve memory for such events. In couples therapy, partners could be encouraged to keep daily records of positive behaviors that the other person did during the day to refocus their attention on positive rather than negative relationship events.

Gotlib and Krasnoperova (1998) also recommended another method for working with information-processing biases: Have clients learn ways of interrupting their memory for negative events, through methods such as learning how to distract themselves, rather than ruminating on the bad things that have happened. As they explained, "Distraction can inhibit processing and rehearsal of the negative events and, consequently, should weaken the representations of these events in memory" (p. 613). As applied to couples therapy, partners could be taught to become aware of when they are ruminating about the negative aspects of their partner or their relationship, and to distract themselves and refocus on something else. For example, following a disagreement with his or her partner, a person might typically ruminate about all the negative things that were said in this and other similar disagreements. Rather than ruminate on the negative, however, the person could redirect his or her attention using distraction such as engaging in another activity (e.g., reading, gardening, listening to music).

Relapse Prevention

Whisman, McKelvie, and Chatav (2005) reviewed research on relapse prevention for the treatment of couple distress. In this review, two major methods for preventing relapse were discussed. First, the risk for relapse may be reduced through the use of booster sessions. In a 2-year follow-up of couples who had been treated with behavioral couples therapy (BCT), Jacobson, Schmaling, and Holtzworth-Munroe (1987) asked participants what could be done to enhance the effectiveness of therapy or make the positive effects of therapy last longer. The most common response, offered by 20% of couples formerly in treatment, was follow-up (i.e., booster) mainte-nance sessions. Those who did not spontaneously recommend the use of booster sessions were asked directly, and 90% responded positively. In a review of treatment of marital conflict, Bray and Jouriles (1995) also recom-mended the use of booster sessions. Furthermore, they calculated the cost effectiveness of increasing the number of sessions of treatment, and found that despite the increase in cost resulting from booster sessions, these costs were still lower than those associated with adverse outcomes such as divorce.

Support for the potential efficacy of booster sessions comes from a study by Braukhaus, Hahlweg, Kroeger, Groth, and Fehm-Wolfsdorf (2003), who evaluated the impact of adding two booster sessions to a cognitive–behavioral psychoeducational prevention program for couples who were committed to their relationship. Compared with couples who didn't receive the additional sessions, couples who received booster sessions reported sig-nificantly higher marital satisfaction and fewer problem areas at a 1-year follow-up. A concept related to booster sessions is the idea of fading the frequency of therapy sessions over time. Bögner and Zielenbach-Coenen

(1984) evaluated the impact of fading sessions by comparing two groups of couples that received BCT. The first group received nine sessions over 8 weeks, whereas the second group received nine sessions over 13 weeks. The group that received sessions on a fading schedule had better outcomes at the end of treatment and at follow-up. Taken together, these findings provide preliminary support for the notion that including booster maintenance sessions or fading the frequency of therapy sessions over time may be effective in preventing relapse.

Another method reviewed by Whisman et al. (2005) for preventing relapse following couples therapy is incorporating some of the techniques advanced by Marlatt and Gordon (1985) in their relapse-prevention program for the treatment of addictive behaviors. For example, one important component of this program is identifying high-risk situations and developing ways of coping with these situations before they occur. High-risk situations might be those that trigger dysfunctional relationship schemas. For example, someone with an anxious attachment pattern might be particularly vulnerable to starting conflicts when his or her partner is away on business. A therapist using a relapse prevention strategy in couples therapy would, toward the end of therapy, discuss with a couple specific kinds of situations that they might encounter in the future that could pose a challenge to their relationship. Once high-risk situations are identified, the therapist would work with the couple on ways of coping with the situation.

OUTCOME RESEARCH

In this section, we review the outcome research on the efficacy of cognitive interventions in work with couple distress. We then offer several suggestions for the obtained results, as well as provide suggestions for future research on treating schemas and core beliefs in couples. The application of cognitive therapy to relationship dissatisfaction has mostly been within the context of adjunctive interventions to enhance the efficacy of BCT. Baucom and Lester (1986) randomly assigned 24 couples to three experimental conditions: BCT alone, BCT plus cognitive restructuring, and a wait-list control group. Results indicated that couples who were randomly assigned to the two treatment conditions demonstrated significant improvements on levels of marital satisfaction at the termination of the 12-week treatment and at 6-month follow-up. A direct comparison of the two treatment groups, however, indicated no significant differences on outcome measures between BCT alone and the enhanced BCT treatment. In a subsequent study, Baucom, Sayers, and Sher (1990) compared a BCT alone condition with BCT plus cognitive restructuring (CR), BCT plus emotional expressiveness training (EET), BCT plus CR and EET, and a wait-list control group among 60 couples. Results indicated that couples assigned to all four treatment groups demonstrated greater improvement in marital adjustment compared with couples in the control condition. However, comparisons between treatment conditions indicated that the addition of CR and EET did not appear to enhance BCT effectiveness. Halford, Sanders, and Behrens (1993) then compared BCT alone with an enhanced BCT (EBCT) condition among 26 couples. EBCT incorporated cognitive restructuring techniques and a component that focused on affect exploration. Halford et al. found that BCT and EBCT were equally effective in generating positive outcomes. Couples in both treatment conditions demonstrated significant increases in self-reported marital satisfaction, as well as decreases in interactional negativity, unrealistic cognitions, and negative affect.

Other investigators have explored the efficacy of cognitive therapy alone in the treatment of marital discord. Huber and Milstein (1985) compared a cognitive-restructuring-only treatment with a wait-list control group and found that efforts aimed at modifying unrealistic beliefs about marriage, the self, and one's partner were effective in increasing marital satisfaction. That is, couples in the experimental group demonstrated greater treatment gains than did those in the control condition. In a similar study, Emmelkamp et al. (1988) compared cognitive restructuring alone with a communication skills training condition, and reported that both treatments were equally effective in decreasing target problems identified before treatment.

From this review of the literature, two conclusions are apparent. First, it appears that cognitive therapy, either alone or combined with BCT, is effective at reducing relationship distress. Second, it appears that cognitive therapy is no more (or no less) effective than are behavioral approaches to treating relationship distress. The findings of equal efficacy may result in part from the fact that because the enhanced versions of treatment had an equal number of sessions as the purely behavioral treatment, the component treatments included in the enhanced treatment were, by necessity, abbreviated. This abbreviation may have resulted in a suboptimal dosage of the behavioral and cognitive components. Furthermore, the findings of equal efficacy may reflect the reciprocal relationship that exists between cognition and behavior, such that changes in one domain are likely to result in changes in the other domain. In fact, results from the studies conducted by Baucom and colleagues (Baucom & Lester, 1986; Baucom et al., 1990) indicated that women in behavioral treatment demonstrated significant change in both behavior and cognition at posttreatment. Moreover, Emmelkamp et al. (1988) reported changes in both cognition and behavior among couples enrolled in a strict cognitive condition and among those enrolled in a communication skills training condition.

Furthermore, investigators have noted that random assignment of participants to study groups within the investigations described earlier might have resulted in diluted treatment effects. Random assignment restricts the matching of client needs to treatments, as is done in most treatment settings. Anecdotal evidence suggests that certain couples might benefit more from an approach that includes a cognitive component whereas others might benefit more from a strict behavioral approach (Baucom & Lester, 1986; Baucom et al., 1990). Additional efficacy studies will be necessary to identify people who are most likely to benefit from cognitive therapy.

It is important to note that no published studies to date have evaluated the efficacy of cognitive therapy specifically devoted to modifying maladaptive schemas or core beliefs. This is an important topic for future research evaluating the efficacy of cognitive interventions for couple distress.

IMPLICATIONS FOR FUTURE RESEARCH

In this chapter, we reviewed basic and applied research on maladaptive schemas and core beliefs in couples. Although there is a growing body of literature on relationship outcomes associated with questionnaire measures of schemas related to assumptions, standards, and attachment styles, we are not aware of any published studies that have evaluated relationship outcomes associated with questionnaire measures of other types of schemas, such as Young's (1990; Young et al., 2003) early maladaptive schemas. Furthermore, research on information-processing measures of relationship schemas and relationship functioning is in its infancy. Some information-processing measures have been evaluated in only one study (e.g., Whisman & Delinsky's, 2002, incidental recall task), and therefore are in need of replication. In comparison, other information-processing measures such as Baldwin et al.'s (1993) lexical decision task have not been evaluated with respect to relationship outcomes such as satisfaction or stability. Additional research is needed in these areas. Furthermore, research is needed to determine if measures of relationship schemas explain incremental variance in relationship outcomes, over and above that which can be accounted for by other known correlates of relationship functioning. Evaluating incremental validity is particularly important for information-processing measures, to justify the added time and expense required for measuring these constructs. Establishing that research on schemas contributes to an increased understanding of relationship outcomes over and above that which can be obtained through more accessible means, such as questionnaires, would go far in promoting continued research in relationship schemas.

We have also reviewed several methods for working with relationship schemas. However, the efficacy of most of these methods has yet to be evaluated in clinical trials. The existing research has shown that cognitive interventions are no more or no less effective than other types of interventions, such as BCT. Additional research is needed to determine whether some of these other methods that are specifically designed for working with schemas may result in improved outcome, as well as whether matching couples to particular kinds of therapy enhances efficacy. In addition, continued advances are needed in developing methods for modifying information-processing components of relationship schemas. As these techniques are developed and refined, we are hopeful that they will lead to an increased array of treatment strategies for couples therapists and better treatment outcome for couples.

REFERENCES

Baldwin, M. W. (1992). Relational schemas and the processing of social information. *Psychological Bulletin, 112*, 461–484.

Baldwin, M. W., Fehr, B., Keedian, E., Seidel, M., & Thomson, D. W. (1993). An exploration of the relational schemata underlying attachment styles: Self-report and lexical decision approaches. *Personality and Social Psychology Bulletin, 19*, 746–754.

Bartholomew, K., & Horowitz, L. M. (1991). Attachment styles among young adults: A test of the four-category model. *Journal of Personality and Social Psychology, 61*, 226–244.

Baucom, D. H., Epstein, N., Daiuto, A. D., Carels, R. A., Rankin, L. A., & Burnett, C. K. (1996). Cognitions in marriage: The relationship between standards and attributions. *Journal of Family Psychology, 10*, 209–222.

Baucom, D. H., Epstein, N., Rankin, L. A., & Burnett, C. K. (1996). Assessing relationship standards: The inventory of specific relationship standards. *Journal of Family Psychology, 10*, 72–88.

Baucom, D. H., Epstein, N., Sayers, S. L., & Sher, T. G. (1989). The role of cognitions in marital relationships: Definitional, methodological, and conceptual issues. *Journal of Consulting and Clinical Psychology, 57*, 31–38.

Baucom, D. H., & Lester, G. W. (1986). The usefulness of cognitive restructuring as an adjunct to behavioral marital therapy. *Behavior Therapy, 17*, 385–403.

Baucom, D. H., Sayers, S. L., & Sher, T. G. (1990). Supplementing behavioral marital therapy with cognitive restructuring and emotional expressiveness training: An outcome investigation. *Journal of Consulting and Clinical Psychology, 58*, 636–645.

Beck, A. T. (1967). *Depression: Causes and treatment.* New York: Basic Books.

Beck, A. T. (1998). *Love is never enough: How couples can overcome misunderstandings, resolve conflicts, and solve relationship problems through cognitive therapy.* New York: Harper & Row.

Beck, J. S. (1995). *Cognitive therapy: Basics and beyond.* New York: Guilford Press.

Bögner, I., & Zielenbach-Coenen, H. (1984). On maintaining change in behavioral marital therapy. In K. Hahlweg & N. S. Jacobson (Eds.), *Marital interaction: Analysis and modification* (pp. 27–35). New York: Guilford Press.

Bowlby, J. (1969). *Attachment and loss: Vol. 1. Attachment.* New York: Basic Books.

Bradbury, T. N., & Fincham, F. D. (1993). Assessing dysfunctional cognition in marriage: A reconsideration of the relationship belief inventory. *Psychological Assessment, 5,* 92–101.

Braukhaus, C., Hahlweg, K., Kroeger, C., Groth, T., & Fehm-Wolfsdorf, G. (2003). The effects of adding booster sessions to a prevention training program for committed couples. *Behavioural and Cognitive Psychotherapy, 31,* 325–336.

Bray, J. H., & Jouriles, E. N. (1995). Treatment of marital conflict and prevention of divorce. *Journal of Marital and Family Therapy, 21,* 461–473.

Brennan, K. A., Clark, C. L., & Shaver, P. R. (1998). Self-report measurement of adult attachment: An integrative overview. In J. A. Simpson & W. S. Rholes (Eds.), *Attachment theory and close relationships* (pp. 46–76). New York: Guilford Press.

Burns, D. D. (1980). *Feeling good: The new mood therapy.* New York: Signet.

Dattilo, F. M., & Padesky, C. A. (1990). *Cognitive therapy with couples.* Sarasota, FL: Professional Resource Exchange.

Eidelson, R. J., & Epstein, N. (1982). Cognition and relationship maladjustment: Development of a measure of dysfunctional relationship beliefs. *Journal of Consulting and Clinical Psychology, 50,* 515–720.

Emmelkamp, P. M. G., Krol, B., Sanderman, R., & Ruphan, M. (1987). The assessment of relationship beliefs in a marital context. *Personal and Individual Differences, 8,* 775–780.

Emmelkamp, P. M. G., van Linden van den Heuvell, C., Rüphan, M., Sanderman, R., Scholing, A., & Stroink, F. (1988). Cognitive and behavioral interventions: A comparative evaluation with clinically distressed couples. *Journal of Family Psychology, 1,* 365–377.

Epstein, N. B., & Baucom, D. H. (2002). *Enhanced cognitive–behavioral therapy for couples: A contextual approach.* Washington, DC: American Psychological Association.

Epstein, N., Pretzer, J. L., & Fleming, B. (1987). The role of cognitive appraisal in self-reports of marital communication. *Behavior Therapy, 18,* 51–69.

Feeney, J. A. (1999). Adult romantic attachment and couple relationships. In J. Cassidy & P. R. Shaver (Eds.), *Handbook of attachment: Theory, research, and clinical applications* (pp. 355–377). New York: Guilford Press.

Fincham, F. D., Garnier, P. C., Gano-Phillips, S., & Osborne, L. N. (1995). Preinteraction expectations, marital satisfaction, and accessibility: A new look at sentiment override. *Journal of Family Psychology, 9,* 3–14.

Fraley, R. C., & Waller, N. G. (1998). Adult attachment patterns: A test of the typological model. In J. A. Simpson & W. S. Rholes (Eds.), *Attachment theory and close relationships* (pp. 77–114). New York: Guilford Press.

Fraley, R. C., Waller, N. G., & Brennan, K. A. (2000). An item-response theory analysis of self-report measures of adult attachment. *Journal of Personality and Social Psychology, 78,* 350–365.

Gordon, K. C., & Baucom, D. H. (2003). Forgiveness and marriage: Preliminary support for a measure based on a model of recovery from a marital betrayal. *American Journal of Family Therapy, 31,* 179–199.

Gotlib, I. H., & Krasnoperova, E. (1998). Biased information processing as a vulnerability factor for depression. *Behavior Therapy, 29,* 603–617.

Halford, W. K., Sanders, M. R., & Behrens, B. C. (1993). A comparison of the generalization of behavioral marital therapy and enhanced behavioral marital therapy. *Journal of Consulting and Clinical Psychology, 61,* 51–60.

Hazan, C., & Shaver, P. (1987). Romantic love conceptualized as an attachment process. *Journal of Personality and Social Psychology, 52,* 511–524.

Hollon, S. D., & Kriss, M. R. (1984). Cognitive factors in clinical research and practice. *Clinical Psychology Review, 4,* 35–76.

Holmberg, D., & MacKenzie, S. (2002). So far, so good: Scripts for romantic relationship development as predictors of relational well-being. *Journal of Social and Personal Relationships, 19,* 777–796.

Huber, C. H., & Milstein, B. (1985). Cognitive restructuring and a collaborative set in couples' work. *American Journal of Family Therapy, 13,* 17–27.

Jacobson, N. S., & Margolin, G. (1979). *Marital therapy: Strategies based on social learning and behavior exchange principles.* New York: Brunner/Mazel.

Jacobson, N. S., Schmaling, K. B., & Holtzworth-Munroe, A. (1987). Component analysis of behavioral marital therapy: 2-year follow-up and prediction of relapse. *Journal of Marital & Family Therapy, 13*(2), 187–195.

Kirkpatrick, L. A., & Davis, K. E. (1994). Attachment style, gender, and relationship stability: A longitudinal analysis. *Journal of Personality and Social Psychology, 66,* 502–512.

Kobak, R. R., & Hazan, C. (1991). Attachment in marriage: Effects of security and accuracy of working models. *Journal of Personality and Social Psychology, 60,* 861–869.

Marcus, H. (1977). Self-schemas and processing information about the self. *Journal of Personality and Social Psychology, 35,* 63–78.

Marlatt, G. A., & Gordon, J. R. (Eds.). (1985). *Relapse prevention: Maintenance strategies in the treatment of addictive behaviors.* New York: Guilford Press.

Mikulincer, M., Florian, V., Cowan, P. A., & Cowan, C. P. (2002). Attachment security in couple relationships: A systemic model and its implications for family dynamics. *Family Process, 41,* 405–434.

Moller, A. T., & Van Zyl, P. D. (1991). Relationship beliefs, interpersonal perception, and marital adjustment. *Journal of Clinical Psychology, 47,* 28–33.

Reifman, A., & Crohan, S. E. (1993). Perceiving one's romantic partner: Schema structure and affective extremity. *Cognition & Emotion, 7,* 473–480.

Safran, J. D., Vallis, T. M., Segal, Z., & Shaw, B. F. (1986). Assessment of core cognitive processes in cognitive therapy. *Cognitive Therapy and Research, 10,* 509–526.

Senchak, M., & Leonard, K. E. (1992). Attachment styles and marital adjustment among newlywed couples. *Journal of Social and Personal Relationships, 9,* 51–64.

Terman, L. M., Buttenwieser, P., Ferguson, L. W., Johnson, W. B., & Wilson, D. P. (1938). *Psychological factors in marital happiness.* New York: McGraw-Hill.

Whisman, M. A., & Delinsky, S. S. (2002). Marital satisfaction and an information-processing measure of partner-schemas. *Cognitive Therapy and Research, 26,* 617–627.

Whisman, M. A., McKelvie, M., & Chatav, Y. (2005). Couple distress. In M. M. Antony, D. R. Ledley, & R. G. Heimberg (Eds.), *Improving outcomes and preventing relapse in cognitive–behavioral therapy* (pp. 380–408). New York: Guilford Press.

Whisman, M. A., & Weinstock, L. M. (2002). Cognitive therapy with couples. In T. Patterson (Ed.), *Comprehensive handbook of psychotherapy: Vol 2. Cognitive–behavioral approaches* (pp. 373–394). New York: Wiley.

Young, J. E. (1990). *Cognitive therapy for personality disorders: A schema-focused approach.* Sarasota, FL: Professional Resource Exchange.

Young, J. E., Klosko, J. S., & Weishaar, M. E. (2003). *Schema therapy: A practitioner's guide.* New York: Guilford Press.

Young, J. E., & Gluhoski, V. (1997). A schema-focused perspective on satisfaction in close relationships. In R. J. Sternberg & M. Hojjat (Eds.), *Satisfaction in close relationships* (pp. 356–381). New York: Guilford Press.

AFTERWORD

LAWRENCE P. RISO

The interest in schema-focused approaches is rapidly growing along with the search for temperamental, personality, and developmental antecedents of clinical problems. Schema theory has enormous potential to enhance understanding of the persistence of psychopathology, uncover its developmental antecedents, and improve psychotherapeutic intervention. The contributors to this book have tailored the general schema-focused approach to specific disorders and couple distress.

The construct of cognitive schemas has several strengths. First, at a theoretical level, schemas provide a way of conceptualizing the cognitive residue from early adversity that later contributes to a broad range of clinical phenomena. Second, at a clinical level, schemas offer a useful tool for clients to organize and understand their thinking and emotional reactions and to help them consolidate a wide range of symptoms. Third, altering cognitive schemas may be one way to attain lasting clinical improvement. Fourth, a growing literature supports the validity of the construct of schemas and suggests that their inclusion in a cognitive case formulation may facilitate the treatment of more chronic problems.

Despite our enthusiasm for the schema concept, some important areas need further study. Theoretical development is inadequate at this time to make a sharp distinction between the schema construct and the notion of core beliefs. Furthermore, the notion of schema activation is a powerful heuristic and this volume presents considerable evidence in support of this idea. However, there is virtually no work on what leads to the deactivation of schemas. Also, although research suggests that schemas contain both cognition and affect, we are far from theoretically modeling and empirically understanding this complex interaction. Researcher's early views of cognition leading to affect, or of affect leading to cognition, need to be developed into more complex models in which cognition and affect structure one another in a reciprocal fashion.

Other areas in need of further study include the hypothesized origin of cognitive schemas in early relationships (including early adversity). The data in support of this hypothesis are rather scant. Additional work needs to follow up on preliminary data indicating the particular importance of emotional abuse (Alloy et al., 2004). Future research may profit from placing cognitive schemas within a larger theoretical context such as adult and early attachment theory. Attachment theory has related internal working models to specific kinds of developmental experiences. The recently developed two-dimensional model of avoidant and anxious attachment dimensions (Brennan, Clark, & Shaver, 1998; Fraley & Shaver, 2000) warrants additional research attention within the clinical–cognitive literature. This powerful dimensional mode is backed by considerable factor-analytic research and the factors are conceptually and empirically orthogonal. Future research also needs to go beyond parental attachment figures and incorporate peer relations (Cole, Jacquez, & Maschman, 2001) and peer victimization (Schwartz et al., 1998).

Another larger theoretical context in which to consider placing cognitive schemas is the five-factor model of personality. For instance, a study of which types of schemas load on which personality dimensions is needed. This effort may help identify higher order factors among Young's (1995) list of 16 schemas, lead to a new taxonomy of these schemas, and improve their discriminant validity.

Although researchers have made advances in the assessment of schemas, much additional work needs to be done in this area. For instance, there are obvious problems with paper-and-pencil assessments, including their inherent mood–state biases and their inability to assess cognitive structure. However, information-processing paradigms may lack clinical usefulness for both theoretical and practical reasons (however, see Palfai & Wagner, 2004, for some notable exceptions). The distance between such unobservable constructs and the experience of clinical phenomena will remain a challenge for years to come.

In this volume, schema theory is used to expand and deepen the knowledge base of a range of different clinical disorders. At present there is no widely accepted theory or unified "schema school." An advantage of this situation is that future work can proceed in multiple directions. However, the lack of a unified schema school or overriding theoretical model may hamper the coherence and stepwise progress in this research. We hope that this volume has contributed to exploring the clinical usefulness, strengths, and weaknesses of schema-focused approaches as well as areas in need of further work, and will promote further development in the area.

REFERENCES

Alloy, L. B., Abramson, L. Y., Gibb, B. E., Crossfield, A. G., Pieracci, A. M., Spasojevic, J., et al. (2004). Developmental antecedents of cognitive vulnerability to depression: Review of findings from the cognitive vulnerability to depression project. *Journal of Cognitive Psychotherapy, 18,* 115–133.

Brennan, K. A., Clark, C. L., & Shaver, P. R. (1998). Self-report measurement of adult romantic attachment: An integrative overview. In J. A. Simpson & W. S. Rholes (Eds.), *Attachment theory and close relationships* (pp. 46–76). New York: Guilford Press.

Cole, D. A., Jacquez, F. M., & Maschman, T. L. (2001). Social origins of depressive cognitions: A longitudinal study of self-perceived competence in children. *Cognitive Therapy and Research, 25,* 377–395.

Fraley, R. C., & Shaver, P. R. (2000). Adult romantic attachment: Theoretical developments, emerging controversies, and unanswered questions. *Review of General Psychology, 4,* 132–154.

Palfai, T., & Wagner, E. F. (2004). Current perspectives on implicit cognitive processing in clinical disorders: Implications for assessment and intervention [Special series]. *Cognitive and Behavioral Practice, 11,* 135–138.

Schwartz, D., Dodge, K. A., Coie, J. D., Hubbard, J. A., Cillessen, A. H. N., Lemerise, E. A., et al. (1998). Social–cognitive and behavioral correlates of aggression and victimization in boys' play groups. *Journal of Abnormal Psychology, 26,* 431–440.

Young, J. E. (1995). *Cognitive therapy for personality disorders: A schema-focused approach.* Sarasota, FL: Professional Resource Press.

INDEX

Early maladaptive schemas (EMS),
    continued
    in substance abuse, 121–122,
        123–124
        alcohol abuse, 123
Eating disorders, 141
    cognitive–behavioral therapy (CBT)
        for, 139–140, 145, 150
        and SFCBT, 149, 169
    maintenance models of, 149
        and case example, 156
    medical monitoring for, 150
    schema-focused cognitive–
        behavioral therapy (SFCBT) for,
        140–141
        case studies on, 145
        and CBT, 149, 151, 169
        course of, 167–168
        formulation from, 154–156
        research on, 169–170
        techniques of, 156–167
    schema-focused models of, 146–149
    schemas in, 141–146
    transdiagnostic model of, 140, 149
    treatment of, 149–155
        assessment in, 149, 151–154,
            154–155
        case example on, 155–156
Eating Disorders Belief Questionnaire,
    144
Ellis, Albert, 115
Emotion
    in conceptualization diagram, 46
    and psychosis, 193
Emotional activation, in CT, 25
Emotional expressiveness training (EET),
    214–215
Emotional reasoning, and OCD, 96
Engagement, with psychosis, 181–183
Enhanced BCT (EBCT), 215
ERP. *See* Exposure and response
    prevention
Evaluation, of eating disorders, 151–154
Evidentiary analysis, 186, 210–211
Evolution, and biological model of
    depression, 24–25
Exercise, dissociation from (eating
    disorder case example), 165
Expectancies, on substance use (relapse-
    prevention model), 113

Expectations, 16
    in Case Formulation Sheet
        (Stephanie), 27
    and marital satisfaction, 206
Experiences in Close Relationships—
    Revised (ECR–R), 208
Exposure-based interventions, for PTSD
    victims, 74, 75, 81, 84, 86–87
Exposure and response prevention (ERP),
    93, 99, 103, 104
    cognitive therapy with, 100
    in vivo, 74, 100, 105
    toleration of strong feelings in, 102

Facilitating–permissive beliefs, 115
Family members, in OCD treatment, 100
Fearful–avoidant individuals, 203
Fears, regarding change (eating
    disorders), 158
Fiona (eating disorder example), 153–154
Five-factor model of personality, 222
Flashcards
    in eating disorder treatment,
        163–164
    in relationship intervention, 212
Frustration tolerance, low
    in REBT model, 115, 116
    in substance use (cognitive therapy
        model), 117
Functional analysis of behavior, 112
    in dual-focus schema therapy, 119

Gemma (eating disorder example), 153
Gender differences
    and eating disorders, 143
    in views of trauma victims, 71
Global meaning, 65, 66
Global thinking, and chronic depression,
    54
Guided imagery, 48
    in chronic depression case
        illustration, 52

Harold (case presentation, chronic
    depression), 50–54
Harry (case example, psychosis), 184–
    185
High-risk situations, 112, 214

Overvigilance, and chronic vs. non-chronic depression, 43

Paranoia, punishment, 191
Paranoid personality disorder, early maladaptive schemas and interpersonal problems with, 124
Paranoid thoughts, images in, 193
Parents
    and child-rearing practices, 123
    in chronic depression, 43–44
    in MDD case presentation (Stephanie), 17–18
Passivity, in therapeutic relationship, 49
Pattern breaking, 212
Perceived benefits, and PTSD, 67
Perfectionism, 98
    in case studies, 14, 52, 120, 158
Performance-based studies, on relationship functioning, 204–206
Personal Beliefs and Reactions Scale (PBRS), 71, 75
Personality, five-factor model of, 222
Personal Significance Scale, 99
Pharmacotherapy
    and major depressive disorder, 13, 22
    and OCD, 93, 94
Piagetian learning concepts, and depressive thinking, 24
Pie charts, for eating disorders, 162
Pleasure seeking, and substance use
    in cognitive therapy model, 116–117
    in REBT model, 115
Point–counterpoint technique, 48, 160–161
Positive data log, 20–21, 33
    for eating disorders, 159
    in psychosis intervention, 192–193
Posttraumatic Cognitions Inventory, 70, 75
Posttraumatic growth (PTG), 67–68
Posttraumatic Growth Inventory (PTGI), 71
Posttraumatic stress disorder (PTSD)
    assessment of, 75, 86
        schema-focused, 70–72
    information-processing studies on, 64
    and assumptions, 64–68

attributions and posttraumatic pathology, 68–70
schema-focused approaches and cognitive interventions, 72–75
schema-focused assessment, 70–72
and psychosis, 193–194
risk factors for, 61
schema concept in cognitive theories of, 60–63
schema-focused treatment of, 75–86, 87
    case illustration on, 76–79, 82–84, 85
    cognitive interventions, 72–75
    future directions in, 86–87
    and psychosis treatment, 193
Prediction log, for eating disorders, 159
Predispositional characteristics, in cognitive therapy model of substance use, 117
Preferential encoding, 70
Prejudices
    psychoses compared to, 189–190
    schemas compared to, 20–21, 157
Preoccupied individuals, 203
Procedural beliefs, 180
Propositional representational system, 63
Psychoeducation
    about eating disorders, 150
    about PTSD, 74, 76, 77, 80
    on substance abuse, 114–115
    on substance abuse treatment, 128
Psychopathology
    developmental antecedents of, 4, 6
    and schemas, 6
Psychosis
    advantages and disadvantages of, 185–186
    assessment of and engagement with, 179, 181–183
    case formulation for, 183–184
        case example of, 184–185
        and schemas, 180
    and CBT, 177–178, 193
    cognitive models of, 177–178
    intervention for, 185
        and accompanying problems, 193–194
        behavior strategies in, 188–189

maintenance of (explaining), 20–21, 157
measuring of, 12–13
and MDD, 23
in OCD model, 95, 95–96
and personality model, 222
and psychosis, 180–181
and case formulation, 180
and relationship functioning, 199, 200
specific criteria for, 20
in substance abuse, 119
types of
abandonment, 153
alternative, 19, 20
core, 95, 96, 101, 117, 120
depressive, 12
dysfunctional, 11, 12, 13, 118
(*see also* Dysfunctional schemas)
implicit, 19
interpersonal, 12, 18
maladaptive, 118 (*see also* Maladaptive schemas)
relationship, 204, 207–210, 212, 216, 216–217
unlovability, 17, 45, 189, 192
vulnerability, 97
See also Cognitive schemas
Schema activation, 222
in eating disorder case example, 155, 156
Schema avoidance, 47
bulimic eating pathology, 147–148
in substance abuse, 119
Schema based CBT, and OCD patients, 100
Schema change, 11, 23
beginning of, 19
continuum methods in, 19–20
Core Belief Worksheet in, 22
Historical Test of Schemas in, 21
outcome research in, 22–23
positive data log in, 20–21
in psychosis intervention, 189–193
Schema compensation, 47, 155
in restrictive eating pathology, 147
Schema construct, vs. core beliefs, 221–222
Schema dialogue, on eating disorders, 160, 160–161

Schema-driven problems, explaining of (eating disorders), 157
Schema-focused approaches, 221
clinical, 4
Schema-focused assessment, of PTSD, 70–72
Schema-focused cognitive–behavioral therapy (SFCBT), 140–141
and eating disorders
case studies on, 145
and CBT, 149, 151
course of, 167–168
formulation from, 154–156
research on, 169–170
techniques of, 156
Schema-focused models of eating disorders, 146–149
Schema-focused therapy, for PTSD, 75–86
Schema Formulation Sheet, Interpersonal, 31
Schema maintenance, explaining of (eating disorders), 157
Schema surrender, 47, 51
Schema theory, 6, 221, 222–223
Schematic, prepositional, analogue, and associative representational systems (SPAARS), 63
Schematic representations, in PTSD, 62, 63
Schizoid personality disorder, early maladaptive schemas and interpersonal problems with, 124
Schizophrenia, National Institute for Clinical Excellence guidelines on, 177–178
Schizophrenic symptoms, and abuse, 179
Schizotypal personality disorder, early maladaptive schemas and interpersonal problems with, 124
Scripts, relationship, 204–205
Securely attached individuals, 203
Self-efficacy, in relapse-prevention coping skills model of substance use, 114
Self-harm prevention plans, for eating disorders, 163
Self-schema, 200
dysfunctional (negative), 121
and eating disorders, 141
Sense of Coherence Scale, 67

Sexual abuse
  and eating disorders, 144
  psychosis as result of, 179
  and treatment for chronic
    depression, 48
Sexual assault
  beliefs affected by, 64
  case illustration on, 76–79, 82–84,
    85
  CPT for, 72
  interventions for, 86
  PBRS for survivors of, 71
  self-blame for, 68
SFCBT. *See* Schema-focused cognitive–
    behavioral therapy
SFCBT clinician, training, supervision
    and support for, 169
SMART (specific, measurable, achiev-
    able, realistic, and time-limited)
    goals, 182
Situational meaning, 65, 66
Social anxiety, with psychosis, 194
Social learning theory, and relapse-
    prevention model, 113
Sociotropic personality, 12, 17
Socratic questioning
  automatic thoughts elicited through,
    15
  in eating-disorder treatment, 152,
    160
  in psychosis interventions, 186, 190
  in PTSD treatment, 73, 74, 75
  in substance use treatment,
    cognitive therapy model, 118
    relapse-prevention model, 115
SPAARS (schematic, propositional,
    analogue, and associative
    representational systems), 63
Standards, 200. *See also* Relationship
    standards
Stephanie (case presentation, MDD),
    13–14
  case formulation sheet of, 27–28
  cognitive processes of, examined, 16
  continuum methods for, 20, 32
  early childhood experiences of, 17
Strategic processing, in OCD treatment,
    104
Stress management skills, and eating
    disorders, 157–158

Submission, in therapeutic relationship,
    49
Substance use disorders, 111–112
  case study on, 120–121
  cognitive–behavioral models of,
    111–113, 128–129
    and automatic negative thoughts,
      122
    cognitive therapy, 116–118
    dual-focus schema therapy
      (DFST), 118–121, 125,
      126–128
    rational–emotive behavior
      therapy (REBT), 115–116
    relapse-prevention coping skills,
      112, 113–115, 128
  dysfunctional beliefs in, 128
  research on
    and core beliefs, 121–124
    and dual-focus schema therapy,
      126–128
    and early maladaptive schema
      questionnaire, 124–126
  treatment of, 114–115
    cognitive therapy as, 117–118
    with DFST, 119–121, 125,
      126–128
    rational–emotive behavior
      therapy (REBT) for, 115–116
    realistic goals of, 122
    relapse-prevention and coping
      skills, 114
Supervision and support, for SFCBT
    clinician, 169
Surveys, in psychosis intervention, 192
Symptom reduction, early, 47

Target problems for therapy, and patients
    with chronic depression, 44
Therapeutic community, in substance
    abuse treatment, 127–128
Therapeutic relationship (alliance)
  and case formulation, 14
  and case presentation (chronic
    depression), 53
  and client's own experience
    (PTSD), 85
  dominance–passivity trap in, 49
  for eating disorders, 150
  and interpersonal schemas, 18

ABOUT THE EDITORS

Lawrence P. Riso, PhD, is associate professor of psychology at the American School of Professional Psychology, Argosy University/Washington, DC. He completed his PhD in clinical psychology at the State University of New York at Stony Brook; his clinical internship at Brown University in Providence, Rhode Island; and his research fellowship at the Western Psychiatric Institute and Clinic. He is author or coauthor of more than 40 articles and book chapters on mood disorders, personality disorders, and cognitive therapy. Dr. Riso served as principal investigator for a National Institute of Mental Health study of early maladaptive schemas in chronic depression. He currently serves on the editorial boards of the journals *Cognitive Therapy and Research*, the *Journal of Contemporary Psychotherapy*, and *Scientific Review of Mental Health Practice*. Dr. Riso is a certified cognitive therapist through the Academy of Cognitive Therapy and has been a practicing psychologist for more than 10 years.

Pieter L. du Toit, MA, has worked as a clinical psychologist in private practice, research settings, and in the National Health Service in the United Kingdom. Most of his published work focuses on anxiety disorders. He currently studies emotion regulation in posttraumatic stress disorder under the supervision of Tim Dalgleish at the Medical Research Council Cognition and Brain Sciences Unit at the University of Cambridge. His clinical expertise is the application of schema-focused cognitive behavior therapy to personality disorders, mood disorders, and anxiety disorders (particularly obsessive–compulsive spectrum disorders).

Dan J. Stein, MD, PhD, is professor and chair of the Department of Psychiatry and Mental Health at the University of Cape Town, South

Africa, and director of the Medical Research Council Unit on Anxiety Disorders. Dr. Stein is also on the faculty at Mt. Sinai School of Medicine in New York. He did his undergraduate training at the University of Cape Town, South Africa, and his postgraduate training in psychiatry and psychiatric research at Columbia University, New York, and the New York State Psychiatric Institute.

Jeffrey E. Young, PhD, is founder and director of the Cognitive Therapy Centers of New York, and the Schema Therapy Institute, New York. He is also on the faculty in the Department of Psychiatry at Columbia University College of Physicians and Surgeons in New York. Dr. Young is the founder of "schema therapy," an integrative approach for personality disorders and treatment-resistant patients. He has published widely in the fields of both cognitive and schema therapies, including two major books: *Schema Therapy: A Practitioner's Guide*, written for mental health professionals; and *Reinventing Your Life*, a popular self-help book based on schema therapy.